WAR *in the* CHESAPEAKE

WAR *in the* CHESAPEAKE

The BRITISH CAMPAIGNS
to CONTROL *the* BAY, 1813–14

CHARLES PATRICK NEIMEYER

NAVAL INSTITUTE PRESS
Annapolis, Maryland

Naval Institute Press
291 Wood Road
Annapolis, MD 21402

Library of Congress Cataloging-in-Publication Data
Neimeyer, Charles Patrick,
  War in the Chesapeake : the British campaigns to control the bay, 1813–14 /
Charles P. Neimeyer.
      pages cm
  Includes bibliographical references and index.
  ISBN 978-1-61251-865-7 (alk. paper) — ISBN 978-1-61251-866-4 (ebook)
  1. United States—History—War of 1812—Campaigns. 2. Chesapeake Bay Region
(Md. and Va.)—History, Military—19th century. 3. Maryland—History—War of
1812—Campaigns. 4. Virginia—History—War of 1812—Campaigns. I. Title.
  E355.1.C485N45 2015
  355.009755'18—dc23

                                                            2014050286

23 22 21 20 19 18 17 16 15   9 8 7 6 5 4 3 2 1
First printing

CONTENTS

ILLUSTRATIONS

IMAGES

MAPS

ACKNOWLEDGMENTS

All historians stand on the shoulders of giants in their field. A number of such individuals stand out for their superb work in documenting the War of 1812 in the Chesapeake Bay. For local history and understanding of what took place during the war, especially in the state of Maryland, no one is more informed than Ralph Eshelman, Scott Sheads, and the dean of all things related to the War of 1812, Don Hickey. These three fine historians collaborated on a superb reference book that should be on the bookshelf of every student of the War of 1812 in the Chesapeake. It is centrally featured on mine. Don Hickey is one of the very best historians on this era today, and his work has stood the test of time as well. Don Shomette's work on Barney's flotilla and the work of all the previously mentioned historians, including that of my former colleague at the U.S. Naval Academy History Department, Bill Calderhead, are must-haves. Their pathbreaking efforts made my research much easier.

I must thank many people, and none more so than a number of Marine Corps History Division interns who assisted me with this project. First and foremost is Ms. Rachel Webb, recently graduated from American University with a master's degree in international relations. Rachel's diligent and thorough research and fact-checking certainly helped me to deliver a better product. Ms. Sara Pappa, Ms. Elizabeth Bubb, Ms. Kamerin Lauren, Mr. Miles Hartl, and most recently, Ms. Susan Brubaker all helped bring this project across the finish line. I was truly amazed at their dedication to duty and quest for accuracy throughout the span of this project. I found Ms. Brubaker's editorial assistance to be especially helpful.

I would like to thank Glenn Williams of the U.S. Army's Center of Military History for encouraging me to expand an earlier commemorative history I had written for him on this subject. His comments and advice on various aspects of the War of 1812 were extremely helpful. I also discovered that he is the go-to person for information about the USS *Constellation*. I likewise must extend my thanks to my friend and mentor Thomas Cutler of the U.S. Naval Institute. I still fondly remember our days teaching history to the midshipmen at the U.S. Naval Academy. Thanks to Tom for sticking with me on this project.

Finally, I need to thank a number of local historians who helped educate me on critical details about the war in the Chesapeake. Mr. Christopher T. George is one of those rare historians who have not only an eye for detail but a way of telling history that is both enjoyable and educational. He volunteered to speak about the War of 1812 at the Department of Defense history speaker series at the Pentagon and received rave reviews. I, of course, took credit for finding such an engaging historian to speak at this event, but the real star was Chris George. He showed me a number of interesting items, such as key documents, maps, and artifacts, at the Maryland Historical Society—a virtual treasure trove of information on the War of 1812 in Maryland. I also would like to thank the reference librarians at the Gray Research Center in Quantico, Virginia, for assisting me in finding hard-to-get books and other pertinent research materials. Mr. Chuck Melson, the chief historian at the Marine Corps History Division, took the time to show me the little known or visited Slippery Hill and Caulk's Field battlegrounds on Maryland's Eastern Shore. Robert Reyes of Dundalk, Maryland (my hometown), was helpful in identifying key aspects of the Battle of North Point and the fighting around Bear Creek, Baltimore County, and provided me with a number of useful maps.

Having been born and raised in Maryland and now living in my adoptive state of Virginia, I found researching this book to be a tremendous amount of fun. One of my earliest memories is going on a family trip to Fort McHenry and Mary Pickersgill's Flag House on Albemarle Street in Baltimore. I still admire the lines of that fine replica sailing vessel the *Pride of Baltimore* and can only imagine the legendary privateer Thomas Boyle standing on the quarterdeck of the *Chasseur* as he ran down yet another British prize. I delivered newspapers on streets named for the boy martyrs of 1814, Daniel Wells and Henry McComas, and often rode my bicycle past the battle monument on the old North Point Battlefield—giving little thought to what took place there just two hundred years ago. Having left my hometown to join the Marine Corps in 1976 and having been gone on my worldwide travels for well over thirty-eight years, I enjoyed seeing some of the old places—at least once more.

1

PRELUDE TO WAR

On 21 October 1805 Lord Admiral Horatio Nelson, age forty-seven, maneuvered the warships under his command toward the combined fleets of France and Spain off Cape Trafalgar. Wearing his standard dark frock coat emblazoned with the stars of various honorific orders, the easily identifiable one-armed admiral paced the quarterdeck of his massive one-hundred-gun flagship, HMS *Victory*. A nearby Royal Marine drummer had already beat to quarters, and Nelson's well-drilled sailors were at their battle stations. As his ships closed in, Nelson turned to Flag Captain Thomas Hardy and casually remarked that he would not be satisfied this day unless he captured at least twenty enemy ships.

This was no idle boast. Nelson intended to put an end to the maritime prospects of Napoleonic France once and for all. By the end of the fighting at Trafalgar, his fleet had taken seventeen enemy ships. Another vessel, the seventy-four-gun French ship of the line *Achille*, blew up during the fighting, so Nelson came close to capturing the twenty ships he was after. However, owing to a severe storm that followed the action, only four of Nelson's prizes ultimately made it back to Great Britain. Moreover, Nelson himself did not live to enjoy the fruits of his decisive victory. Struck down by a sniper's bullet at the height of the fighting, he died shortly thereafter and instantly passed into history as his nation's greatest naval hero.

Nevertheless, the one-sided result of Trafalgar gave Great Britain a tremendous strategic opportunity to use its mastery of the sea to its advantage in the struggle against Napoleon. But not all was lost for the emperor of France. While his admirals were no match for the likes of Nelson, Napoleon continued to reign supreme on land. By December 1805, with his resounding victory over the Third Coalition at Austerlitz, Napoleon completed his iron grip over much of the continent of Europe.

Britannia Triumphant: The Most Decisive and Glorious Naval Victory shows an 1805 broadside celebrating Admiral Horatio Nelson's victory against the French at Trafalgar. Royal Navy Museum

Although future U.S. president James Madison did not realize it at the time, the respective British and French victories at Trafalgar and Austerlitz factored into why the United States ultimately declared war against Great Britain in 1812. While the American reasons for going to war in 1812 are far more complex than these two battles, there can be no doubt that after Trafalgar Great Britain intended to leverage its dominant position on the high seas. This meant trouble not only for France but for neutral nations as well. Just as ominous for neutral states, Napoleon's defeat of the Third Coalition enabled him to freely experiment with economic warfare, and both Britain and France had trump cards to play. Britain saw its pathway to wartime success against Napoleon connected to its near-total control of the seas and the commerce that traveled on them (to include that of neutral nations). On the other hand, Napoleon's military dominance on land enabled him to create an exclusionary anti-British economic apparatus that became known as the continental system. Such a system would not have been possible if the emperor had lost at Austerlitz.

However, even before Trafalgar the Royal Navy had grown obnoxious to the commerce of most neutral states. Throughout the early 1800s, to offset the continued string of victories Napoleon had wrested from each and every coalition formed against him, the British issued increasingly more aggressive orders in council to its seagoing forces. An order in council was emitted directly by the king's Privy Council and is akin to an executive order issued by the U.S. president today. For example, during the wars of the French Revolution, an order in council resurrected the maritime Rule of 1756, used the last time the British had fought an extended war against the French. This rule—unique to Great Britain—forbade neutral nations such as the United States from engaging in commerce with colonial ports during war when such ports had been normally closed to them in peacetime. While the Rule of 1756 was designed to ensure British dominance at sea, it wreaked havoc on the trade and economies of neutral states like Denmark and the United States.

Nevertheless, enterprising Yankee sea captains and other neutrals figured a way around the Rule of 1756 by employing the practice of broken voyages. During a broken voyage, a neutral American commercial vessel would load up on noncontraband goods in a colonial port not under an actual physical blockade. The vessel would then proceed to "break" its voyage by stopping at a neutral location, such as Marblehead, Massachusetts, or Charleston, South Carolina. The ship then paid customs duties, unloaded and reloaded its cargo, sailed to other countries or colonies, and sold the products as neutral "American" goods. However, this practice also allowed belligerent nations to mitigate any naval deficiencies of their own by using neutral hulls to transport their commerce for them. It also allowed merchant houses in the United States to profit greatly from this carrying trade. In years past the British government had tolerated broken voyages and occasionally allowed its own merchant vessels to use this practice. After Trafalgar the British decided that strict observance of neutral rights and the practice of broken voyages no longer served their national interest.[1]

Even in Europe neutral maritime trading rights were a major issue. Twice within a span of six years (in 1801 and 1807), neutral northern European states attempted to form a "league of armed neutrality" as a potential hedge against growing British naval dominance. However, heavily reliant on free trade in the Baltic for critical naval stores and foodstuffs, Great Britain sent a fleet to successfully break up each armed league of neutrals that formed. Lord Nelson himself brought down the 1801 league with his audacious victory over the Danish fleet in Copenhagen Harbor. In 1807 British vice admiral Sir James Saumarez attacked the city of Copenhagen with a new weapon called Congreve rockets. Invented in 1804 by Sir William Congreve, these rockets were essentially iron tubes filled with highly combustible gunpowder. Wildly inaccurate, they still made an effective incendiary device, and this is exactly how the British used them against the Danes. Saumarez's attack destroyed about a third of the city of Copenhagen and killed a significant number of civilians. While the Copenhagen fire brought down international scorn on Great Britain, it nonetheless effectively ended the second Armed League of Neutrality. From a foreign policy view, however, the 1807 Copenhagen attack was a major mistake because it provided a pretext for Russia, long concerned about unfettered sea access for its lone Baltic seaport of St. Petersburg, to declare war against Great Britain. If the British were going to defeat Napoleon, they needed a continental ally with a powerful land army. Needlessly antagonizing Russia did not help their cause.

Luckily for the British, Napoleon was no less myopic when it came to foreign policy. In 1806 he moved to defeat yet another coalition formed against him. This time Prussia sought to regain its former preeminence as a central power and allied itself with Russia. Not waiting for the massive Russian army to link up with its Prussian allies, Napoleon moved his army into Prussia, fought a series of engagements, and won them all. He then went after the Russian army and defeated it as well, at the Battle of Friedland on 14 June 1807. Thus, at that particular moment and despite Great Britain's ham-handedness at Copenhagen, the czar remained more concerned about the threat posed by the emperor than about prosecuting a vigorous war against the British. Consequently, between 1807 and 1812, fighting between Great Britain and Russia was confined purposely by both sides to minor naval skirmishes in the Baltic and Barents Seas.

As for America, there can be no doubt that the issue of neutral trade was at the heart of its grievances with Great Britain. Inflammatory pamphlets flew back and forth across the Atlantic, with each side accusing the other of violating maritime and international law. One pro-British pamphleteer, James Stephen, wrote a lengthy treatise titled *War in Disguise; or, The Frauds of the Neutral Flags* (1806). Stephen argued,

> Never was our maritime superiority more decisive than in the last and
> present war. We are still the unresisted masters of every sea . . . yet we do

not hear that the merchants of France, Spain, and Holland are ruined or that their colonies are distressed, much less that their exchequers are empty. The true solution is this—the commercial and colonial interests of our enemies, are now ruined in appearance only, not in reality. They seem to have retreated from the ocean . . . but that is a mere *ruse de guerre*. They have, in effect . . . only changed their flags, chartered many vessels really neutral, and altered a little the former routes of their trade. Their transmarine sources of revenue, have not been for a moment destroyed by our hostilities, and are at present scarcely impaired.[2]

Although he had not yet seen Stephen's manuscript, Secretary of State James Madison exhausted every classic and contemporary source on maritime and international trade law while writing his own ponderous 217-page "pamphlet" in an attempt to represent the neutral-state point of view (although he published the pamphlet anonymously). Madison worked on his treatise, titled *An Examination of the British Doctrine, Which Subjects to Capture a Neutral Trade, Not Open in Time of Peace*, a full three months in Philadelphia while he waited for his wife, Dolly, to recover from knee surgery. In it he emphasized that no nation in the world recognized the validity of the Rule of 1756 except, of course, Great Britain. In condemning the aggressive British policy regarding neutral trade, Madison remarked that international law favors nations at peace vice those at war. He believed Great Britain was actually using the Rule of 1756 as an excuse to crush neutral trade and, more specifically, the American competition. Madison concluded,

Finding no asylum elsewhere, it at length boldly asserts, as its *true foundation, a mere superiority of force*. It is right in Great-Britain to capture and condemn a neutral trade with her enemies, disallowed by her enemies in time of peace, for the sole reason that her force is predominant at sea. And it is wrong in her enemies to capture and condemn a neutral trade with British colonies, because their maritime force is inferior to hers. The question no longer is, whether the trade be right or wrong in itself, but on which side the superiority of force lies? The law of nations, the rights of neutrals, the freedom of the seas, the commerce of the world, are to depend, not on any fixt principle of justice, but on the comparative state of naval armaments.[3]

Madison's anonymous pamphlet, with its overly legalistic arguments on the subject of neutral rights, was so difficult to comprehend that few congressmen took time to read it. Administration critic John Randolph believed that Madison's arguments bordered on the ridiculous and scoffed that the secretary of state was throwing a "3 shilling pamphlet" against an "800 ship" Royal Navy.[4] Although Randolph exaggerated the number of British ships then in commission by several hundred vessels, his sarcasm was to the point. Without a navy the United States could not do much about the increasingly restrictive British trade policies that emerged just before the War of 1812.

Two landmark Admiralty court case rulings vividly illustrate how British policy changed and why the situation between the United States and Great Britain was growing acrimonious. In 1800 the American brig *Polly* was captured at sea by the Royal Navy on a voyage from Marblehead, Massachusetts, to Bilbao, Spain. The *Polly* had traveled from Havana, Cuba, where it had loaded sugar and cocoa. These goods were brought back to Marblehead, where customs duties were paid and the cargo was off-loaded. Some repairs were made to the vessel, and the cargo was reloaded, fully documented, and insured. Only then did it leave port for Spain. When the *Polly* was captured by the British, they argued at an Admiralty court that "landing the goods and paying duties did not prove a bona fide importation." However, famed Admiralty law expert Sir William Scott retorted, "If these criteria are not to be resorted to . . . I should be at a loss to know what should be the test." At that time the duties paid at Marblehead, new insurance, and other documentation were enough to establish the *Polly*'s voyage and cargo as thoroughly American—the ship and its contents were restored to the owners, thus upholding the tradition of broken voyages.[5]

However, just five years later, when England's maritime supremacy was much stronger, an Admiralty court reversed the *Polly* ruling and declared that a captured American brig, *Essex*, had been legally seized and condemned by the Royal Navy. In this case the *Essex* originally set sail with its cargo from Barcelona, Spain, and arrived at Salem, Massachusetts, where it was unloaded and received new documentation, as in the *Polly* case. The *Essex* then departed for Havana, Cuba, but was captured en route by the Royal Navy. The court ruled that the cargo had been intended for the Port of Havana all along (Spain was then in alliance with France), and therefore the voyage was not "broken" but direct, making the cargo liable for seizure as a legal prize of war. It now seemed the ultimate destination of the ship mattered more than what it actually carried in its hold. This reversal abruptly ended the tradition of broken voyages. It also effectively curtailed the ability of neutral states to use their vessels as intermediaries for nations at war. This especially hurt the United States, since a substantial portion of its overseas commerce was devoted to the colonial West Indies trade. In fact, "more than 50 percent of [all] U.S. exports in 1805" became instantly liable for seizure under this new interpretation. It was now open season on neutral shipping. Within a fortnight of the ruling, insurance rates on American shipping quadrupled.[6] Jefferson and Madison both believed that this outcome was exactly what the British had intended all along.

Thanks to the policy change, some Royal Navy captains and privateers erroneously seized any American ships that strayed across their path. The American commercial shippers along the Eastern Seaboard howled with indignation. There was also no doubt that the change of policy was indirectly related to growing American competition with English commerce. Throughout the early 1800s, while the maritime resources of Great Britain were tied down trying to contain Napoleon, American merchant vessels moved rapidly to fill the vacuum and began to dominate trade with the British West Indies. Many in Britain now saw America as a growing economic threat. American ships had replaced British hulls carrying their own colonial goods to market in Great Britain and other parts of Europe.

Lord Henry Mulgrave, foreign secretary under William Pitt the Younger (1805–6) and later first lord of the Admiralty, mused, "The great advantage of possessing colonies [in the first place] was the enjoyment of an exclusive trade with them." During the Napoleonic era conservatives in Britain believed that protection of their commerce was the principal reason behind their nation's rise to greatness. Many in Parliament were convinced that the main purpose of a dominant navy was to regulate trade for their own benefit and to crush the competition. One pamphleteer wrote, "Commerce is connected to the strength and glory of England, and he who respects the strength and glory of England, will contemplate her Navigation and Colonial System, but with the sentiment . . .—ESTO PERPETUA."[7] Even Thomas Jefferson was convinced that the British sincerely believed rising American prosperity had been "filched" from theirs.[8]

By 1807 the situation between Great Britain and the United States over neutral trade was reaching a boiling point. To make matters worse for America, that same year Napoleon promulgated his Berlin and Milan decrees, which put the continental system into full operation. No longer just the Royal Navy but now French privateers and other allied vessels also seized American ships in increasing numbers. Fully caught between the warring superpowers, Secretary of State James Monroe in 1812 issued a report on the number of vessels lost to both Britain and France. His computations were highly revealing. From 1803 until the Berlin decree, the French took 206 American vessels. During roughly the same period, the British seized more than two and a half times that amount (528). From 1807 until 1811, when Napoleon essentially repealed the decrees as they pertained to American shipping, France took another 307 American ships. An additional 45 American vessels were taken after the rollback of the decrees for a grand total of 558 ships taken by the French from 1803 to Napoleon's invasion of Russia in 1812.[9] If the French were also taking a significant quantity of Yankee merchant ships, why then was American outcry over this issue so one-sidedly anti-British?

The answer to this important question can be traced directly to new orders in council that the British issued in November 1807 and perhaps the Jefferson administration's intrinsic antipathy toward Great Britain. The new orders in council went further than even Napoleon's decrees in targeting neutral shipping. Moreover, they were emitted after the controversial June 1807 *Chesapeake-Leopard* affair and at a time when the British still had not provided the United States with an explanation or apology for the Royal Navy's precipitous attack on the USS *Chesapeake*. In fact, over the entire course of the Napoleonic era, the British had taken 917 American ships—nearly double the number taken by the French. After the 1799–1800 Quasi-War with France had been resolved, French ships never again during the Napoleonic era committed a direct attack on a major U.S. Navy vessel along the lines of the HMS *Leopard*'s attack in 1807. Moreover, the emperor had rescinded the negative effects of his decrees against America by November 1810. On the other hand, the British were not moved to change their own restrictive orders in council until their merchant class was hit with a sharp trade recession in mid-1812—too late to avoid America's declaration of war. Although it was true that the 1807 orders in council did not stop Americans from trading with ports not under French control, Napoleon dominated nearly all of Europe at the time, so this concession meant little to vulnerable American merchant vessels. Thomas Jefferson only slightly exaggerated the problem for American shippers: "[Great Britain] forbade us to trade with any nation without entering and paying duties in their ports on both the outward and inward cargo. Thus, to carry a cargo

The USS *Chesapeake*, one of the superfrigates of the War of 1812, by F. Muller.
Courtesy of the Naval History and Heritage Command, #NH 59556-KN

of cotton from Savannah to St. Mary's, and take returns in fruits, for example, our vessel was to go to England, enter and pay a duty on her cotton there, return to St. Mary's, then go back to England to enter and pay a duty on her fruits, and then return to Savannah, after crossing the Atlantic four times, and paying tributes on both cargoes to England, instead of a direct passage of a few hours."[10]

During the Napoleonic era the two most important commodities the United States traded with Great Britain were grain and cotton. However, American wheat and corn actually accounted for only a quarter of all food imported by England. Neutral Baltic States sold grain to Great Britain when supplies from America became scarce. As for cotton, while Britain imported around 80 percent of this particular commodity from American planters, in an emergency there were alternative sources to be had—most notably Brazil. Further, in anticipation of a crisis with America, commercial houses in London had been stockpiling cotton for a number of years. The chimera of British textile mills screaming for American cotton was as ephemeral in 1812 as it proved to be in 1861. On the other hand, in 1806 "Britain sent to America cottons and woolens worth $41 million, more than half her textile exports and nearly one-quarter of all British exports of whatever kind. American citizens needed British cloth almost as much as British factories required a market."[11] In reality, the British held a stronger economic hand than the Jefferson administration realized at that time. Although a trade war or embargo hurt the economies of both nations, the British clearly had a greater depth of resources with which to stand the pain.

The British fear of a rising America as an economic competitor may have been well founded. Beginning in the early 1790s, American overseas trade seemed on the increase, although how much of this largesse was actually reexported, broken voyage goods is difficult to ascertain. Nonetheless, by 1806 the sum total value of American exports "had grown from $20,750,000 in 1792 to $101,550,000"—a whopping 400 percent increase in trade in just fourteen years. Even if half this trade can be credited to broken voyages, the increase still represented a significant jump in overall American economic activity.[12]

Another way to determine how well America was doing is not to overly fixate on the export bottom line but to look at the increase in the number of American-flagged vessels from 1793 to 1806. The small shipping firm of George Crowninshield & Sons of Salem, Massachusetts, is an excellent case in point. In 1792 the Crowninshield firm operated just 3 small merchant vessels—each one rated at less than 100 tons. Just 12 years later, the firm had tripled its number of operating vessels to 9—all rated between 250 and 500 tons apiece. George Crowninshield's son Jacob was one of the few merchants in coastal New England who claimed to be both a Republican and a supporter of President Thomas Jefferson. Jacob Crowninshield had done so well as a captain that he was able to retire from the sea by the age of 29. In 1804 he was confident enough to run for Congress against a former secretary of state, Timothy Pickering, and he won the bitterly contested election. Jacob Crowninshield's rise to social and political prominence was directly related to his economic success. In the years before his untimely death in 1808, Crowninshield became a confidante to both Jefferson and Secretary of State James Madison. He had even been nominated by Jefferson and confirmed by the Senate to replace Robert Smith as Secretary of the Navy, but he apparently never served in this capacity—although his younger brother, Benjamin, later did after the War of 1812 had ended.[13]

Writing to Madison in 1806, Crowninshield pointed out the dilemma of American merchants trying to do business in and around the British West Indies:

The first observation that occurs is that this commerce is held upon the most uncertain nature. Our merchants know not what articles will be admitted into the English islands from day to day. . . . At no time during the war are the British ports in the West Indies open for more than six months and then only for articles of the first necessity. They are occasionally shut. One island admits fish; another excludes it at the same time. Beef and pork are occasionally excluded. Rice is not always admitted. It is the same with lard and butter. Large live cattle are often refused at the same time that small live stock is received. By proclamation boards, planks, and certain kinds of timber will be admitted when other woods will not be. . . . The merchants of the United States can seldom tell whether the trade is open or shut at Jamaica or Barbados.[14]

Crowninshield argued that without the onerous orders in council, American merchants could easily outmatch rival British or even Canadian firms. He noted, "We sail our vessels cheaper than most other nations; we make shorter voyages; we are more economical in our expences. Our vessels stay but little time in port. The captains transact their own business seldom going consigned. Here [in America] two commissions are saved one on the sales and another on the purchase." Crowninshield observed that the British allowed American merchant captains to be paid in molasses and rum only. "Sugar and coffee cannot be touched. [Thus] the [West Indian] planter suffers. The supplies for the Islands [become] less abundant, more uncertain and sometimes a scarcity ensues. The planter endeavors to make up for his losses by selling his rum at the highest possible price. The American must take it, or leave his debt." When multiple ships were in port, as was frequently the case, this caused the price of molasses and rum to rapidly increase as various merchant captains bid on these commodities in exchange for their cargoes. Hence the Americans were often forced to sell their goods "for a trifle and not being allowed to make a choice of produce, being forced to buy rum, they sometimes sink half their capitals."[15]

The one-sidedness of trade with the West Indies and the limits placed on this trade by Great Britain made it clear to commercially minded men like Jacob Crowninshield that something must be done to change the status quo:

Great Britain will calculate . . . [her] shipping can come to our ports, take our lumber, beef and pork, fish, flour, rice, etc., and supply her own islands. She will attempt this while our vessels will not be admitted. She will expect us to receive her ships destined to her own colonies with American produce while our ships will not be allowed to export to them a single barrel of beef or flour. This would be a ruinous system for us to put up with. We could not long put up with it. We should be obliged to refuse the exportation of supplies to her Colonies in her bottoms until the two flags were placed on an equal footing. She can have no claim to a trade under her flag which she would deny to others.[16]

Nevertheless, lacking a blue-water navy to guard its merchant fleet, the United States could do little about the situation. During this time Jefferson occasionally pondered an alliance with Great Britain as a means to resolve the problem of neutral trade. However, Madison quickly reminded the president that Great Britain remained the mortal enemy of the United States. He pointed out that an alliance with Britain would require America to give up much without getting anything in return. Moreover, at some point such a deal would no doubt force the United States to become involved in England's continual wars against Napoleon. Madison argued that the British had no real interest in seeing American commerce succeed. He believed that the British were just like his arch Federalist political enemy Alexander Hamilton—in a word, untrustworthy. As historian Garry Wills artfully noted, "Madison looked at England and saw only so many thousands of Hamiltons. Why ally oneself with the source of one's own corruption?"[17]

Consequently, both Jefferson and Madison remained highly suspicious of British economic intent throughout the Napoleonic era. To make matters worse, transatlantic communication between the two nations, always difficult in the early nineteenth century, became confused. The *Essex* broken voyages ruling greatly alarmed American envoys in London, James Monroe and William Pinkney. The situation became so bad that the king's advocate, Sir John Nicholl, felt compelled to relay to American merchants via the Board of Trade that "some vessels were seized . . . under a notion that it was illegal for an American ship to convey Colonial Produce from America to Europe; and this misapprehension became so strong, that it was fully believed by many here, and by more in America, that special Instructions to that Effect had been issued by His Majesty's Government." Many of these ships would be restored to their owners after a hearing before an Admiralty court, but this might take years. Meanwhile, the American merchant lost thousands of dollars as he waited for his day in court. Moreover, the British reaffirmed their post-*Essex* policy with the Admiralty court ruling in the case of the ship *William* in May 1806. This time, the British announced well in advance that broken voyages were a thing of the past and American commerce could no longer claim trade protection by performing "mere voluntary ceremonies."[18]

A second significant maritime issue that angered many Americans in the years leading up to the War of 1812 was the impressment of sailors from American merchant vessels. As a neutral nation, America did not overly object to having its vessels searched for contraband goods while they were in international waters. Such searches happened all the time during this era of nearly constant warfare. However, involuntarily seizing crew members and forcing them to serve on board a Royal Navy man-of-war was another matter altogether.

The issue of impressment had long been anathema to most Americans, and the presence of a press gang in a seaport such as Boston or New York usually meant trouble. In 1747, for example, Admiral Charles Knowles famously ordered the impressment of men from a number of British colonial ports. However, when a British press gang visited Boston, Massachusetts, and seized forty-six dock-workers, three days of rioting ensued and forced the royal governor, William Shirley, to flee the city for the protection of Castle William in the middle of the harbor. Eventually, fellow dockworkers and sailors were able to gain the release of their impressed comrades.

Even in Canada, the presence of press gangs occasionally caused local turmoil. In 1805, in Halifax, Nova Scotia, Vice Admiral Andrew Mitchell authorized press gangs from the HMS *Cleopatra* to rove the streets of the city armed with bayonets in an effort to impress desperately needed sailors. The press took nearly anyone it found, violating laws regarding who might be pressed and under what conditions, and rioting broke out that resulted in one man being killed and dozens of others injured. The unrest was so severe that long-serving lieutenant governor of Nova Scotia Sir John Wentworth remonstrated with Admiralty officials in London to order Halifax press gangs to confine their activities to what was allowed by local law. In the past a press had been reasonably tolerated by Crown officials in Nova Scotia. For example, from 1793 to 1805 "the Nova Scotia Council issued thirteen impressment warrants, all with limits on time (usually two weeks or less) and the number of men that could be taken (most ranged between twenty and seventy). The longtime exemption for the colony's permanent residents also remained in place. During the period, only two requests were denied." However, owing to the 1805 riot, the council did not approve another single warrant until the War of 1812.[19]

"Manning the Navy," a political cartoon of a British press gang. Originally published by Bentley and Co. in *Attic Miscellany*, 1 June 1790

Two significant underlying issues complicated the impressment issue: nationality and legal protection from a press. Just who was an American citizen in 1812? Who was legally eligible to be impressed? How a person became a naturalized citizen of another country was still evolving as an international legal concept, and in the years following the American Revolution, the United States had certainly received its fair share of immigrants. Although the British recognized the right of nations to naturalize immigrants and conferred such citizenship themselves, they did not believe at that time that a British subject could ever totally renounce his or her birth obligations to the British sovereign. In essence, once a British subject, always a British subject. Sir John Nicholl succinctly summed up the commonly held British position on the matter:

> Individuals owe an Allegiance and Duty to that State of which they are natural born subjects. From this Allegiance and Duty they cannot, without the consent of the State, release themselves. A most important part of this Allegiance and Duty is to assist their Country when engaged in War. This Duty to their Country is prior and paramount to any Contract or Engagement they can enter into with another State or its

Inhabitants. Hence arises the right to compel natural born Subjects by Punishment or Impressment to return to their Duty, notwithstanding they may have been admitted Burghers or Citizens, or engaged as Mariners in the service of another State. The Principal had been put in Practice by this Country since time immemorial. The Practice has been admitted on the part of other States by acquiescence in it, and in the Public Proclamations enforcing it.[20]

Further, the international character of the Atlantic seafaring community made it hard to sort out what sailors belonged to which nation at any given time. To add to the complexity, the idea that a vessel in international waters was an extension of a nation's territorial sovereignty had not yet been fully established in international law. The British believed that once on the high seas, a mariner of British birth, regardless of whether he claimed to be a naturalized citizen of another country, enjoyed no special protection from impressment. The Americans argued the opposite view and held that their vessels at sea were a direct extension of their national sovereignty. In fact, Madison strongly pressed this point with American envoy James Monroe when he wrote on 5 January 1804, "We consider a neutral flag, on the high seas, as a safeguard to those sailing under it." In essence, Madison believed the flag itself constituted adequate protection, although in the same letter he admitted that Great Britain had "not yet adopted, in the same latitude with most other nations, the immunities of a neutral flag." Madison was convinced that he was in the right. He challenged the British to consult international treaties on the subject of freedom of the seas. He argued that such documents all focused on contraband cargo, "enemies serving in war," and "articles going into blockaded ports," but nowhere included language "which justifies the taking away of *any* person, *not an enemy in military service* [emphasis in the original], found on board a neutral vessel."[21] Madison stated that if the situation and conditions were reversed and British citizens, naturalized or native-born, were taken by an American press gang, England would certainly never stand for it.

Nevertheless, to avoid being pressed into the Royal Navy, merchant sailors working on a vessel flying the American flag were sometimes given written legal protection from a local magistrate or notary that verified they were native-born or naturalized citizens of the United States. They were supposed to carry this documentation with them at all times. The documents provided their place of birth, the town in which they resided, and a physical description of the sailor in a halfhearted attempt to circumvent any attempts at forgery. However, at least according to the British, forgery was rampant, and anyone could buy a legal protection from a notary for as little as a quarter of a dollar—money well spent if it saved you from forcible service on a British man-of-war.

In the years leading up to the War of 1812, it is estimated, nearly 30 percent of the 70,000-man American merchant fleet was British-born sailors. Only a handful of these men (1,500) ever went to the trouble of becoming legally naturalized citizens of the United States.[22] Most preferred to remain international citizens of the sea, working vessels of various nations that best served their personal interests at any given time. Thus, it was possible but unlikely that naturalized American citizens were taken by the press. However, legitimate native-born Americans were occasionally taken and forced to serve long terms on notoriously lethal British warships. These instances seemed to especially provoke the American political establishment. Moreover, in an era during which hypernationalism was not uncommon, impressment of native-born citizens was seen by many as an especially gross violation of national honor—a violation that demanded a response.

There can be no doubt that the British were desperate for naval manpower throughout the Napoleonic era. By the War of 1812, the Royal Navy had more than tripled in size and listed 584 ships of varying size on its active register list. Such a robust navy required about 114,000 men, up from the 36,000 it had formerly needed in 1793, at the beginning of the wars of the French Revolution. Life on a Napoleonic-era man-of-war was notorious for its brutality, and men would go to great lengths to avoid serving on such vessels. Moreover, unlike more lucrative merchant vessels, Royal Navy vessels did not "pay off" or muster out sailors after an extensive voyage. Instead, navy sailors were required to remain part of a ship's company unless they died in the service from shipboard disease, accident, or battle wounds. The crew was normally discharged only when a warship was laid up "in ordinary" (mothballed until the next conflict), placed in dry dock for extensive repairs, or entirely stricken from the active register. The lengthy wars of the French Revolution and Napoleonic era thus meant years of servitude for the average British tar. Service was so onerous that in 1797 the British experienced two large-scale sailor mutinies that ended with many of the principal conspirators of the second mutiny being publicly executed. If required to remain in service, most Royal Navy sailors were not likely to see their thirtieth birthdays. A survey of British naval casualties in 1810 revealed that a full 50 percent of the 5,183 fatalities that occurred that year were caused by disease. Another 31.5 percent were killed in accidents, and an additional 10.2 percent died when ships were lost at sea or blown up. Only 8.3 percent of all casualties were caused by enemy action. Nevertheless, many saw extended time on a Royal Navy man-of-war as a virtual death sentence. It was disease they feared, not necessarily a French man-of-war.[23]

To get enough men to replace those lost to combat, disease, accidents, and desertion, Great Britain had long used impressment to supplement the numbers gained by volunteers and men ordered by a magistrate to serve on board a navy vessel in lieu of a prison term. Even Horatio Nelson noted that "without a press" he had "no idea how our Fleet can be manned."[24] Impressment was an established and recognized tradition used throughout the British Atlantic community. Other European nations had similar systems. During the Napoleonic era the Royal Navy received an estimated 50 percent of its manpower from impressment alone.[25]

Ashore, a press gang was often commanded by a Royal Navy officer who, along with trusted boatswain's mates and hired street toughs, would rove through various communities in search of able-bodied males who could be tricked, beguiled, or, if necessary, forced to become part of a ship's company. While the press preferred to focus on communities with populations that likely possessed a modicum of seagoing skill, during times of war it would take just about anyone who was unfortunate enough to fall in with it. This especially included sailors from the British merchant fleet and those who Royal Navy officers suspected were British subjects or deserters working for neutral nations. Classes of people—such as overage sailors, merchant ship master's mates, officers, and apprentices—often had written legal protection from the press. Such people were required to carry their "protection" documentation with them at all times. However, during wartime, a "hot press" was occasionally authorized to take men regardless of the category of protection they fell under.

In truth, still-at-sea England-bound merchant vessels were primary targets for most press gangs because seized men were likely to be skilled sailors vice unskilled or semiskilled landsmen caught in an inland town or coastal village. There was also little to no opportunity for these pressed sailors to escape. Although the press gang was technically required to leave a merchant ship with a minimum number of able-bodied seamen to navigate the vessel to its destination port, this number was subject to wide interpretation by the officer in charge. The press gang was not legally authorized to molest merchant ships on the outward-bound legs of their voyages, but this rule was also not always faithfully observed. Consequently, when a press gang did take a merchant sailor, it often substituted "ticket-men," or "men-in-lieu," for those being taken for royal service. Ticket-men were given papers, or a "ticket," that described their appearance and provided written notice that they were serving the merchant vessel in place of a pressed man and should be allowed to return to the Royal Navy upon reaching port. These men seemed to come in two categories: exceptionally trustworthy (since the opportunity for desertion was quite high) or essentially valueless, meaning that the Royal Navy was ambivalent over whether they returned or not. Thus, a captain often unloaded a troublemaker or chronically sick or injured sailor and gained a skilled, healthy mariner in return—a good deal for the Royal Navy but a bad one for a merchant trying to get his ship into home port.

The practice of impressing American seamen throughout the wars of the French Revolution and Napoleonic era was a long-smoldering problem. Estimates widely vary over just how many "American" sailors were impressed, but a figure of ten thousand total sailors (of various nationalities) seems reasonable.[26]

From 1796 to late 1805, the United States and its principal trading partner, Great Britain, were bound by the Treaty of Amity, Commerce, and Navigation (commonly called the Jay Treaty after its chief American negotiator, Chief Justice of the United States John Jay). This treaty served to mitigate tension between Great Britain and the United States, and while it did resolve a number of issues left over from the American Revolution—most notably the removal of British military outposts in the Old Northwest and the establishment of American commercial rights as a neutral nation—it did not contain any provision for ending impressment. To get around this thorny issue, Lord William Grenville promised Jay he would write new orders in council and direct the Royal Navy to avoid impressing legitimate American-born sailors. Again, determining just who was an American proved to be extraordinarily difficult.

The treaty itself was only slightly favorable to the American commercial sector (as Treasury Secretary Alexander Hamilton hoped it would be), but it did dampen the Royal Navy's pretreaty enthusiasm for taking American merchant vessels and impressing some of their sailors. However, the treaty remained unpopular with the rising, agrarian-leaning Republican Party since it seemed to benefit the Federalist commercial sector most. Moreover, antislavery envoy John Jay did not press the British to compensate American slave owners who had lost their slaves to British forces during the Revolution; hence, the Republicans in the southern states viewed the treaty with disdain. In a large number of American cities and towns, the news of the treaty's ratification was greeted with mobs burning Jay's effigy from a makeshift scaffold. Once again, the issue of impressment remained unresolved.

No sooner was the ink dry on the Jay Treaty than Republican Party newspapers—and even some with Federalist credentials—began printing stories of the Royal Navy's continued abuse of American sailors. Many Republicans, including Thomas Jefferson, saw impressment as a key wedge issue that could discredit and embarrass their rival Alexander Hamilton and the Federalist Party. While such politically motivated newspaper accounts need to be taken with a grain of salt, the sheer number of them revealed that even if magnified, the hated and continued practice of impressment was still alive and well.

Many of these impressment newspaper stories began with a sarcastic reference to the Jay Treaty, such as "Evidences of British Amity, More British Amity" or simply "British Piracy."[27] British West Indian ports seemed to be the worst places for alleged impressment abuse. The 4 July 1795 edition of the *Jersey Chronicle*, edited by Philip Freneau, a notoriously pro-Republican editor, published several firsthand accounts from American merchant captains who stated that the British frigate HMS *Success* at St. Jeremie had impressed two-thirds of the Americans in that port and that one American vessel had all her hands taken. On 22 August 1795 the *Jersey Chronicle* continued with more stories reporting that the British frigate HMS *Hermione*, also in port at St. Jeremie, had pressed 60 American sailors. However, the port with the worst reputation by far was Kingston, Jamaica. One American merchant, Captain Brown of the *Nancy*, reported via the 22 March 1796 *Jersey Chronicle* that during his time in Kingston, at least 150 American vessels had come into port, and most of them had their sailors taken in large numbers—a few allegedly had all their men seized. Brown stated that pressed men often had their printed certificates of protection taken or tossed into the harbor. One merchant captain told of being boarded by British frigate press gangs on three separate occasions.

Captain Figsby of the American brig *Fan Fan* reported via the New York *Argus* on 8 June 1796 that he had sailed in April 1796 from Jamaica for Guadeloupe and was boarded by the British privateer *Sea Nymph*, whose press gang proceeded

John Jay Burned in Effigy by Felix Octavius Carr Darley. Courtesy of the New York Public Library, 814266

to generally abuse him and seize two of his crew. But they did not stop there. The *Sea Nymph* gang then allegedly "robbed [Figsby] of a great part of his poultry, suffered him to proceed, though not without taking away his colours and damning the American Flag." Two days later, the American vessel was boarded by yet another British warship, this time "called the *Unicorn*, of 18 guns, who treated him at first very politely, but before they left the vessel robbed him of four sheep, three hogs, and the remainder of his poultry; and taking from him by force, another of his crew (Josh White) of Massachusetts and sending in his room two disabled American seamen [who ha]d been wounded in a late engage[ment,] whom [Captain Figsby] landed in Philadelphia."[28] Again, even if this account is only partially true, it appears aggressive impressment situations continued and occasionally devolved into a form of legalized piracy.

By 1805, about the same time the Jay Treaty was set to expire, the situation between Great Britain and the United States on the high seas rapidly deteriorated. Following the *Essex* ruling, President Thomas Jefferson urged Congress to pass the first of two nonimportation acts directed at Great Britain. In truth, both Jefferson and his ubiquitous secretary of state, James Madison, were consistent disciples of economic coercion as means to force policy change on powerful Great Britain. Jefferson also instructed his envoys in London, James Monroe and William Pinkney, to craft a new treaty that might resolve the growing chasm between the two nations.

Known as the Monroe-Pinkney treaty, this document will forever remain a historical "might have been," primarily owing to the failure, once again, of American envoys to convince the Crown to modify its impressment policy for naturalized or native-born sailors employed on American vessels. In early March 1807, when British ambassador David M. Erskine received a final draft of the treaty, he rushed it over to the secretary of state's office so that Madison could submit it to the Senate for ratification before the senators adjourned. While hopeful the treaty would meet with the secretary's approval, Erskine was crestfallen when Madison "expressed the greatest astonishment and Disappointment" in the document.[29] In fact, both Madison and Thomas Jefferson believed that the treaty overly favored the British point of view. Jefferson decided to not even submit the treaty for ratification, much to the ire of his Federalist opposition. A Federalist newspaper, the Boston-based *Columbian Centinel*, considered it "extraordinary" that the president rejected the work of his own appointed ministers. As the outbreak of armed conflict approached in 1812, Federalist complaints rose to a crescendo, as many were convinced that the stillborn Monroe-Pinkney treaty might have avoided war with the British altogether. As the editors of the 31 January 1812 *Alexandria Daily Gazette* artfully wrote, "The rejection of that treaty, the responsibility of which act Mr. Jefferson has boldly taken to himself, has been the fruitful source of all the evils, which we have suffered from embargoes and non-importation acts, and may soon suffer from war."[30]

In reality, the Monroe-Pinkney treaty might have extended the commercial benefits the United States had previously derived from the defunct Jay Treaty. While it required greater American restriction on trade to India and forbade the

United States from employing future economic sanctions against Great Britain, it allowed a modified form of broken voyages that had so benefited the American commercial sector before the *Essex* ruling. Most important, the treaty indemnified American shippers from losses incurred while they waited for an Admiralty court ruling. Nevertheless, Jefferson decided to return the treaty to London for revision but held no real hope that the British would entertain his new conditions.[31]

The 1807 establishment of a new Tory government in London proved to be the final nail in the coffin of Monroe-Pinkney. To make the situation worse, it was well-known throughout the Atlantic maritime community that the Americans offered wages that were nearly twice the going rate for British vessels. This disparity encouraged numbers of British sailors to desert the Royal Navy and even their commercial ships for more lucrative Yankee vessels. The British naval officer in charge of the North American station, Vice Admiral George Cranfield Berkeley, was quite chagrined over the matter. He declared, "The high wages given both in their Men of War and trading Ships cannot be withstood by the Men." Berkeley believed that American ships were providing a safe haven for British deserters and that he could easily press "above 10,000 English Seamen . . . [who] are at present employed in the Service of the Americans." Even U.S. treasury secretary Albert Gallatin estimated that approximately "9000 men, or one-half of the able seamen aboard U.S. merchantmen employed in foreign commerce, were British subjects."[32] While it is impossible to corroborate either Berkeley's or Gallatin's estimates, contemporary writing on the subject made clear that the British believed large numbers of their valuable sailors were jumping ship for American employment. Further, owing to the failure of the Monroe-Pinkney treaty to normalize U.S.-British maritime relations, Secretary of State Madison could truthfully use the argument that the United States was under no treaty obligation to assist Britain in the recovery of deserters. This lack of communication quickly led to further difficulty.

In December 1806 the British consul at Norfolk, Virginia, Colonel John Hamilton, received a request from the Americans to release three men they believed had been erroneously pressed by the Royal Navy's Chesapeake Squadron. This squadron was in the region because several French warships, damaged by an August hurricane, were known to have sought refuge in the ports of Annapolis and Norfolk. Hamilton sent the request to the commanding officer of the station, Royal Navy captain John Erskine Douglas. Douglas responded that two of the men were not impressed and were being held until their vessels were released. He refused to release the third man because Douglas claimed that the man had volunteered for service and taken a bounty for enlisting in the Royal Navy.

Douglas' ships put into the Port of Norfolk to replenish their water casks, but the visit also created an opportunity for a number of British sailors and marines to desert. A few of the marines were allegedly later seen wearing U.S. Army uniforms at nearby Fort Nelson. Five sailors from the frigate HMS *Melampus* escaped after commandeering their captain's gig. British consul Hamilton contacted local U.S. Navy representative Captain Stephen Decatur because he believed some of these deserters were attempting to join the USS *Chesapeake*, then also in port. Decatur merely referred Hamilton back to the local Norfolk authorities and was of no further help. Five more sailors from the eighteen-gun sloop HMS *Halifax*, commanded by Captain Lord James Townshend, commandeered another longboat from a midshipman. Only one of these five men had been born in America: William Hill of Philadelphia. The other four were British born. One of them, Jenkin Ratford, immediately changed his name to John Wilson once ashore. Ratford quickly enlisted for service on board the USS *Chesapeake*. This sailor would be at the center of what became known as the *Chesapeake-Leopard* affair.

Captain Townshend tenaciously tried to recover his missing men. He encountered one of his five deserted sailors, Henry Saunders, on the streets of Norfolk and convinced him to return to the *Halifax*. However, before either man got very far, Jenkin Ratford appeared and, grabbing Saunders by the arm, loudly declared that "he would be damned if [he or Saunders] should return to the ship; that he was in the Land of Liberty; and that he would do as he liked, and that [Townshend] had no business with him."[33] Ratford then allegedly proceeded to use abusive language toward his former commanding officer. This in turn caused Townshend to directly complain to Consul Hamilton, whereupon Hamilton appealed to Decatur, the mayor, and Lieutenant Arthur Sinclair, the recruiting officer of the USS *Chesapeake*—all to no avail. The mayor was advised by his attorney, Littleton Tazewell, not to assist the British in the recovery of their men "on the grounds that the case was not covered by either federal treaty or state law." Hamilton appealed to Ambassador Erskine in Washington, and Erskine took the matter up directly with Secretary of State Madison. Madison reminded the ambassador once again that no formal treaty between the two nations existed; hence, he had no legal grounds or reason for helping the British recover their deserters.[34]

All of this information was forwarded by Captain Townshend to Vice Admiral Berkeley at Bermuda. Townshend told Berkeley that he firmly believed at least thirty-five men on board the USS *Chesapeake* were British deserters. Townshend added that these deserters were now "patrolling the Streets of Norfolk in triumph." This news enraged Berkeley, who was still upset over the banning of some of his ships from American ports owing to the previous activity of the HMS *Leander*. Of little note to many historians today, the *Leander* affair had far-reaching implications for the future of American-British relations leading up to the War of 1812. The incident occurred off the coast of New York and involved the refusal of the American merchant vessel *Richard* to stop in order to be inspected for contraband by the HMS *Leander*. This refusal caused the captain of the British ship to fire into the *Richard*. American merchant seaman John Pierce was subsequently killed by a large wooden splinter. The British boarding party found no contraband. However, Pierce's death caused a public uproar in New York City. Angry anti-British crowds paraded the deceased man's body throughout the dockside areas. The American government responded by ordering that the *Leander* and other ships (but not all) of Berkeley's North American squadron were no longer allowed to put into American ports.[35]

The *Leander* incident was followed in rapid succession by a second incident caused by the sloop of war HMS *Driver*'s putting into port at Charleston, South Carolina, on 2 May 1807. The *Driver*'s captain, William Love, claimed the locals had given him a hard time over getting his water casks filled. Love threatened to use force to get what he needed. This caused the captain and his ship to quickly become persona non grata with the citizens of Charleston. He was given twenty-four hours' notice to leave town and wisely complied, but he also dutifully reported the incident to Berkeley. These issues likely helped form the peremptory decision by Vice Admiral Berkeley to order the interception of the USS *Chesapeake*, then known to be readying for an extended cruise to the Mediterranean, and its inspection for the deserters he was sure were on board. Berkeley was also considerably upset that the Americans denied his vessels the use of their ports while the damaged French ships continued to have this privilege.

Berkeley lamented to Ambassador Erskine that he had no specific instruction on what actions he was authorized to take regarding the increasing number of incidents between his ships and the American ones. Anxious to make a statement about deserters and perhaps to respond forcefully to the *Leander* and *Driver* incidents, Berkeley sent out a fateful proclamation:

Whereas many seamen, subjects of his Britannick Majesty, and in his majesty's ship and vessels ... while at anchor in the Chesapeake, deserted and entered on board the US frigate *Chesapeake* and openly paraded in the streets of Norfolk, in sight of their officers, under the American flag, protected by the magistrates of the town, and the recruiting officer belonging to the above mentioned American frigate, which magistrates and naval officer refused giving them up, although demanded by his Britannick Majesty's consul, as well as the captains of the ships from which said men deserted.

The Captains and commanders of his majesty's ships and vessels ... [are] hereby required and directed, in case of meeting with the American frigate *Chesapeake*, at sea, and without the limits of the U. States, to shew to the captain of her, this order, and to require to search his ship for the deserters ...; and if a similar demand shall be made by the American, he is to be permitted to search for any deserters from their service.[36]

In response to Erskine's constant hectoring over alleged deserters on the USS *Chesapeake*, Madison somewhat relented and ordered Secretary of the Navy Robert Smith to have Commodore James Barron, senior naval officer in Norfolk, look into the issue of the alleged HMS *Melampus* deserters: William Ware, John Little, Daniel Martin, and John Strachan. Barron quickly responded that he believed that three of the four men in question were indeed American citizens (Ware, Martin, and Strachan) who had been previously impressed off merchant vessels by the Royal Navy. Strachan and Ware claimed they carried protections that had been ignored by the press gang. Martin said he had lost his paperwork. Barron added that John Strachan, who claimed to be a resident of Maryland's Eastern Shore, had been taken by a press gang from the *Melampus* two years earlier in the Bay of Biscay while he was employed on board a British-owned merchant vessel. The British truthfully countered that Strachan had volunteered for service on board the British frigate on 15 March 1805. They also admitted that the other two Americans had originally been pressed men but said they served on board the *Melampus* for only a few weeks before they returned to port at Plymouth, whereupon they joined the commercial brig *Neptune*.

This activity was corroborated by the *Neptune*'s American master, Captain Crofts. In 1807, following the *Chesapeake-Leopard* affair, Crofts testified to Albert

Gallatin that his brig had been stopped by the *Melampus* in the Bay of Biscay and that the British had in fact pressed a number of his crew, Ware and Martin among them. However, Crofts further stated that both these men later deserted the *Neptune* after he had confronted Ware about a stolen bag of coffee. The accusation had caused Ware to swear "he would do no more duty on board [the *Neptune*]." On 3 January 1806, while they were ashore to fill water casks, both Ware and Martin made good on their promise and enlisted as volunteers on the HMS *Melampus*. These especially enterprising sailors remained with the *Melampus* until they deserted a third time and joined the USS *Chesapeake*, then at Norfolk, Virginia.[37] Thus, it can be said that Ware and Martin were impressed Americans, Royal Navy volunteers, and serial deserters all at the same time.

The USS *Chesapeake* set sail for a cruise to the Mediterranean on 22 June 1807. Not expecting trouble from any of the ubiquitous British vessels lingering around Cape Henry, Commodore James Barron was initially unconcerned when Captain Salusbury P. Humphreys of the HMS *Leopard* hailed the *Chesapeake* soon after she had cleared the light at Cape Henry. Humphreys requested that Barron stop for a short conference. Because the *Chesapeake* had earlier sailed past larger British warships, such as the powerful seventy-four-gun HMS *Bellona*, without incident and because the commodore was unaware of Berkeley's inspection order, Barron complied.

At this point Barron was shown Vice Admiral Berkeley's orders to search his ship for deserters. Impressing merchant seamen was one thing, but national honor, then or now, did not tolerate a warship being forcibly searched for anything, much less deserters from another nation. When Barron naturally refused the demand, Humphreys decided he was required by his order to force compliance. The *Leopard* was very close to the *Chesapeake*, with its lower gun ports open and tampions (gun muzzle plugs) removed. But the *Chesapeake* was not ready for any sort of response. Its magazine was in disarray, with lumber, cargo, canvas, and other gear strewn about. After he had repeatedly hailed Barron to allow the inspection, Humphreys proceeded to fire a broadside directly into the *Chesapeake*. Round shot smashed into the ship's hull primarily amidships and sprayed jagged wooden splinters all around. Barron himself was wounded in the leg by at least two pieces of wood. The commodore hailed Humphreys that he was going to send a boat over. This was a ruse to buy more time; the British commander saw it as such and fired a second broadside into the American vessel. The British fired at least one more broadside, although the Americans later claimed a total of five were fired. Amazingly, owing to the confusion on board the *Chesapeake*, only a single return shot was ever fired, and this for "honor's sake," which required an officer to carry a live coal from the galley in his bare hands in order to fire the weapon. With three men dead and sixteen more wounded (one of whom would later die), Barron struck his colors, and the British ceased firing. The action lasted approximately fifteen to twenty minutes. British officers and sailors, now on board the *Chesapeake*, seized Jenkin Ratford, who loudly protested that he was John Wilson, an American sailor. The *Leopard*'s purser knew better and positively identified Ratford as a British deserter. The other alleged deserters from the *Melampus*—William Ware, John Strachan, and Daniel Martin—were also set aside. Interestingly, only Ratford received a court-martial death sentence for mutiny, desertion, and contempt. He was hanged from the foremast of his former ship, the HMS *Halifax*. Before he died, he admitted he had been born in Yorkshire. The other three prisoners were indeed American, but since they had "volunteered" for Royal Navy service, they were convicted of desertion and sentenced to receive five hundred lashes. However, before the sentence was carried out, the lashes were remitted "in consideration of their former good conduct," and the men were ultimately restored to the U.S. Navy. Unfortunately, William Ware died of disease while in temporary captivity. Strachan and Martin rejoined the *Chesapeake* at Boston in 1812.[38] In 1811, after much negotiation, the British finally disavowed the attack and promised some amount of restitution—restitution that was never paid.

Although it can be said that the *Chesapeake-Leopard* affair did not directly cause the War of 1812 since the issue was peaceably resolved before the war, the affair's aftereffects resounded throughout the Atlantic community. While the Americans and British argued over the finer points of international maritime law, a directed search for deserters on a foreign warship had no precedent and was indisputably outside acceptable norms, even in 1807. Anti-British fury erupted in America, especially so in the *Chesapeake*'s home port of Norfolk. The town passed a series of punitive resolutions that called for an end to all assistance (meaning food and water) to British ships still in the region and asked that its citizens wear black crepe for a ten-day mourning period. A mob proceeded to destroy two hundred water casks intended for the HMS *Melampus*. When a British naval officer of the HMS *Bellona* named Manderson tried to deliver messages for Consul Hamilton, his presence ashore caused an angry mob to gather at Hamilton's residence. If it had not been for the mayor reluctantly sending local militia to restore order, Manderson may have possibly been torn apart by the angry crowd.

President Thomas Jefferson ordered defensive preparations made throughout the United States in the event war broke out over the incident. Amazingly, the British refused to back off and sent their warships into American territorial waters both at Hampton Roads and inside Sandy Hook off New York City. There was an actual clash between a landing party in search of water and a Virginia militia company near Norfolk that resulted in the surrender of British sailors who were eventually restored to their ship. Cooler heads finally prevailed on both sides of the Atlantic when in October 1807 the British government emitted a proclamation that stopped future searches for deserters on board other nations' warships. The Admiralty recalled both Berkeley and Humphreys. However, Berkeley, who likely had better political connections than former frigate captain Humphreys, was later given another command and a promotion, much to the ire of Secretary of State Madison. Humphreys was treated more harshly: he was put on half pay in 1808 and would largely remain in that status for the rest of his long naval career. Although promoted to rear admiral in 1840, he never again commanded at sea. Humphreys went to his grave haunted by his role in the *Chesapeake-Leopard* affair.[39]

Throughout these tumultuous prewar years, some were convinced that the Americans made a bigger issue of impressment than was actually merited. British chargé d'affaires Edward Thornton was squarely in this camp. He believed that his nation suffered as much from seduction and desertion of its seamen as the United States did from impressment. Thornton felt that Jefferson made much of impressment to curry political favor with maritime-oriented New England. He also believed Jefferson purposely stirred up trouble over impressment to coax France to pressure its ally Spain to cede East Florida (at some point) to the United States. On 3 December 1805 Phineas Bond, the British consul in Philadelphia, wrote to Foreign Secretary Lord Mulgrave, stating that the Americans had wrongly combined the "recent detention of American ships" as a result of the *Essex* ruling with "the Impressments of American Seamen, and endeavor to excite universal Resentment against us." Thornton, Ambassador Anthony Merry, and Merry's successor, David Erskine, believed the true bone of contention between Great Britain and the United States was sailor desertion and not impressment at all.[40]

Jefferson now decided to play what he perceived to be his remaining trump card against the British: economic sanctions. In 1807, thanks to the anti-British feelings generated by the *Chesapeake-Leopard* affair, Jefferson convinced Congress to pass the Embargo Act, which extended the provisions of the Nonimportation Act of 1806. The embargo, which technically lasted until 1809, can only be seen as an unmitigated economic disaster for the United States and the worst idea that Jefferson and Madison ever had. The embargo became a source of great suffering for an American economy already beset by the reinvigorated orders in council and Napoleon's continental system. Jefferson was forced to use his own military to stop rampant smuggling from taking place inside the United States. Part of a larger program of Republican Party economic coercion, eventually called the restrictive system, Jefferson's various nonimportation and embargo acts combined to send the previously thriving American economy into a severe tailspin. While in his final days in office, Jefferson replaced the Embargo Act with a nonintercourse measure that affected only Britain and France; it was clear that economic coercion as a policy was not as effective as he and Madison had previously supposed. Even after war broke out in 1812, Madison continued to propose various economic measures against Great Britain, but Congress was no longer in the mood for such experimentation and denied them all.[41]

Within weeks of Madison's inauguration in 1809, there was a brief opportunity for the United States to avoid conflict with Great Britain, but time and circumstances worked against this possible outcome. On 23 January 1809 British foreign secretary George Canning wrote instructions to David Erskine in Washington, D.C., telling him to offer the withdrawal of the November 1807 orders in council if the Americans would modify the Nonintercourse Act as it pertained to Great Britain but leave it in place for France. Canning's instructions also provided an avenue for resolving the *Chesapeake* affair in the United States' favor that included monetary reparations for damages and to the families of those killed. Canning advised Erskine not to countenance any American requests for further punishment of Admiral Berkeley, the originator of the *Chesapeake* affair, beyond his recall from the North American station, and asked the United States to disavow Commodore Barron's enlistment of British deserters and to express disapproval of the treatment of British officials in Norfolk following the *Chesapeake* affair. In addition, the Americans were to discourage future desertion from His Majesty's vessels. Finally, the American government was to "renounce, during the Present War, the pretension of carrying on, in time of War, all Trade with the Enemies Colonies, from which she was excluded in Peace."[42] In sum, the Americans were to relent

"Ograbme, or the American Snapping-Turtle," a cartoon from 1807 that
shows American frustration over Jefferson's embargo, by Alexander Anderson.
Reprinted from Harpers' *Popular Cyclopaedia of United States History from the Aboriginal
Period*, by Lossing, page 438

to the British demand that they officially adhere to the Rule of 1756. From the
American point of view, yielding to this demand was not ideal, but it would enable
Yankee vessels to resume their lucrative carrying trade, at least with the British
West Indian colonies.

Unfortunately, Erskine did not receive these instructions until April 1809.
Nevertheless, he faithfully carried them out and concluded on 10 June 1809 what
became known as the Erskine Agreement. This agreement was a clear diplomatic
breakthrough for America, and although some policy dissonance still existed
between the two nations, especially as it related to the Rule of 1756, a path for
the resolution of their chief differences had been created. However, Canning did
not receive the agreement until July 1809, and by this time the U.S. Congress
had repealed the Embargo Act, just as it seemed to be having an effect on British
policy. Senator Samuel Smith of Maryland stated in Congress on 19 March 1809,
"The people were impatient under the embargo, and you [Congress] repealed it.
Yes, sir, it was repealed at the very moment when Great Britain, smarting under

its effects, was modifying her Orders in Council; and she would have done us complete justice but for the wavering indecisive conduct that she saw we were pursuing."[43] No longer worried about the effects of the embargo, Canning repudiated the Erskine Agreement, even though Erskine had largely followed his instruction letter of 23 January. Then Erskine was recalled home and replaced by Francis James Jackson. The demise of the Erskine Agreement ended the last best hope for immediate reconciliation between Great Britain and the United States.

There are several other issues historians cite as contributing to America's decision to go to war in 1812. The most important is related to the continued unrest in the Old Northwest Territory (including Ohio, Indiana, Illinois, Wisconsin, and Michigan), which many believed was generated by the British to keep Americans from consolidating their grip on the territory and to ensure that the American Indian tribes remained British allies in the event of a war with the United States. Although British Indian agents did actively keep the tribes supplied with trade goods (including weapons, shot, and powder), Great Britain did not exert actual direct control over the tribes' activities. At best the relationship between the British and the American Indians was indirect, and the individual tribes of the Old Northwest (including the Shawnee, Sauk, Kickapoo, Potawatomi, and Miami) went to war or declared peace according to their interests at any given time.[44]

Nevertheless, most Americans at the time were not blind to the rise of a pan-Indian confederacy in the region being organized by the Shawnee tribal leaders, the Prophet and his brother Tecumseh. The confederacy arose in direct reaction to increased American land encroachment and lawlessness, but this fine point was lost to most whites who lived on the frontier. Most were firmly convinced the British were behind the unrest. The Prophet and Tecumseh were indeed supported by British arms, and this was enough to form the American Indians and British into a single monolithic entity in the minds of men like Indiana territorial governor William Henry Harrison.

At Harrison's request President Madison, seven months before the outbreak of war with Great Britain, authorized the governor and soon-to-be major general to destroy the native confederacy before it became too powerful. Harrison marched a thousand-man force of regulars and militia deep into Shawnee territory on 7 November 1811. They set up camp near Prophet's Town (modern-day Lafayette, Indiana)—considered the heart of the native confederacy—and were soon surprised by an attack from a smaller Indian force. Harrison's men managed to hang on and ultimately claimed victory over the Indians at the Battle of Tippecanoe, although they lost far more men defending the camp than the Indians did attacking it. Harrison was later criticized for the action at Tippecanoe, but still, the battle served to cement in the minds of Americans that the Indians of the Old Northwest—armed with British weapons, supplied with British goods, aided and abetted by British trade agents—were a perpetual security threat that needed to be resolved once and for all. Furthermore, while the Battle of Tippecanoe was just the opening round in a series of battles between native tribes and the Americans, it was important in forming the perception that by 1811 the British were somehow up to no good in the Old Northwest Territory.[45] It did not help that the British took years to abandon their military posts in the region—posts they had originally agreed to vacate in 1783.

2

THE WAR BEGINS

*D*uring the long, hot summer of 1812, James Madison, fourth president of the United States, out of options and perhaps patience, decided the time was right to declare war on Great Britain. In his war message to the Twelfth Congress, he asked whether "the United States shall continue passive under these progressive usurpations and these accumulating wrongs, or, opposing force to force in defense of our national rights, shall commit a just cause into the hands of the Almighty Disposer of Events."[1]

Madison's final decision to go to war against the militarily superior nation of Great Britain was based on several basic premises. First, thanks to the threat posed by Napoleon Bonaparte, the bulk of British military strength remained tied down in Europe and its surrounding seas. As long as Napoleon continued in power, Great Britain was never fully secure. Further, on 16 June 1812 Napoleon led a massive army on an ill-fated invasion of Russia. While no one at the time had any idea how Napoleon's gambit might turn out, it was clear to even an amateur strategist like Madison that this invasion would occupy the affairs of all the European powers for some time to come. Finally, domestic politics played a role. Many of Madison's own political party demanded a response to years of British abuse relating to maritime affairs and trade and Britain's continued support of the American Indian tribes that violently resisted American settlement in the Ohio country. By 1812 Madison, having tried since 1806 to deliver positive results for the United States using economic leverage that America really did not hold, believed the time was right to use military means. The British, of course, did not have quite the same perspective. They believed that they alone were holding the line against Napoleonic tyranny and that an American war declaration, coming at such a time, was nothing more than a treacherous stab in the back.

President James Madison's presidential portrait, 1829–30, by Chester Harding.
Courtesy of the National Portrait Gallery, NPG.68.50

Throughout the War of 1812, the British press and Tory politicians alleged wartime collusion between Madison and Napoleon. Although no evidence could confirm the validity of this claim, British political cartoonists such as George Cruikshank still went after America for declaring war. In his cartoon titled "A Sketch for the Regents Speech on Mad-Ass-Son's Insanity," Cruikshank depicts Great Britain in female form thrusting forth a shield toward the outstretched arm of an American Indian warrior. Madison is shown simultaneously appealing to both Napoleon and the devil exclaiming, "Tis you two that have brought this Disgrace upon me—Support me or I sink." To which Napoleon replies, "I suffer greater hardships than you! But the Devil will help us both." Hovering over both men is the angel Gabriel blowing a horn with the words "Bad news for you" coming out of it.[2]

This alleged French connection is repeatedly referred to in British newspapers. Much of this angst may have been due to British frustration with Madison's

"A Sketch for the Regents Speech on Mad-Ass-Son's Insanity," a political cartoon by George Cruickshank. Originally published in 1812 by Walter and Knight. British Cartoon Prints Collection, Prints and Photographs Division, Library of Congress, LC-USZC4-5917.

failure to understand the British view that the United States had far more to fear from an unchecked Napoleon than from its former mother country. British foreign secretary Lord Castlereagh, in the months leading up to the American declaration of war, constantly remonstrated with his minister in Washington, D.C., Augustus Foster, about the absolute necessity of convincing Madison that France, not Great Britain, was his true enemy. Castlereagh even sent Foster clippings from French newspapers advertising the sale of captured prize goods and vessels taken from the American merchant fleet under Napoleon's continental system so that he could show them to U.S. State Department representatives. Firm in their belief that only Great Britain and its "wooden walls" (the Royal Navy) stood between world freedom and Napoleonic tyranny, British politicians came to view Madison's Republicans, and Americans in general, as a body of grasping, opportunistic Francophiles who needed to be taught a hard lesson.[3]

Despite this British attitude Madison desired to take advantage of the time and space delay presented by the Atlantic Ocean. After all, Madison knew he was at war, whereas it would be over a month before the British government in London could be apprised of this same situation. Much might be accomplished in the interim—before the superior military might of Great Britain was assuredly brought to bear. The only possible way for the Americans to immediately and meaningfully affect Great Britain was to invade neighboring Canada. A rapid military victory there might achieve several political results in a single year. First, such a campaign could put an end to the continued and bloody hostility between American settlers in the Northwest Territory and American Indian tribes, now led by a formidable military leader, Tecumseh. Next, temporary occupation of Canadian soil could allow the United States to achieve some concessions from Great Britain—although the American political leadership never articulated what it intended to do with Canada if it indeed fell into American hands. Finally, attacking Canada would largely negate the one major military advantage the British possessed in the North American theater in 1812: its superb navy. An American army did not need to enlist its own miniscule navy to get to Canada or to worry about a British fleet potentially disrupting any invasion plans.

While some, like the acid-tongued John Randolph of Roanoke, characterized any move against Canada as nothing more than a naked land grab, nearly all the political documents of the time ignore this argument and focus instead on "Free Trade and Sailors' Rights" as the real cause for war. Nonetheless, this did not stop Randolph, leader of a Republican splinter group in Congress sometimes called Tertium Quids, or more accurately, Old Republicans. Randolph was a former ally of Jefferson and Madison but now believed that Jefferson's "heir" was leading the country to ruin. In refuting an 1811 Foreign Affairs Committee report, Randolph dramatically stated that all he now heard in Congress was "but one word—like the whip-poor-will, but one eternal monotonous tone—Canada! Canada! Canada!"[4]

Randolph's speech was high theater for the times, but he could not have been more wrong. In reality, Canada as a military objective was never well conceived by American military commanders. Even the notorious war hawk Speaker of the House Henry Clay candidly wrote in late 1813, "Canada was not the end but the means, the object of the War being the redress of [British inflicted] injuries [on the high seas], and Canada being the instrument by which that redress was to be obtained."[5] It should be noted that Clay spoke these words after the first American offensives in Canada had ended in dismal failure. A pro-war New York newspaper pointed out that taking Canada from Great Britain made eminent military sense. The writer of an editorial signed "Whig" believed going after Canada was important if only to deprive the British of "her supplies of naval stores . . . so necessary to her gigantic navy." With no small amount of hyperbole, the writer continued, "With our occupation of the Canadas . . . the savages would lose an instigator that offers gold for innocent scalps; and we should be relieved on our borders from a brace of enemies, savage and British, the one excelling in cruelty, the other in perfidy."[6]

As "Whig" indirectly noted, "the Canadas" were not a single political entity but actually six interconnected but separate colonies that stretched well over a thousand miles from the Great Lakes to Cape Breton (Newfoundland was considered separate from Canada). Attacking either end of this lengthy chain of sparsely populated provinces offered the United States no real military advantage. However, not knowing what else to do and lacking any sort of expertise in war planning, the American military leadership designed a three-pronged invasion of Upper and Lower Canada emanating from the Detroit and Niagara areas as well as the traditional, two-way Lake Champlain invasion route. A successful invasion might temporarily interdict the St. Lawrence River and possibly give Madison the leverage with Britain he so desperately sought.

As events turned out, the first few months of the war in the west found the Americans bogged down around Amherstburg on the north shore of Lake Erie and not all that distant from Detroit—a far cry from what had originally been envisioned. Almost as soon as the war began, the situation began to unravel for the Americans. Not only did the British and Canadians mount a credible resistance to the invasion, but the very capable British commander, Major General Isaac Brock, ordered a British detachment at Fort St. Joseph to attack the key American outpost at Michilimackinac, located at the confluence of three of the Great Lakes. Surprisingly, this crucial fort was weakly defended, and its American garrison had not yet even been notified by William Hull, general of the Army of the Northwest, that war had been declared. Fearful of Britain's Indian allies, the Americans surrendered Michilimackinac without a fight. Since they were surrounded by tribal warriors only loosely controlled by the British, this decision likely saved their lives. However, the loss of Michilimackinac had far-reaching consequences for the Americans. The fort's location was considered sacred ground to many of the still-wavering neutral tribes, and the Americans' defeat caused the tribes to abandon their earlier promise to remain neutral. Moreover, the loss of the post meant that the American Indians and other British forces could now threaten the rear of Hull's Army of the Northwest, raid his critical logistical support inside Michigan, and ultimately force him to retreat back to Detroit—which is exactly what happened.

The tribes' loyalty proved to be the center of gravity for the entire western campaign. Whoever they fought for was likely to prevail—at least at the beginning, before American wartime recruitment could fully kick in. The presence of a large body of American Indians at the siege of Fort Detroit was a major factor in Hull's ignominious 16 August 1812 surrender of the bastion. The day before Hull capitulated, Brock had sent the American a note stating that unless Fort Detroit was surrendered immediately, he could not guarantee control over his Indian allies—meaning they would likely butcher wounded and surrendered Americans if Brock were required to take the fort by storm. Having the Indians, far more numerous than the handful of British regulars in the region, as allies often proved to be a double-edged sword. Fighting in their traditional way and only loosely controlled by their British benefactors, the terrifying American Indian warriors were never loath to kill or scalp surrendered prisoners. In turn American soldiers would sometimes scalp fallen native warriors. The conflict between the two groups was brutal and had been this way in the region for decades—at least since Americans had begun moving into the Ohio territory en masse after the Revolution. Whereas the far fewer British regulars and Canadian militia might recognize the niceties of European-style warfare, in which surrendered prisoners were usually given quarter and a captured officer's private baggage and arms were often returned to him, the tribes followed no such conventions. If a captive was unable to replace a warrior lost in battle or to disease or if the opportunity to ransom him was not immediately at hand, the prisoner was more of a liability than an advantage to a fast-moving warrior in the still-rugged Great Lakes region.

Several early engagements illustrate the sheer brutality of the fighting in the northern American territories of Michigan, Indiana, and Illinois. On 5 August 1812 several dozen warriors, led by Tecumseh and Wyandot leader Roundhead, ambushed a detachment of approximately two hundred Americans, led by Major Thomas Van Horne, as they crossed Brownstown Creek. Seventeen Americans were struck down and scalped, "their corpses staked into the ground to terrify future expeditions." The lone native casualty was an interpreter known as Logan Blue Jacket. Blue Jacket's death caused Tecumseh to select two Americans for summary execution. Both men were dispatched by tomahawk blows to the head. Later, Dayton militia captain Robert Gilcrest was also killed as he was being conveyed by boat to Malden, Ontario: "A sqaw [sic] came up behind him and struck him with a tommyhauk [sic] to revenge the death of a son she [lost] in a fight."

Although British observers were clearly shocked by the behavior of their native allies, they hesitated to stop them. Thomas Vercheres de Boucherville summed up why this was so: "Our garrison was weak and these warriors were numerous enough to impose their will upon us."[7]

A little over a month later, the American garrison at Fort Dearborn (Chicago) was massacred by Potawatomis. The fort's commander, U.S. Army captain Nathan Heald, had been ordered by Hull to abandon Chicago and make his way toward Fort Wayne, Indiana. But the Potawatomis discovered his preparations to leave and began to gather around the fort. Thinking they might be assuaged if he gave them a significant portion of the fort's abandoned stores (except for the gunpowder and liquor supplies, which he ordered destroyed), Heald and most of his column—which included the women and children of the garrison, among them Heald's wife (who survived being wounded numerous times)—were killed or captured almost as soon as they left the fort.

The most sensational massacre of American soldiers occurred in early 1813 near present-day Monroe, Michigan, at a place called the River Raisin (the conflict was also known as the Battle of Frenchtown). Here a body of Kentucky militia was attacked by a mixed force of British and American Indians under Colonel Henry Procter. After a lengthy fight the American commander, Brigadier General James Winchester, was captured along with about five hundred of his men. About eighty Americans were seriously wounded in the fighting and unable to travel with their British captors back to Canada. It being winter, Procter promised to send sleighs back to retrieve these men the next day. However, during the night the Indians fell upon the wounded and killed about thirty of them. Some were burned alive in the houses that had been their temporary refuge. Roundhead had Winchester garishly tattooed across his face and upper body and forced the American to march around the camp to both the shock and merriment of nearby British officers.

The Americans held Procter personally responsible for what took place during and after the Battle of Frenchtown. "Remember the River Raisin" became an American rallying cry and highly effective recruiting slogan for the rest of the war. The battle on the river was certainly a factor in Major General William Henry Harrison's 4 October 1813 defeat of the charismatic Tecumseh and most of his immediate followers at the Battle of the Thames (Moravian Town). Both Tecumseh and Roundhead were killed in this engagement, and the carefully crafted Indian confederacy dissipated soon afterward.

"A View of Winchester in North America Dedicated to Mr. President Mad-I-Son!" a political cartoon showing captured Brigadier General James Winchester in Canada, 1813. Courtesy of the War of 1812 Collection, Lilly Library, Indiana University

Throughout the war Indian atrocity accounts flooded newspapers, and although they were frequently embellished, these incidents resonated with an American public raised on such stories. Moreover, once the British had imposed an effective blockade on American commerce in mid-1813, the issue of "Free Trade and Sailors' Rights" became moot. At that point very little trade was taking place. Instead, Madison turned attention toward the Indians, remarking in his March 1813 inaugural address that the British "let loose the savages . . . and carried them to battle by their sides, eager to glut their savage thirst with the blood of the vanquished, and to [inflict] the world of torture and death on maimed and defenseless captives."[8] The *Baltimore Whig* in May 1813 went even further: "Hang *four or five* Indians for every American massacred," the editors exclaimed, "and if it does not bring them to their senses it will at least go some way toward their *extermination* [emphasis in the original]."[9] Thus, the American public focus shifted, and the new demand was for retribution against the British and Indians around Detroit and Niagara. This served to keep the Canadian border as the primary focus of the American war effort—even when other parts of the United States later came under direct attack.

Bring me the Scalps
and the King our Master
will reward you

Reward for
the Scalps

Arise Columbia's Sons and forward press
Your Country's wrongs call loudly for redress
The savage Indian with his scalping knife
Or tomahawk may seek to take your life

By bravery aw'd they'll in a dreadful fright
Shrunk back for refuge to the woods in flight
Their British leaders then will quickly shake
And for those wrongs shall restitution make

"A Scene on the Frontiers as Practiced by the 'Humane' British and Their 'Worthy' Allies," in which the British officer says, "Bring me the scalps and the King our master will reward you." Etching by William Charles, 1812. Prints and Photographs Division, Library of Congress, LC-DIG-ppmsca-31111

Not to be outdone, the Americans did their share of raiding into Canada, although without the assistance of terror-inducing native warriors. On 21 September 1812 Captain Benjamin Forsyth and a hundred men successfully raided a Canadian supply depot at Gananoque, Ontario, driving out a small force of Canadian militia. The Americans seized supplies, burned the government warehouse, and withdrew back across the border. On 7 February 1813, thanks to the St. Lawrence River being solidly frozen, about two hundred Americans, again under Benjamin Forsyth, successfully raided Elizabethtown (modern-day Brockville), Ontario, to seize supplies and liberate some American prisoners known to be lodged in the town jail. Forsyth's raids prompted a sizable force of British regulars and Canadian militia, under Lieutenant Colonel "Red George" MacDonnell, to conduct a large-scale counterattack against the American operating base at Ogdensburg, New York, on 22 February 1813. Forsyth and his men resisted the British for a short while before being driven from town. The British seized military supplies and some cannon, burned two schooners and two gunboats frozen in the river ice, and returned to Canada for the rest of the winter. In sum, with neither side able to inflict a decisive blow on the other and with naval control of the Great Lakes still undecided, by February 1813 large-scale raids and punitive counterattacks had become wartime de rigueur.

By early spring of 1813, all three American land offensives were clearly in tatters. It was no wonder that the Yankee press made much ado about a few notable ship-to-ship victories won earlier that year by their tiny but now thoroughly respected U.S. Navy. These victories at sea certainly helped shore up sagging American morale once it became clear that taking Canada was not going to be as easy as many first thought. Soon after Madison had signed the declaration of war, Thomas Jefferson penned a foreboding letter to his friend William Duane, the editor of the pro-war Philadelphia-based newspaper *Aurora*. Jefferson argued, "The acquisition of Canada, this year, as far as the neighbourhood of Quebec, will be a mere matter of marching." Few get past Jefferson's misplaced overconfidence about Canada to see other key components of his letter. Most notably, the former president warned that owing to the deplorable state of American military readiness and experience, "we should expect disasters." Furthermore, Jefferson foresaw the vulnerability of America's great eastern ports to British sea power and wrote, "Their fleet will annihilate our public force on the water. . . . Perhaps they may burn New York or Boston. If they do, we must burn the city of London."[10] In sum, Jefferson envisioned a war with Great Britain verging toward a totality not yet seen on the continent of North America, even during the American Revolution. By the early spring of 1813, raids and retaliations were well established along the Canadian border; this type of warfare emerged to a slightly lesser degree during the summers of 1813 and 1814 in the Chesapeake Bay region.

One city not specifically mentioned in Jefferson's letter was the rapidly growing Baltimore, Maryland. By the War of 1812, Baltimore had taken on the character of a boomtown, or "mob town," as some would soon call it. Growing in population and economic importance since the 1790s, by 1804 trade from Baltimore surpassed that from Philadelphia, then the second-largest city in America. Baltimore had at least "1000 sailors" registered in port in 1806. In the years leading up to the war, Baltimore merchant houses profited and suffered from both British and American maritime policy. Although the Maryland maritime community, like the rest of America, was greatly harmed by Jefferson's embargo, many shippers offset their losses by investing in the new textile mills being established along the fall line north and west of the city.[11] Baltimore also benefited from geography. Unlike the vulnerable city of Norfolk, Virginia, Baltimore was located far enough up the Chesapeake Bay to make it more defensible from any seaborne assault force. Moreover, in these years before the Erie Canal and railroads, Baltimore's deepwater port was far closer to the Ohio country than any other eastern American seaport, thus making it an ideal central location for trade with the American interior.

There can be no doubt that in 1812 Baltimore was largely a pro-war Republican town. However, the rest of the state of Maryland, including its sitting governor, Levin Winder, was mostly pro-Federalist. During the 1812 presidential campaign, the incumbent James Madison had received just a single electoral vote more from Maryland than his Federalist Party opponent, DeWitt Clinton (the electors were split six to five). The city of Baltimore, however, did possess a small but vocal minority of Federalists. This faction was led by Alexander Contee Hanson Jr., the editor of the *Federal Republican*.

Hanson was not native to the city. A grandson of the prominent John Hanson, the first man selected by Congress as president under the Articles of Confederation, Alexander Hanson originally hailed from Annapolis and lived for a while in Montgomery County, Maryland. He had come to the city of Baltimore a few years before the War of 1812 to further the cause of the Federalist Party following an 1807 riot that broke out after fellow Maryland Federalists Luther Martin and Robert Goodloe Harper successfully defended Aaron Burr in his trial for treason. Since that time Hanson had made himself extraordinarily unpopular in Republican Baltimore. For example, he was a volunteer in one of Baltimore's Republican-dominated militia companies but was court-martialed for expressing his strong Federalist views.[12] Hanson was fond of referring to President Thomas Jefferson as "His Gallic Majesty." He later accused Madison of being "a dupe" of "Irish immigrants" for declaring war against Great Britain. These charges were not well received by Baltimore's dock and yard workers, many of whom had recently arrived from Ireland. In an editorial titled "Thou Hast Done a Deed Wherat Valour Will Weep," Hanson wrote,

> Without funds, without taxes, without a navy, or adequate fortifications—with one hundred and fifty millions of our property in the hands of the declared enemy, without any of his in our power, and with a vast commerce afloat, our rulers have promulgated a war against the clear and decided sentiments of a vast majority of the nation. . . . We mean to

represent in as strong colors as we are capable, that it [the war] is unnecessary, inexpedient, and entered into from a partial, personal, and, as we believe, motives bearing upon their front, marks of undisguised foreign influence which cannot be mistaken. . . . We are avowedly opposed to the presidency of James Madison, and we never will breathe under the dominion, direct or derivative, of Bonaparte, let it be acknowledged when it may. Let those who cannot openly adopt this confession abandon us; and those who can, we shall cherish as friends and patriots worthy of the name.[13]

Hanson was so reviled in Baltimore that within days of Congress' war declaration, a mob wrecked his newspaper office on Gay Street. The Republican Party mayor, Edward Johnson, made a halfhearted attempt to stop the crowd from destroying the paper. One rioter told the mayor, "Mr. Johnson, I know you very well, nobody wants to hurt you; but the laws of the land must sleep, and the laws of nature and reason prevail; that house is a temple of Infamy, it is supported with English gold, and it must and shall come down to the ground!"[14]

Hanson was forced to print later editions of his paper in Georgetown and travel about armed with a brace of loaded pistols. When he returned to Baltimore in July with his Georgetown-based paper, he denounced the Baltimore mob and Madison and boldly informed people that he had brought along "friends" to help him distribute his newspaper.[15] In truth, Hanson's activities did not have the general approval of other Federalists, who believed his hyperbolic diatribes against Madison and the war were overly inflammatory. Nevertheless, Hanson's views do indicate how divided the state of Maryland was in 1812—a fact not overlooked by the British when they first visited the region in the spring of 1813.

The situation soon deteriorated for Hanson and his Federalist allies in Baltimore. For days following the mob's 22 June 1812 destruction of the *Federal Republican*, Baltimore Federalists and others were increasingly attacked by violent mobs. Among the mob's targets was the home of a free black named James Briscoe and that of his daughter. The Republicans also beat up a free man named Remier. Briscoe was rumored to have made pro-British comments, but in reality harassment of free blacks was more likely motivated by race and class than by any sense of misplaced patriotism on the part of the mob. Another man named Hudgins narrowly missed being tarred and feathered for allegedly making disparaging remarks about George Washington. The mob physically dismantled several ships rumored to be bound for pro-British Portugal and Spain, including the *Josepha*, whose rudder was cut off once it had cleared customs and was headed down the bay. Returned to Baltimore, the crew of the *Josepha* could not find a ship's carpenter to repair their ship, and the vessel remained tied up at the dock. Another man named Alexander Wiley, an immigrant of Protestant Irish descent, was accused of having helped Hanson's coeditor, Jacob Wagner, as an express rider. However, Wiley believed he was attacked because of the animosity of working-class Irish Catholics, who used the unrest to settle private scores having nothing to do with the declaration of war against Great Britain.[16]

All this activity elicited little to no response from the Republican city authorities. This nonresponse encouraged further mob activity, and at this point many noted Federalists wisely decided to leave town. Former secretary of war James McHenry was one. Departing for Allegany County, Maryland, McHenry wrote that other Federalists "walk the streets at the mercy of the secret instigators of misrule; that the air of Baltimore is the air of a prison; that houses are no places of safety; that there is a mine under them ready to explode, the moment they shall either by word or by look give offence to their masters. I lament I am obliged to leave the City."[17] Federalists in the Maryland House of Delegates decried the activities of the Baltimore mob as "machinations" of Irish and French interests.[18] This view played perfectly into the stereotype that Maryland Federalists already held about Madison and his Republicans as "dupes" of Napoleon and therefore by extension friend to vehemently anti-British Catholic Ireland.

Undeterred, Hanson decided to strike a blow for the freedom of the press and distribute the paper in the town of Baltimore anyway. He sent Wagner ahead to scout out a new location for the distribution of the now Georgetown-based *Federal Republican*. Wagner found a stout brick house at 45 South Charles Street and reassigned it to Hanson on 22 July for the grand sum of one dollar. Hanson invited a number of friends to assist him in his endeavor. This group eventually grew to over twenty people, including Revolutionary War heroes Major General Henry "Lighthorse Harry" Lee (the father of Robert E. Lee) and Maryland-born Brigadier General James Lingan. In case of violence and as a means of self-defense, Hanson authorized another adherent to procure weapons and bring them to the house. He hoped that the gravitas represented by the two Revolutionary War heroes (along with the weapons) would be enough to dissuade the mob from further attacks on his newspaper or himself. Another cohort named John Lynn urged that "a store of tomahawks and hatchets, with dirks for every man be provided." Just in case no tomahawks could be found in urban Baltimore, Lynn further advised that "lathing hatchets would be a good substitute for tomahawks if they cannot be had."[19] Although Lynn later stated it was his intention to accompany Hanson, he never made it to Baltimore.

Hanson's strategy did not work. Someone noticed that Hanson had brought weapons to the Charles Street house. This served to convince many in town that the editor and his confederates were planning more than just the distribution of his newspaper. Many Republicans in town believed that Hanson, by bringing in people from outside the city, who the mob was convinced were well armed (as indeed they were), was actually trying to instigate a civil war. During the late afternoon of 26 July 1812, Hanson and a contingent of followers, including several members of the prominent Gaither family of Montgomery County, arrived at the Charles Street residence. They quickly established a watch for the evening, but nothing happened. The next morning, Hanson's newspaper, which the denizens of the Baltimore docks found so incendiary, arrived around 9:00 from Georgetown via an express wagon. Toward dusk on 27 July, a group of boys and some men showed up at the Charles Street house and began to threaten Hanson and his friends still inside.

At this point the situation rapidly devolved. With the crowd beginning to grow around 45 Charles Street, boys began throwing rocks at the building, breaking every window and even shattering door frames and sashes. The crowd also hurled insults at the men inside. Hanson posted several confederates on the central stairway to cover the front door, now being battered with pieces of brick and even cobblestones pulled up from Charles Street. From the upper-story windows Hanson shouted for the mob to disperse, but he was ignored. Ephraim Gaither threw an iron stove plate out a window, and it cut off part of onlooker Dennis Nowland's foot. Thoroughly besieged, some house members brandished weapons out of the upper-story windows and fired several blank-charged muskets in hopes that this would intimidate the mob. Instead, it only sent the men into a greater frenzy. Many began arming themselves. Someone even found an artillery piece and pointed it at the house, but no one in the crowd seemed to know how to load and fire the weapon. An angry apothecary named Dr. Thaddeus Gale led a rush on the front door. This time Hanson's musket men fired ball cartridges. Gale

The Conspiracy against Baltimore or the War Dance at Montgomery Court shows the confrontation between Federalists and anti-Federalists in 1812 in Baltimore. Engraving by an unidentified artist. Courtesy of the Maryland Historical Society, SMPR P322

was killed, and several of the rioters were wounded as they attempted to drag his body back outside the house. Firing continued, and a second man, a stonecutter named John Williams, was accidentally struck by a musket ball.

As they had been when Hanson's newspaper office was wrecked on 22 June, the civil authorities were slow to respond to the rapidly escalating mayhem on Charles Street. The commander of the city militia, Brigadier General John Stricker, lived just a few blocks from the scene of the commotion. When frightened citizens appeared at his door and pleaded with him to restore order in the city, Stricker claimed he could not call out the militia until he had a signed order from two magistrates requesting that he do so. Citizens then rushed about to find the judges, but it was tough to find one willing to risk the ire of the mob by putting his signature to the document. After considerable delay two brave souls were finally found, but several hours elapsed before two companies of Colonel James Sterett's Fifth Maryland Regiment were ordered to turn out—and then only around thirty to forty men actually reported for duty.

Stricker did have a nearby contingent of cavalry under the command of Major William Barney available. Barney was prepared to disperse the mob, but before he moved his troops to the scene, Stricker recommended that he remove his aristocratic Order of the Cincinnati eagle and ribbon from his uniform and the white feather from his hat (a symbol of the elite hussars). As a further precaution,

Barney placed his lower-class red-feathered chasseurs in front of his own hussars, thinking that the mob might recognize friends in their ranks and be less inclined to do anything to them. In reality, Barney's tiny force, which caused the mob to withdraw temporarily, was not large enough to keep it away for long. The group soon returned, shouting "blood for blood" and demanding that Barney allow it to seize the defiant men inside the house and avenge the deaths of Gale and Williams. Instead, Barney stalled for time, hoping that Stricker might arrive with more militia. However, like the timid judges, most of the militia men, at least on this night, were not willing to stick their necks out for a group of people they intensely disliked in the first place. With no more troops in sight, Barney decided that discretion was the better part of valor, and he opened negotiations with the mob leadership rather than confront the group outright.

Hanson and others inside the house suspected that Barney was actually in league with the mob. This made them hesitant to leave their fortified residence. Indeed, Barney let it be known to the mob leaders that he was their "political friend" and loudly declared he would not allow Dr. Gale's killers to escape justice. He was equally determined that the mob not take Hanson and his men by force. He positioned himself and his horsemen between the mob's cannon and the house. The tension was finally broken when Mayor Johnson arrived. Earlier that day— probably aware there might be trouble in Baltimore that evening—he left town for his country estate. Now returned and in company with General Stricker, he brokered a compromise in which the militia would escort the men inside the Charles Street house to the city jail to await further justice. After some debate as to whether carriages would be provided to convey Hanson and his followers to jail, it was decided that they had better walk. The militia formed a hollow square, and the men in the house, including Lee, Lingan, Hanson, the Gaithers, and others, marched in the center of the formation until they arrived at the jail.

The trip to jail did not mollify the crowd. Someone found a fife and drum to play "The Rogue's March" while the growing crowd hurled insults and stones at both the prisoners and their unenthusiastic guards. Early on 28 July, the prisoners were finally ensconced in the jail, and the Republican town leaders were relieved that they had not been forced to use their largely anti-Federalist militia against their own comrades. During past town disturbances, daylight had normally been the moment when riots had ended owing to fear that mob members might be recognized by the authorities. On this day, however, the mob showed no inclination of going home and in fact soon doubled in size.[20] Some estimated the mob to be between three thousand and five thousand people.

Despite their earlier promises to leave the now-empty residence alone, the mob completed the destruction of the Charles Street house throughout the day— the looters scuttling off into alleyways and side streets with whatever they could carry. Toward evening a crowd gathered in front of the jail and hurled insults and made threats against the inmates. Because Stricker had been able to muster only a minuscule portion of the militia that should have reported for duty, he decided that the few uniformed soldiers near the jail were simply serving to further inflame the mob. He dismissed the soldiers. This was a major mistake on Stricker's part: the mob took the withdrawal of the militia as a sign it could now storm the jailhouse with impunity. In the growing darkness the people surged toward the door. Mayor Johnson tried to bodily block their passage but this time was roughly swept aside by several violent men. One swore at him, "You damn'd scoundrel, don't we feed you, and is it not your duty to head and lead us on to take vengeance for the murders committed?"[21]

According to prisoner John Thomson, who became a victim of the mob: "[Earlier that day] two butchers, one named [John] Mumma and the other Maxwell, came into our room, the former having a key in his hand. Mumma asked me the names of several of the prisoners. I told him. Mr. Hoffman [a fellow prisoner] said he wondered [why] Mr. Bently [the jailer] should suffer so many men to come into their room who had no business there. Mumma answered that he came there on Mr. Bently's business . . . we suspected their intentions were not good, and I inquired of Mr. Bently if Mumma was a friend of his—Bently answered he pretends to be so."[22]

Thomson believed that Mumma's true intention was to determine the exact location of the prisoners inside the jail in preparation for an assault on the building later that evening and to identify his intended targets. Hanson had wisely planned for this possibility and advised his followers inside the jail to snuff out all the candles and torches in the cell area in the event of an assault. The idea was for the prisoners to rush past the mob in the darkness and confusion. However, once the assault on the jail began, Mumma stationed himself at the exit and physically beat down those he recognized from his earlier visit, although at least some of the prisoners did make their escape by blending in. Otho Sprigg was one. He testified that he owed his life to a French cellmate named Du Prat, who was already in jail when Sprigg arrived. He stated that once the mob broke in, he tried to make himself as inconspicuous as possible. When the mob came to his cell door, Du Prat said that all the inmates in his particular cell were not the Federalists they were looking for. Sprigg believed that many of the mob members were "Irishmen," and when they passed by Du Prat's cell, others called out to leave him alone because "he is a Frenchman. He has no tories in with him."[23] The mob's frequent use of the word *tory* is important as it placed Federalists among those who collaborated against the Americans during the Revolutionary War and even in 1812 was considered a highly derogatory term.

According to John Thomson, his cell door was opened by "someone having the key." Although he did not say so, it may have been Mumma the butcher. Thomson, along with another Federalist prisoner named Murray, had somehow been able to arm himself with two pistols and dirks. He said that as he was being dragged from his cell, he was talked out of shooting "Henry Keating," a man "who keeps a print shop," by General Henry Lee. Thomson then tried to implement Hanson's original plan to rush into the mob in the darkness and nearly made it when he was clubbed from behind and sent rolling down the front stairs of the jail. He stated that the mob "beat me about the head until I was unable to rise." The mob seemed to single out Thomson for especially brutal treatment, and the crowd dragged him down the street, violently beating him with clubs the whole way. He was placed in a cart, his clothes were torn off, and he was tarred and feathered on his "bare body." Thomson stated that the mob then dragged him around in the cart and called him "traitor and tory and other scandalous names; they did not cease to beat me with clubs, and cut me with old rusty swords. I received upon my head, arms, sides, thighs and back upwards of eighteen cuts of the sword. On my head one cut was very deep, beside which my head was broken in more than twelve places by other instruments, such as sticks and clubs."[24]

The worst was yet to come for John Thomson. He had sustained repeated beatings by the mob before one of the men from the crowd attempted to gouge out Thomson's eyes. The man was ironically prevented from doing so by the hardened tar that now covered most of Thomson's face. Thomson said a "fellow struck both of my legs with a bar of iron, swearing 'damn my eyes, I will break your legs.'" Thomson acted as if he had broken them, and the man went away exultant that he had accomplished such a deed. At this point, Thomson decided that playing dead was his only chance of survival. He did not move or flinch even when another man twice stuck him with a pin. However, another was not convinced. Pulling a patch of tar and feathers off Thomson's body, he set it on fire and put it back on him. At this Thomson rolled on the ground to put out the flames and begged the mob, "For God's sake be not worse than savages." He asked for them to stop the torture, to just kill him and be done with it.

Finally, a man told Thomson they would spare his life if he would tell them the names of all Hanson's adherents in the jail. To this he agreed, since he estimated the names were already known by the mob. He was then taken to Bull's Head Tavern in Fells Point, where he was further questioned and then forced to stagger to the watch house. On the way to the watch house, a man threatened to decapitate him. The mob leaders said they would return at 9:00 a.m. to make Thomson swear to what he had told them that evening. A doctor came and stitched up his head wounds and removed as much of the tar as he could. Some trousers and a shirt were found for Thomson to wear. The mayor and Thomson's friend Lemuel Taylor ultimately rescued Thomson from the watch house, and he was taken to the hospital and placed in a room next to the severely injured Henry Lee. Thomson said he could hear Lee's "groans" through the wall. Afraid that the mob might return to finish its work, friends found a carriage and eventually took both Thomson and Lee to York, Pennsylvania, where they believed the men could be more safely cared for.[25]

Hanson and around seven or eight of his friends were treated in similar fashion by the mob: rolled down the jailhouse stairs and viciously beaten. One of Hanson's adherents, John Hall, tried to run through the crowd but was captured by two large men who led him back to the scene, where the others were in the process of being beaten senseless. Trying to again run away, Hall was immediately set upon by a group of men who beat him unconscious. He awoke only to find someone "jumping on his arm [most likely in an effort to break it]."[26] Trying to escape once more, he was again violently assaulted. Hall then realized that any attempt to move brought on a harsher beating from the crowd, so he decided to play dead. This strategy likely preserved his life. Once their targets stopped moving and were assumed to at last be dead, the mob members moved on. At length they piled the unconscious bodies into a bloody heap in front of the jail. Some stuck penknives into the faces of the brutalized prisoners or dripped hot candle wax into their eyes.

The elderly Revolutionary War veteran James Lingan did not try to run. Instead, he remonstrated with the mob, reminding them of his past patriotic service to the country and of the large family that depended on him for support.

None of this mattered to the mob, and several men violently attacked the old man with fists and clubs. Just before Lingan was knocked unconscious, one of the rioters hit him with a rapid series of hard blows to his head and then stamped on his breast exclaiming, "the damned old rascal is the hardest dying of all of them."[27] These last blows were enough to kill Lingan, and his body was added to the growing pile of unconscious forms in front of the jail. Fortunately for Hanson and some of the others, they had been so bloodied and deformed from what they endured that in the darkness the mob could no longer tell who was who in the pile of bodies and eventually left them alone. Only the approach of dawn ended the mob's bloodlust. Doctors rushed to the scene to save those they could. Lingan was already dead. The others in the pile were just barely alive. The more seriously injured victims, like General Lee and John Thomson, were initially sent to medical locations in the city. Those considered more mobile were sent to homes of friends near Ellicott Mills in an effort to save them from further attacks by angry men with clubs still roaming the streets of Baltimore.

Even the Republican authorities in Baltimore realized that the mob had spun dangerously out of control on the evenings of 27 and 28 July 1812. While Hanson recuperated from his injuries, instead of personally delivering his newspaper, he mailed it to his Baltimore subscribers. On 4 August, when the mob again threatened to attack Federalists in town, General Stricker did not wait for any magistrates to approve his callout of the militia—and this time his men largely reported for duty. When the mob threatened to attack the U.S. Post Office because it was the new means of delivery for Hanson's hated newspaper, Stricker had upwards of "700 men in uniform" patrolling the streets of Baltimore.[28] His cavalry unhesitatingly charged the mob, and no attempt was made to negotiate with its members. Eventually some of the July mob ringleaders were arrested. When their confederates gathered outside the prison and openly threatened to break the ringleaders out of jail, an artillery piece was placed in the central hall of the facility, this time manned by people who knew how to use it. This was enough to cool the mob's ardor. It was not long before the Baltimore mob's power had fully dissipated.

Later that year, largely owing to fallout over the riots, Maryland Federalists regained control of the state House of Delegates. They immediately ordered a full-scale investigation of the July riots. Predictably, the committee found fault with the actions of Mayor Johnson and General Stricker. They especially condemned the conduct of militia brigadier general Tobias Stansbury, a well-known Republican, who arrived at the jail just as the mob was breaking in. Witnesses testified that instead of trying to stop the mob, Stansbury urged them on. Others refuted this charge. The committee did admit that "private revenge" also likely played a role in the late July disturbances. The targeting of innocent blacks and the mob's predominantly Irish membership support this observation. Much evidence shows that most of the mob members were poor whites who had come to the central part of town from the Federal Hill area or the West Side precincts— places "where a large percentage of Baltimore's poor immigrants resided." Unlike those who wrecked Hanson's newspaper office on 22 June 1812, of the twenty-nine rioters charged in court for the disturbance on Charles Street, "only six appeared on the militia rolls, none were assessed at more than $100 in the tax records, and only two had residences in Baltimore Town [the inner harbor area east of Federal Hill]. Most of the rioters were tinsmen, plasterers, and carters— members of the working class often in direct competition with African Americans for jobs."[29] Thus, it seems that at least a portion of the mob likely used the political disagreement of the time to its own advantage. The class distinctions also indicate why the mob showed no deference to the pleas of General Lee and General Lingan and treated the Republican mayor, a political ally, with such disdain. Nevertheless, the 1812 riots earned Baltimore the dubious title of "Mob Town" for decades to come.

During the summer of 1812, some in Great Britain, such as Foreign Secretary Lord Castlereagh, thought that war could have been easily avoided if the Americans had only been aware that the British government had rescinded its long-reviled orders in council. What Castlereagh failed to understand was just how adamant Madison was about the issue of impressment. Furthermore, in the interim two U.S. Navy superfrigates, the USS *Constitution* and the USS *United States*, had won ship-to-ship victories against their British opponents. These victories were a tremendous psychological boost to the American cause—coming at a time when the illusion of an easy conquest of Canada was being demolished by Major General Isaac Brock at Fort Detroit. Moreover, no one alive could recall an instance in which a Royal Navy man-of-war had lost to an opponent in single combat. It did not matter that the American ships were larger and carried more ordnance than their Royal Navy challengers. British newspapers were nearly unanimous in their opinion that their nation needed to teach the surprisingly successful Americans a hard lesson as to the true power and reach of the mighty Royal Navy. As a further precaution the Admiralty ordered that unless the situation was unavoidable, British frigates were no longer authorized to take on larger American superfrigates alone.

Adding to the concerns of the Admiralty, the declaration of war had unleashed swarms of privateers into the North Atlantic shipping lanes. By October 1812 American privateers had taken an estimated 150 British ships. One of the first privateer commissions offered by the U.S. Department of State went to a "group of Baltimore businessmen." In the way they might own stock in a company, men with money would buy "shares" in fitting out a privateer in hopes that the prizes and goods captured would more than make up for their original capital investment. One Baltimore privateer captain was Revolutionary War hero Joshua Barney. Barney commanded the *Rossie*, and on his first war patrol, he met with spectacular success, taking "18 British merchant vessels" and defeating the *Jeannie*, a British letter-of-marque vessel rated at twelve guns, and the eight-gun British packet *Princess Amelia*. However, Congress heavily taxed the value of his condemned prizes—so much so that the disgusted Barney did not return to sea in the *Rossie* and retired, temporarily as it turned out, to his Maryland farm.[30] Barney argued that congressional taxation had made the risk not worth the reward.

The summer's intense U.S. naval activity caused the Crown to replace its North American station commander, Vice Admiral Herbert Sawyer, with fifty-nine-year-old Knight of the Bath, baronet, and Vice Admiral of the Blue Sir John Borlase Warren. Warren was not only an experienced and respected officer but a diplomat who had once served as Great Britain's ambassador to Russia. During the summer of 1812, with Napoleon marching deep into Russia, the British desperately searched for a solution to their North American problem so that they could more properly focus on the activities of the emperor. Before leaving England, Warren had met with the first lord of the Admiralty, Viscount Dundas Melville, who instructed him to attempt to resolve the matter with the United States via diplomatic means. Melville also warned Warren to be ready to wage an aggressive war if the talks failed. Any spare ground forces were to defend Canada and provide garrison troops for colonies such as Bermuda and Jamaica. At the same time Melville enlarged Warren's North Atlantic command, making him responsible for all naval activity from the Great Lakes to New Orleans. It was a huge task for the new station commander.

Reaching Halifax, Nova Scotia, on 27 September 1812, Warren wrote Melville to say that the situation in North America was worse than they both had previously supposed. It seemed to him that the war had taken on a "more active and inveterate aspect than before." Moreover, he had discovered that Madison and his secretary of state, James Monroe, were thoroughly dug in on the issue of impressment. From the British standpoint, impressment was nonnegotiable and intertwined with their ideas about national survival. With both sides once again deadlocked over impressment, Warren prepared his command to do "far more fighting than talking."[31]

In the early spring of 1813, Dundas Melville again wrote Warren and succinctly laid out what he expected him to do: "We do not intend this to be a mere *paper* blockade [emphasis in the original], but as a complete stop to all trade & intercourse by Sea with those Ports, as far as the wind & weather & the continual presence of a sufficient armed Force, will permit & ensure." Warren thought that opening operations in and around the Chesapeake Bay would be a good way to relieve pressure on the Canadian border. He fully expected Madison to pull back regiments headed for Canada in order to protect the national capital and the rich port cities of Norfolk and Baltimore. However, Melville warned Warren, "If you find [a complete blockade] cannot be done without abandoning for a time the interruption which you appear to be giving to the internal navigation of the Chesapeake, the latter object must be given up, & you must be content with blockading its entrance & sending in occasionally your cruisers for the purpose of harassment & annoyance."[32] Melville further instructed the admiral to ensure that Jamaica and the Leeward Islands be left with enough force to deter privateers from operating there and to guard convoys sailing between Quebec and Halifax and the West Indies. In sum, Warren was asked to do the near impossible with just a hundred ships at his disposal.

Previously, when Warren had pleaded with the Admiralty for more resources, he had done so by setting up a false comparison of the force levels Great Britain had sent to North America during the Revolution and those that he now had at his disposal. The acerbic Admiralty Secretary John Croker responded by pointing out to Warren that unlike Sir Richard Howe back then, he did not have to worry about a French fleet helping the Americans and that in the unlikely event that the French did send ships to help the Yankees, the Admiralty would certainly respond in kind. Croker closed by reminding Warren of the smallness of the American Navy as compared to the nearly one hundred "pendants" and seventeen hundred men he had at his disposal.[33] Both Croker and Melville were convinced that Warren had more than enough force to be effective in this still secondary theater of operations. Nevertheless, the Admiralty did agree to send Warren four more ships of the line and some frigates from the Cadiz station off Spain. Arriving

Portrait of Vice Admiral Sir John Borlase Warren, North American Station commander in chief, in the beginning of the War of 1812. Etching by James Fittler. Published by John and Josiah Boydell, 1 October 1799. Courtesy of the National Portrait Gallery, Greenwich, London, NPG D37851.

in command of these reinforcements was the fiery Scottish-born rear admiral George Cockburn. Cockburn would serve as Warren's second in command. By February 1813 Warren had already ordered Cockburn to take his Cadiz squadron and scout out the Chesapeake Bay in anticipation of Warren's arrival with naval reinforcements in the coming summer months. The British were coming to the Chesapeake in force.

3

———

THE BRITISH ARRIVE—1813

$\mathcal{W}$ith the War of 1812 beginning its second campaign season, Sir John Borlase Warren was in a quandary. Ordered by the Admiralty to produce a quick end to the nearly yearlong war with the United States, he was expected not only to support British and Canadian land forces then contending with repeated American invasions of Canada but also to conduct a limited blockade of the American coast, defeat or blockade American superfrigates such as the USS *Constellation*, and finally deal with rising American naval power on the Great Lakes. Warren had to do all this with less than adequate military support since Great Britain remained focused on the military threat still posed by Napoleon in Europe.

In late April 1813 the Americans launched yet another invasion of Upper Canada (lower Ontario). On 27 April the provincial capital of York (modern-day Toronto) fell to superior American forces commanded by Brigadier General Zebulon Pike. During the assault Major General Sir Roger Hale Sheaffe, commander of the British and Canadian forces in the town, ordered the destruction of his grand magazine at the exact moment that Pike was entering into surrender negotiations with a local Canadian commander. The blast created by the simultaneous ignition of over three hundred barrels of gunpowder killed or wounded dozens of American soldiers, including the popular Pike, who was crushed by a large stone that had been flung high into the air by the blast. Pike died shortly thereafter from his wounds. Enraged by the loss of their comrades and popular commander, soldiers of the U.S. 16th Infantry and sailors from the supporting American flotilla burned much of the town, including the brick Parliament House.[1]

Today, historians usually point to the destruction of York, Canada, as one of the primary reasons why the British came to the Chesapeake Bay. However, the Royal Navy was already in the Chesapeake in force by the time York was attacked on 29 April 1813. While the destructive activity conducted by the British during their 1814 campaign was partially related to what took place at "Little York," stronger evidence suggests that the British commanders were more concerned about the continued, overarching American threat to Canada. They believed that if they opened a new theater of war in the Chesapeake, a panicked Madison would order valuable regular Army regiments southward to defend the valuable port cities of Norfolk and Baltimore, thereby relieving pressure on Upper Canada. To heighten the sense of fear, the British wished to engage in a punitive campaign involving raids and destruction as part of the overall strategy. A Chesapeake campaign also served a secondary purpose. The arrival of British men-of-war in the lower Chesapeake would put an immediate stop to the swarms of Baltimore- and Norfolk-based privateers that used the bay as a safe haven in order to devastate British commercial shipping, especially in and around the West Indies. The Admiralty in London was determined to do something about them.

Since 1805 Thomas Kemp, formerly of St. Michaels, Maryland, had oper- ated a small shipyard at Fells Point in Baltimore. Kemp's yard and that of his principal competitor and neighbor, William Price, turned out some of the fastest sailing sloops the world had ever seen. Moreover, in anticipation of future conflict, Kemp shrewdly advertised his vessels as "privateer-built" or "finished privateer fashion." It was not long before Kemp's yard was turning out nearly five vessels a year—an incredible rate of production for the time.[2] Kemp's and Price's sloops were extraordinarily fast and hence in high demand for service once war did break out. Speed was the chief hallmark of the sharp-ended Chesapeake privateers, and speed ensured they survived on the high seas against the more numerous and powerful ships of the Royal Navy. It is important to note that out of approximately "55 Baltimore schooners that embarked on one or more privateer cruises during the War of 1812, only about ten failed to return to their owners." Of those vessels actually taken, most were caught while also heavily laden as blockade runners.[3]

Baltimore built and Baltimore based, the Fells Point privateers were a sight to behold and represented "the highest development of small American sailing craft, a widely copied vessel with long, light, and extremely raking masts; very little rigging; low freeboard; great rake to the stem and stern posts, with a great deal of drag to the keel, aft. Its deadrise was great, and bilges slack. The beam was rather great for its length. Nearly always flush-decked, it had a wide, clear deck suitable for handling the guns. Built for speed with easy lines, light weight and a large rig, the Baltimore clipper's excellent design was far in advance of its times."[4] Privateer captain George Coggeshall noted, "Baltimore had sent to sea since the declaration of war forty-two armed vessels, carrying about three hundred and thirty guns, and from 2,800 to 3000 men."[5] Soon Baltimore privateers such as the *Rossie*, commanded by future commodore Joshua Barney, and Thomas Boyle's *Comet* were taking dozens of British prizes on the high seas. When confronted by a heavier escort or man-of-war, these fast ships simply outsailed their pursuers. While many captured prizes were frequently recaptured from their prize crews, a "generally accepted estimate is that Baltimore privateers took approximately 550 British ships." This meant that Maryland-based schooners, which represented "12 percent of the total commissioned, captured or sunk more than 40 percent of the British merchant ships lost!"[6] On the other hand, of "the 41 privateers that sailed from Salem, [Massachusetts], only 15 remained uncaptured by the end of the war."[7] The large difference between the privateer survival rates for Baltimore and Salem illustrates just how important speed and design were to such vessels. The superfast Chesapeake schooners were clearly a better investment.

Scholars of the War of 1812 have long argued that the British merchant fleet was never seriously hampered by the American Eastern Seaboard privateer effort. While privateering had the potential to be an enormously profitable venture for individual investors and ship captains alike, reality was often quite different. Of the "2,500 prizes taken during the war by American warships and privateers," 400 had to be burned, which meant they lost most if not all of their value as condemned prizes for their investors. Moreover, "some 750 [prizes] were recaptured" before they reached a friendly port.[8] More often than not, privateering expeditions were renowned for delivering little, especially for the poor sailors risking life and limb on such cruises. George Little of Norfolk, Virginia, thought that signing on board the privateer *George Washington* offered him "an opportunity of making a fortune." However, he also noted that his decision "was counterbalanced by the possibility of getting [his] head knocked off, or a chance of being thrown into prison for two or three years." Indeed, British prisons were soon bulging with the restive crews of captured American privateers. Moreover, many of these prisoners of war (POWs) were no strangers to the inside of a prison. Little noted that his *George Washington* shipmates "appeared to have been scraped together from the lowest dens of wretchedness and vice," and he referred to them as a "band of ruthless desperadoes."[9] Nevertheless, the occasional single-prize grand slam could still be made, such as when the privateer *Yankee* took the *San Jose Indiano*, loaded with silks and other high-value goods worth a half million dollars. The payout for the investors and crew was so valuable that even the ship's two cabin boys (who happened to be black) received a cash payment of "$1,121.88 and $739.19," a huge sum in 1812 dollars.[10] Like winning the lottery, extraordinary but rare payouts convinced many unemployed or underemployed maritime workers to sign on for privateer duty.

Thomas Boyle of Baltimore had one of the more successful careers as an 1812 privateer commander. Originally from Massachusetts, Boyle first appeared in Baltimore around 1792. A skilled sailor with no physical property to his name at the time, he was most likely lured to Baltimore by the economic boom the town was beginning to enjoy. Boyle sailed the commercial vessel *Theresa*, among other ships, for owner-merchant John Carrere. He did so well with Carrere's firm that he was able to marry a local woman named Mary, and they built a small house on a lot at 63 Albemarle Street. Carrere held the mortgage on the property. One of Boyle's neighbors, at 60 Albemarle Street, was Mary Pickersgill. (Mary was the soon-to-be-famous seamstress who sewed the "Star Spangled Banner" flag of Fort McHenry.) By 1804 Boyle was prosperous enough to buy his own vessel, the *Traveller*, a 72-foot brig of approximately 100 tons burthen. He entered into a semipartnership with his former boss, Carrere, and both men outfitted various merchant ships. Boyle personally commanded them at sea. His seamanship was superb, and he evidently had Carrere's complete trust. Boyle made enough money to buy about two-thirds of a choice Baltimore town property formerly owned by Declaration of Independence signer Samuel Chase called Ridgely's Delight. He also invested in a local tannery and was for a time named to the board of the Mechanics Bank of Baltimore, originally located at the "southeast corner of Calvert and Fayette streets." Boyle was so well respected that he was appointed a company commander in the Fifty-First Maryland Regiment. By 1812 Thomas and Mary Boyle had moved with their five daughters to 94 Granby Street. When war was declared, Boyle took command of the Thomas Kemp–built privateer *Comet*.[11]

Boyle armed the *Comet* with a number of 9- and 12-pounder long guns. These weapons ideally engaged an opponent at three hundred yards but could be fired at elevation all the way out to eighteen hundred yards. The *Comet*, as was true of most privateers of the era, also carried a number of 12-pounder carronades.

Named for Carron Ironworks in Scotland, where this particular weapon design had originated, the short, stubby carronades were akin to a monster sawed-off shotgun and especially devastating at close range. Most privateer captains also overmanned their vessels and carried a crew that was three to four times larger than that of a typical merchant vessel. A privateer preferred to rapidly overtake a slower, less-well-manned merchant target and fire just a few cannon shots before getting close enough to capture the vessel by boarding. The idea was to take the vessel and its cargo with as little destruction as possible; the captors hoped that an intact prize would garner a greater profit once the captured vessel and its cargo were legally condemned by an Admiralty court.[12]

Privateering was simultaneously both a lucrative and a risky business. Congress attempted to strictly regulate privateers but also expected the federal government to profit from sanctioning such activity. Once shipowners or investors raised enough money to purchase and outfit a privateer, they then applied to the secretary of state for a letter of marque and reprisal. To prevent privateers from becoming pirates, the owners were usually required to provide a cash bond to ensure that their vessel obeyed all the laws of the United States, and most important, they themselves were made liable for any illegal activity their crew or vessel might engage in.

The cost of a privateer was often covered by selling shares in a particular vessel, and proceeds from captured prizes were split among the investors, captain, and crew. For example, Thomas Boyle's *Comet* was jointly paid for by "Francis Foreman, Jeremiah Sullivan, Thomas Shepherd, Levi Hollingsworth, Christian Keller, Peter Karthaus, Andrew Clopper, Levi Clagett, Elie Clagett, and Thorndike Chase." Boyle was named captain, Thomas Ring was his lieutenant, and they hired 110 sailors and marines from the Baltimore maritime community as crew. By 26 July Boyle and the *Comet* were already out to sea, and *Comet* had taken its first prize, the British merchant vessel *Henry*. With an eleven-man prize crew on board, the *Henry* was sent to Baltimore and condemned in court as a legal prize. The profit from the sale of the vessel and its cargo enabled the investors, Boyle, and his crew to split $100,000. The federal government realized $50,000 in customs duties alone. Boyle took other prizes in quick succession. He was at sea for just eighty-two days, and upon his return to Baltimore in October 1812, *Comet*'s prizes amounted to over $400,000 before taxes and fees. Boyle had personally made enough money during his first voyage to become a *Comet* shareholder by the time he was ready to take the vessel back to sea in November. Including Boyle as a shareholder also ensured that he would continue to serve as the *Comet*'s highly successful captain.[13] Being both shareholder and captain made Thomas Boyle an especially aggressive commander.

Not all shareholders of a privateer were men of means. Often groups of marginal investors would pool their resources without having to risk too much of their own fortunes. Grocers, ship's chandlers, flour vendors, and other maritime-industry craftsmen would buy shares in a privateer or be paid for their goods via the shares system vice an exchange of any currency. Once the British blockade of the Chesapeake took full effect, the share system simply provided these men another way to generate income. Some would do double duty as a ship's husband, a person who managed the vessel's financial affairs and records, in order to qualify for a share. For example, "oil and paint store proprietor John Kipp, a mariner in early life, was ship's husband for the [privateer] Wasp."[14] Even shipyard owners Thomas Kemp and William Price often retained shares in the vessels they built for other private investors. Privateers needed constant infusions of capital in order to pay for ordnance, powder, rigging, and advance money to attract enough able-bodied sailors and marines willing to risk their necks on a cruise. An average-size privateer sold for approximately $14,000. Letters of marque went for around $10,000. The number of investors the vessel attracted determined the cost per share. The fewer the investors the greater the possible reward. On the other hand, sole owners and groups of four or fewer shareholders could be financially devastated if their ship was taken by the enemy or lost at sea.

Once a captured ship and its cargo were legally condemned in a federal district court as enemy property, the cargo, at least at the beginning of the war, was treated as if it were imported goods and was subject to customs duties and other fees. A severe fine of $1,000 could also be levied against privateer captains for sloppy or improperly kept logbooks. These practices, including an additional 2 percent federal fee for the support of the widows and children of slain and disabled sailors, cut so deeply into any possible profit margin that captains like Joshua Barney of the *Rossie* believed the reward was not worth the risk. Although the *Rossie* took eighteen British prizes, Barney realized little financial gain for his efforts and temporarily retired.[15]

The Baltimore privateers were not just seagoing predators but effective blockade runners as well. One such vessel was the letter-of-marque *Lynx*. Built in Thomas Kemp's yard and paid for by Levi Hollingsworth and two brothers,

John and James Williams, for approximately $10,000, the *Lynx*, commanded by Sailing Master Elisha Taylor, made a cargo run to Bordeaux, France, and brought back to Baltimore hard-to-obtain goods such as silk, gloves, tin, and champagne in January 1813. Letter-of-marque vessels differed slightly from true privateers in that they also engaged in merchant trade missions, were less well manned, and were powerful enough to overtake and capture enemy vessels. Nevertheless, both types of vessels carried documentation from the government that allowed them to take enemy shipping.[16] By early February 1813, however, the situation for Chesapeake privateers and letter-of-marque vessels was about to change for the worse.

Pursuant to orders from the British secretary of war, Lord Henry Bathurst, by February 1813 Admiral Warren had moved a large naval task force to the Chesapeake Bay. Amazingly, the arrival of his ships off Cape Henry did nothing to stir James Madison, who ordered the majority of the American regular Army troops to remain at their posts on the Canadian frontier. But not all were so calm. For example, once Warren's ships appeared in the Chesapeake, nervous citizens of St. Mary's County, Maryland, petitioned Secretary of War John Armstrong for regular troops to defend them against British raiding parties. Armstrong cavalierly responded, "It cannot be expected that I can defend every man's turnip patch." Consequently, the unpopular Armstrong left the 1813 defense of the Chesapeake Bay primarily in the hands of the governors of Maryland and Virginia and their respective local militia commanders.[17]

Warren's advance frigates effectively closed the Chesapeake to American shipping, and even the most courageous Baltimore-based privateer had a difficult time getting past the British men-of-war. To increase the number of ships taken entering the bay, the British used the ruse of fake pilot boats. The brig *Two Marys* was taken in this fashion. Having been chased by the HMS *Belvidera*, the *Two Marys* was approached by what its captain thought was a friendly pilot boat. Noting only three men above deck, the *Two Marys* captain was shocked when "twenty men, well armed, sprung out of her hold, and boarded us and took posses-sion."[18] The first phase of the Crown's Chesapeake strategy had been carried off without a hitch. Warren soon reinforced his Chesapeake squadron with four larger ships, the HMS *Marlborough*, *Poictiers*, *Victorious*, and *Dragon*. All these ships mounted seventy-four guns each and were considered third-rate ships of the line. The diminutive American Navy had nothing like them. Arriving in *Marlborough* was Warren's second in command, the highly aggressive Rear Admiral George Cockburn (pronounced Co'burn).

On 8 February 1813, near Hampton Roads, "the frigates HMS *Belvidera*, *Maidstone* (36 guns each), *Junon*, and *Statira* (38 guns each)," confronted an unknown schooner. The vessel turned out to be the privateer *Lottery* (six guns), commanded by Captain John Southcomb of Baltimore. The *Lottery* was attempting to speed past the slower British blockade vessels when the wind suddenly died. The British quickly deployed a large number of oar-driven ship's boats with Royal Marines and bluejackets to board the becalmed privateer. Captain Southcomb led a gallant defense against the boarders until he and his men were overwhelmed by superior numbers. Southcomb was heard to shout, "If they do take us, they must pay for her." Mortally wounded in the engagement, Southcomb was taken on board the *Belvidera*, and he died a week later. His *Lottery* was the first of many prizes taken by the Royal Navy in the Chesapeake Bay. Renamed HMS *Canso*, the vessel was recaptured by the USS *Constitution* about a year later. A few days after *Lottery* had originally been taken, the British captured the *Cora* (eight guns) and her forty-man crew in much the same manner. The *Cora* fought off a large number of British barges for about an hour and a half until a pilot boat with an 18-pounder on board maneuvered into a position to rake the American vessel while other British boats closed in for the kill. The Americans decided to surrender with the loss of one sailor killed.[19]

Just a month earlier, the HMS *Poictiers* (seventy-four guns) and the frigate HMS *Acasta* (forty guns) had captured the Baltimore privateer *Highflyer* off the mouth of the Chesapeake Bay. The *Highflyer* was held in such high regard that it was immediately reflagged as a British tender and soon created quite a reputation for itself for capturing a number of other privateers and for leading raids in the upper reaches of the Chesapeake Bay. The *Highflyer* later had an especially bloody engagement against another American privateer, the Norfolk, Virginia–based *Roger Quarles*. Badly damaged in this fight, the vessel returned to the Chesapeake Bay for further repairs and, by the fall of 1813, was being used to run dispatches to British ships off the New England coast. In September 1813, in a fog bank off Nantucket, the *Highflyer* mistook John Rodgers' frigate USS *President* for the HMS *Seahorse* and thus the ubiquitous Chesapeake raider returned once again to American hands—not an unusual consequence for many of these small vessels throughout the War of 1812.[20]

In reality, the capture of these fast-sailing, light-draught vessels proved to be a boon to the British cause in the Chesapeake. While Warren's blockade squadron was more than a match for any American naval vessel, what he really needed at that moment was lighter-draught vessels and schooners that could safely operate on most of the bay's numerous rivers and creeks. Even the smallest British frigate needed considerably more water under her keel than a Fells Point schooner. The capture of the *Lottery* and *Cora* via boarding not only served to reduce the privateer threat but also strengthened the ability of the British invasion force to attack farther inland than anyone on the American side thought possible.

During late March 1813, attempting to use the cloak of stormy weather to pass the British blockade, Captain William Stafford of the Baltimore-based privateer *Dolphin* was forced to turn back when an incompetent local pilot nearly ran the *Dolphin* aground near the mouth of the Rappahannock River. With his boat suddenly becalmed and certain to be captured, Stafford's pilot became so distraught that he allegedly jumped overboard and killed himself. Stafford ordered his men to the oars, or "sweeps," and they painstakingly rowed the *Dolphin* out of immediate danger. But the *Dolphin* was soon chased up the Rappahannock River by two unknown vessels. These ships turned out to also be American letters of marque: the *Arab*, commanded by Captain Daniel Fitch, and the *Lynx*, under the aforementioned Captain Elisha Taylor. Finding that the strange sail they had been chasing was actually a fellow American, the two captains conferred with Stafford as to what to do next. The following day, a fourth American schooner, the *Racer*, under Captain Thomas West, joined the trio. Ominously, West reported that he had not entered the river on his own accord but had been chased there by a British frigate and other vessels.[21]

Thinking that the river and their numbers were enough to deter the British from molesting them any further, the captains waited for the weather to change so that they might make another attempt to run the British blockade. But Warren took the offensive and sent a number of his ship's boats under the command of Lieutenant James Polkinghorne, including the recently captured American privateer *Highflyer*, now under British colors, into the Rappahannock. On 3 April 1813, after having rowed nearly fifteen miles, the Royal Marines and bluejackets of Polkinghorne's flotilla force, which included approximately seventeen barges and other assorted craft, rounded a point in the Rappahannock and caught the Americans by surprise. Some of Polkinghorne's boats mounted swivel guns, light cannon, and even a 12-pounder carronade, on rails amidships.

Like a line of ducks, the smaller British barges followed behind the *Highflyer*. Stafford edged the larger *Dolphin* toward *Highflyer*, thinking it was another American privateer fleeing the British blockade. However, the captain soon saw the rest of Polkinghorne's assault force rowing furiously toward the four American vessels. Putting the *Dolphin* about, he decided to rejoin his three erstwhile compatriots near Carter's Creek and fight it out. By sticking together, the American privateer commanders believed that they could hold the line against Polkinghorne.

The problem for the Americans was that of the four schooners in the river, only the *Dolphin* was a true privateer. The other three were letter-of-marque vessels, and their crews lacked the discipline needed for action on the water against a determined or near-equal foe. As the British closed the distance, the situation began to unravel for the Americans. Instead of joining the other schooners, Captain Fitch's *Arab* remained anchored and fired a few cannon at the British barges. Fitch then cut his anchor cable and drifted toward the Rappahannock shore. He and his crew leapt overboard and waded ashore to escape capture. When a British pinnace pulled alongside *Lynx*, Elisha Taylor ordered his colors to be struck and quickly surrendered. The *Racer* did slightly better, driving back an initial boarding attempt, but it too was eventually forced to surrender. The British now turned *Racer*'s captured guns against the *Dolphin*. Stafford held off the British for just slightly longer until he was wounded and enemy boarders physically ripped down his colors. In fifteen minutes of fighting, the Americans had lost four valuable schooners along with two hundred prisoners and thirty-one pieces of ordnance. The British suffered just two men killed and eleven wounded.[22]

This largely one-sided Rappahannock River affair was a tremendous shock to the entire Chesapeake Bay maritime community. It was not long before recriminations began flying back and forth between the four schooner captains over who was responsible for the 3 April debacle. Stafford was especially condemnatory of the conduct of Captain Fitch of the *Arab*. In the end it did not matter who was at fault. The British had successfully carried off a daring attack far up one of the bay's numerous rivers, and this made them extremely threatening to the hundreds of bay towns that heretofore believed they were protected by creeks and rivers too shallow for even the smallest British frigates. Furthermore, Warren and Cockburn made immediate plans to reflag and use the *Dolphin* and *Racer* elsewhere in the Chesapeake.

In truth, the American schooners had fallen victim to an increasingly effective British naval tactic known as a cutting-out operation. Just a few years earlier,

Captain Stephen Decatur of the American Navy had vaulted to fame for his successful cutting out of the captured USS *Philadelphia* in Tripoli Harbor. Such high-risk operations typically worked best in confined harbors or narrow rivers, such as the Rappahannock, where oar-powered vessels were more maneuverable than those dependent on the wind to get under way. While most schooners could resort to oars, they were difficult to move in this manner; smaller vessels, such as barges, cutters, or even a pinnace, were usually more agile in confined waters. This maneuverability enabled Polkinghorne's boats to swarm the more stationary schooners and overwhelm them one at a time—especially when Fitch's *Arab* neglected to join the other three American schooners. Further, Polkinghorne's men were disciplined fighters, whereas most of the Americans were from the commercial maritime community. These men were not combat sailors. Rather, they went to sea hoping for an easy score against British merchant shipping and were not accustomed to fighting extremely violent naval engagements at such close range.

For reasons of national pride, Warren was strongly interested in capturing one of the vaunted American superfrigates, the USS *Constellation*, known to have slipped into Norfolk, Virginia, moments before Warren's advance squadron arrived in Hampton Roads on 4 February 1813. Immediately before the War of 1812, the *Constellation* (originally laid down as a thirty-eight-gun frigate) had been rearmed with forty-four guns: twenty-four 18-pounder and two 32-pounder long guns and eighteen 32-pounder carronades.[23] Capturing an American forty-four would be a tremendous coup for British naval prestige (as well as Warren's own professional reputation)—prestige that had been shaken by recent American frigate victories on the high seas. However, taking this particular forty-four might be easier said than done. Not counting the guns, sailors, and Marines of the *Constellation*, Norfolk was defended by over three thousand Virginia militia, numerous partially manned gunboats, and two major fortifications—Fort Norfolk and Fort Nelson. Warren had just a few Royal Marine ship's detachments that could act as land troops. If he was going to take a major city like Norfolk, he was going to need the assistance of the British army.

Warren was warned by the British Admiralty not to overly fixate on the Chesapeake Bay. At the time the Crown preferred a general blockade of the entire American coast vice amassing precious naval resources in a single location. Still, Norfolk was too much of a major prize to be ignored, and the Crown eventually reinforced Warren with the 102nd Regiment of Foot, two battalions of Royal

Marines, and two companies of soldiers called Independent Foreigners. The Independent Foreigners were commanded by British officers but were mostly men of various nationalities captured on European battlefields who elected to serve in the British army rather than spend the rest of the war in a fetid POW camp.[24] Before the arrival of these additional troops, the energetic Cockburn had expertly used the few small boats and barges at his disposal to attack a growing number of valuable American sloops located far up the bay tributaries. He soon had more than enough shallow-draught ships to add to the British invasion fleet.

During March 1813 Warren and Cockburn made at least three attempts to cut out the *Constellation*, now firmly blockaded in the shallow Elizabeth River near Norfolk. The *Constellation*'s captain, Charles Stewart, wisely had his vessel kedged closer to protection offered by Fort Norfolk and Fort Nelson. Secretary of the Navy William Jones ordered Captain John Cassin, commanding officer of the Portsmouth Naval Yard, to provide gunboats to assist *Constellation* with fending off British cutting-out operations. These Jefferson-era gunboats were roundly detested by the American maritime community, poorly manned, and difficult to maneuver, whether under sail or by oar power. To avoid being dragooned into service on board one of these vessels, numerous Virginia militiamen deserted their posts.

From this point forward, with few regular American Army troops—or even organized militia—available, the British largely raided the region at will. However, the enemy's sudden appearance in various bay tributaries did finally galvanize the political leadership into taking action. One such leader was Major General Samuel Smith of the Maryland militia. Spurred by the appearance of Cockburn's ships off the mouth of the Patapsco River near Baltimore, Maryland, Governor Levin Winder, a staunch Federalist and longtime political opponent of Republican president James Madison, appointed the capable Smith to take charge of Baltimore's then-decrepit defenses. During the American Revolution Smith had been a Continental army officer who had achieved some amount of fame for his dogged 1777 defense of Fort Mifflin, Pennsylvania. In 1813 Smith was once again tasked with defending a fort—this time Fort McHenry, guarding the entrance to the harbor of Baltimore. Unlike in 1777, when he had been a mere lieutenant colonel, Smith was now a sitting U.S. senator for the state of Maryland and a major general of militia. When Smith spoke, people in Washington and Annapolis listened.

In 1813 Smith's immediate problem was finding enough men to adequately defend the fort. He warned Governor Winder that there were fewer than fifty

Portrait of Major General Samuel Smith by Rembrandt Peale. Courtesy of the Maryland Historical Society, CA681

regular soldiers on duty at Fort McHenry—mostly artillerymen operating the fort's guns. Smith recognized that if Baltimore was to mount a credible defense, the responsibility would largely fall on his Maryland state militia. At the time the port itself had a single gunboat (No. 138), commanded by Maryland-born master commandant Charles Gordon, for its naval defense. According to Gordon, even No. 138 was scheduled to be sent to defend the Potomac. He reminded Secretary of the Navy Jones that Baltimore's allocation of gunboats was nine but all had been sent south to defend Norfolk. Gordon strongly urged the secretary to purchase or lease some of the idle privateers now blockaded in the Patapsco River, and Jones ultimately procured some of these vessels.[25]

If Smith remained in firm command on land at Baltimore, then Charles Gordon clearly was his Navy counterpart and partner. Because of Gordon's hectoring of the Navy Department, Secretary Jones agreed to lease four idle privately owned vessels that were temporarily trapped by the British blockade in the Port of Baltimore. It was something of a historic first for the secretary and the nation. The creation of a privately owned naval squadron meant that the captains of the privateers would be temporarily commissioned into the regular Navy and their crews could be tried for violations of U.S. naval regulations as if they were regular U.S. Navy sailors. As privateers they had largely avoided the military's disciplinary system. Gordon recognized that the approaches to the inner harbor were far too shallow for the larger British men-of-war (such as one of their ubiquitous seventy-fours) to navigate; hence, the shallow-draught privateers would be perfect to defend the narrow confines of Baltimore.

Job West's *Revenge* was the strongest idle privateer then in port. Mounting fourteen 12-pounder carronades, two long 12-pounder naval guns, and one long 18-pounder gun amidships on a pivot (so that it could fire to either side of the ship at all times), the *Revenge* also came with a crew of about 100 to 140 men. However, since the tight blockade had begun, the *Revenge*'s complement of available sailors was substantially less than what was needed, and Gordon had to conduct a vigorous recruiting campaign to adequately man his leased privateers. In fact, recruiting proved to be a problem for Gordon because regular Navy pay was just twelve dollars a month; in contrast, Baltimore City's Defense Committee was offering sixteen dollars a month and Army and militia units paid five dollars a week. Still, there were enough surplus sailors around the Baltimore docks to finally man the privateers. Gordon was able to convince the now-famous Thomas Boyle and his privateer *Comet* to temporarily sign up for regular Navy service. The *Comet* was slightly lighter, with 9-pounder guns being its heaviest ordnance, but probably sailed faster than the *Revenge*. Gordon took personal command of the *Patapsco*, which carried guns similar in size and armament to those of the *Revenge*. The smallest of the four vessels was the *Wasp*, which mounted only three light guns.[26] Gordon rounded out his ersatz flotilla with the despised gunboat, No. 138.

On 16 April 1813 Cockburn had a number of his vessels sail into the Patapsco River and take soundings of the channel (approximately nine miles from the inner harbor). The British were noticed lightening their heavier vessels as if they intended to move in toward the city in preparation for a bombardment. The

Americans in Baltimore had only just begun to prepare the town for defense. To make matters worse, a local commander had foolishly allowed a British schooner under a flag of truce to anchor right next to Fort McHenry. Gordon "peremptorily" kicked this vessel out of port, but the damage had likely been done, and the British schooner commander reported back to Cockburn on the level of defensive activity both in the harbor and on land. As a result, Cockburn immediately withdrew his vessels from the Patapsco and sailed for the upper bay area. This may have been his plan all along, but the appearance of the British squadron did much to energize capable defenders like Samuel Smith and Charles Gordon.[27]

Once the British left for the upper bay, Gordon took his four privateers and No. 138 out of the Patapsco to harass Cockburn's raiders and, if possible, cut out any smaller British vessel that could be lured into shallow waters without support. Gordon and his makeshift flotilla ultimately followed Cockburn's squadron back down the bay and raided the temporary British naval base on Tangier Island, recapturing a number of escaped slaves the British had taken there. By late August 1813, when the British evacuated their temporary base on Kent Island, the crews of Gordon's privateers began to clamor for their discharges so that they could return to the far more lucrative practice of privateering. The Navy Department settled the leases of the *Comet*, *Revenge*, and *Patapsco* after some amount of wrangling with their owners over additional wear-and-tear claims they had levied against the government. Nonetheless, the leasing scheme proved to be a bargain for the country. The total fee for the three largest privateers was $4,800. Considering that the asking price for a single, large, privateer-built schooner was approximately $15,000, Gordon and the U.S. Navy had done quite well in keeping these valuable vessels gainfully employed and likely saved the most valuable prize in the entire Chesapeake Bay region—the Port of Baltimore. Moreover, Charles Gordon had demonstrated that not all privateer squadrons were like the ill-prepared ad hoc Rappahannock River group that had performed poorly in April 1813. In fact, with proper discipline and training, privateer sailors could more than hold their own against their British adversaries.

Throughout the spring and summer of 1813, Samuel Smith embarked on a whirlwind of activity. He requested and promptly received from the federal government fifteen hundred muskets to arm his rapidly growing but poorly armed Maryland militia. He picketed Patapsco Neck, the most likely eastern land approach to the city. He ordered the construction of a small battery, later called

Fort Covington, about a mile behind Fort McHenry. He had another battery built on the Ferry Branch, called Battery Babcock and named for the engineer Captain Samuel Babcock, who had supervised its construction. Smith even managed to get Fort McHenry's irascible regular Army commanding officer, Major Lloyd Beall, replaced by a more cooperative officer, Major George Armistead. Smith had the fort's supporting water battery rebuilt by civilian work gangs and manned it with many of his own militia and other volunteers he scrounged up from the idle Baltimore waterfront. Through a Herculean effort, Smith was able to mount sixty heavy cannon retrieved from a wrecked French man-of-war donated by the French ambassador. He even helped organize a unit of U.S. Sea Fencibles to assist with various duties around Baltimore Harbor. These men were merchant sailors beached by the British blockade. They could man guard boats and, if called on, form experienced cannon crews. Finally, Smith prepared hulks to be sunk in the shipping channels leading to Baltimore's inner harbor. All these improvements made a great difference when the British returned to the region in 1814.[28]

By mid-April 1813, while a portion of Warren's fleet lingered off Norfolk on fixed blockade duty owing to the *Constellation*'s presence in the port, Cockburn planned a series of large-scale raids against the nearly defenseless upper Chesapeake Bay area. As previously noted, on 16 April 1813 he had his entire squadron demonstrate off the entrance to the Port of Baltimore. However, Cockburn had no intention of attacking Baltimore at this particular moment since the only landing forces at his disposal were his small shipboard Royal Marine detachments. Nevertheless, he hoped that this activity would at least hold Smith's militia forces in place in and around Baltimore. Instead of attacking this city, Cockburn moved to the far northern end of the bay. Much of the militia from this part of the state had been sent west to assist in the defense of Baltimore. Cockburn's appearance off Baltimore did send the town into a temporary panic. Lydia Hollingsworth, daughter of a leading Baltimore merchant and major privateer vessel shareholder, wrote to her cousin in Elkton, Maryland, that "rumors" of an enemy landing "were altogether without foundation.... All who could remove their effects, either hurried them off; or put them in trunks, to be sent away as speedily as possible." Hollingsworth continued, "There seemed at first a panic through the city, then a decided resolution to save what conveniently could be done, from a future attack."[29]

Smith kept various companies on duty and had them frequently alternate locations so as to keep them constantly on alert and to avoid complacency. Some days they would do duty at Fort McHenry, at other times they would be ordered forward to picket Patapsco Neck. Smith decided to begin to fortify Hampstead Hill east of the city but still did not have enough men or funding to begin the project. However, he did help convince the Baltimore City government to improve Dulany Street (now East Baltimore Street) for the cost of "$65.49" so that the road toward Hampstead and North Point was made "passable for the Artillery, Militia, etc." Defensive activity seemed to be happening all around the town. Baltimore attorney David Hoffman, however, was not so sanguine about the city's future prospects. He was convinced that "party rancor" had so divided Baltimore that the defensive preparations were "much *form* and *show* and no *spirit* except in party violence and animosity. . . . The only way in which we can oppose the enemy appears to be entirely overlooked viz. on the water. We have no *fortifications*, no gun boats, no sloops of war, no barges, nothing which could protect the city from bombardment [emphasis in the original]."[30]

From 23 April to 6 May 1813, Cockburn's forces savagely punished the upper bay towns. Their complete mastery of the Chesapeake Bay provided them with unprecedented mobility, and Cockburn used this advantage to its fullest. He had forces appear nearly simultaneously at multiple locations and then rapidly maneuver to a designated target location (this time the upper bay region). This masterful use of the bay as a high-speed avenue of approach served to freeze part of Smith's Maryland militia in place and caused the rest to be erroneously sent to locations that were not actually the primary target of the British.

Meanwhile, on 28 April 1813 Cockburn ordered the tenders *Fantome, Mohawk, Dolphin, Racer,* and *Highflyer* to anchor at the mouth of the Elk River. Using tactics similar to those of his earlier successful raids in Virginia, Cockburn directed Royal Navy lieutenant George A. Westphal, along with approximately 175 Royal Marines in thirteen barges, to row up the Elk River and make a predawn attack against the small village of Frenchtown, Maryland. Westphal's raiders were followed closely in support by the schooner *Highflyer*. However, even with the aid of a local guide, Westphal's flotilla managed to get temporarily disoriented and row up the Bohemian River rather than the Elk. It was not until dawn that Westphal discovered the error, and it was midmorning when the flotilla finally rowed its barges within sight of the docks of Frenchtown. As the barges approached the shore, the Cecil County militia, commanded by Major William Boulden, opened a brief but ineffectual fire on Westphal's marines with small arms and a few poorly manned cannon emplaced near the town dock. Once ashore the British quickly drove off any remaining militia and proceeded to burn most of the small town and a number of ships at anchor near the town docks. They seized a schooner loaded with flour; spiked the abandoned cannon, since they were too heavy to transport in the barges; burned several warehouses; and carried off some military stores. While the loss of Frenchtown was fairly inconsequential, the raid did establish Cockburn's intended modus operandi for the rest of the war. As he saw it, if a town meekly submitted to him, then its structures and homes were mostly left intact. However, if any resistance whatsoever was encountered, the town was not only looted but burned as well, and its male citizens of military age were subject to arrest. As Cockburn informed his superior, Vice Admiral Warren, "should resistance be made, I shall consider [what I take] as a prize of war."[31]

While Cockburn could rightfully claim that he often paid for what he took from the towns, he failed to mention that these debts were not redeemable until after the war. One British midshipman, Frederick Chamier, illustrated Cockburn's confiscation methods: "A bullock was estimated at five dollars, although it was worth twenty and sheep had the high price of a dollar attached to them, they being in reality worth six at least. . . . But supposing, and I have seen it one hundred times, that the farmer refused the money for his stock; why then we drove sheep, bullocks, and geese away, and left the money for the good man to take afterwards."[32]

At least one senior officer, Lieutenant Colonel Charles Napier, second in command of the 102nd Regiment of Foot, felt a bit ashamed of how the campaign was waged and later wrote, "Strong is my dislike to what is perhaps a necessary part of our job, viz. Plundering and ruining the peasantry. We drive all their cattle and of course ruin them; my hands are clean, but it is hateful to see the poor Yankees robbed, and to be the robber. If we should fairly take it would not be so bad, but the rich escape; for the loss of a few cows and oxen is nothing to a rich man, while you ruin a poor peasant if you take his only cow."[33] Chamier was more direct and noted, "If by any stretch of argument we could establish the owner of a house, cottage, hut &c. to be a militia-man, that house we burnt." He wrote that if, in searching a building, weapons, including "duck guns" (fowling pieces), were found, that was pretext enough for the British to set a house on fire. Chamier stated that the Americans were punished "for the unnatural sin of protecting their own country."[34]

Soon after they had leveled Frenchtown, Cockburn's Royal Marines tried to take the town of Elkton, Maryland. However, this was one of the few occasions (at that time) in which the militia manning a local fortification successfully defended a town. Undeterred, Cockburn doubled back toward the western shore of the bay, and on 3 May his men raided farmsteads up the Susquehanna River and anchored near the coastal town of Havre de Grace, then a prosperous village of about fifty to sixty mostly wooden dwellings. As he did at Frenchtown, Cockburn used Royal Marines in barges who approached the town at night in preparation for a dawn attack. Like other northern bay towns, Havre de Grace's defenses were entirely reliant on the local militia. However, having seen Cockburn's squadron pass by earlier on its way toward the Elk River, the local militiamen had been allowed to return to their homes. The dismissal of the militia proved to be a major mistake. When Cockburn's squadron suddenly reappeared, many militiamen decided not to return to their posts. Being only slightly larger than most of the surrounding villages, the town had one known gun battery to command the water approaches at Concord Point. This primary position was located on a bluff on the southern edge of the town and was called (for reasons unknown) the Potato Battery.

Although the British were known to be just offshore, the Potato Battery remained weakly manned. In fact, according to a contemporary observer, the situation shortly before the British attack on Havre de Grace was one of complacency:

> The inhabitants, wearied with continual excitement and laborious exercise, [relaxed] from their exertions, and as the English had [been] tranquil for some time . . . they fancied themselves in less danger, than they had apprehended. By some unaccountable want of foresight, all the cavalry and some of the infantry were suffered to return to their homes, and those which remained became uneasy and disorderly. The officers were often absent, and even at the time of the attack, the commanding officer was several miles from town, and did not arrive there, till after the work of destruction was accomplished, and the authors of it [the British] had retired.[35]

At daybreak on 3 May 1813, twenty barges containing Royal Marines and a rocket boat were spotted moving rapidly toward the Concord Point battery. A few militiamen on duty there opened fire, and the noise threw the sleeping town into complete chaos. Civilians rushed hither and yon trying to escape. Officers tried (often in vain) to locate their missing men. To silence the battery, Royal Navy guns fired grapeshot directly into the American position. As a result, the militia members quickly abandoned their guns. The exceptions were Irish-born militia lieutenant John O'Neill and two other men, who continued to resist the British until they were captured. O'Neill might have escaped had he not been injured by the recoil of one of the guns. During the bombardment the Royal Navy launched Congreve rockets into the town. While this noisy missile effectively induced terror, it rarely killed people outright. More often, it was used as an incendiary device, and such was the case at Havre de Grace. Hissing Congreves and Royal Marines with torches soon had much of the town's wooden buildings in flames. One unfortunate militiaman named Webster *was* killed by a Congreve when the iron projectile hit him in the head—only one of two recorded instances during the entire war when a rocket directly caused a personnel casualty.

The Reverend James Wilmer was an eyewitness to the attack. At that time he was temporarily residing in town at the Columbian Inn, operated by a Mrs. Sears. He ran out into the inn's backyard and was nearly killed by "a full volley of canister shot [which] appeared to fall in every direction." Along with other citizens he continued "to the heights, a little above the farm of Mr. Dutton" and observed at least 150 British troops in town "plunder without distinction." Wilmer believed the British burned Havre de Grace because the town fathers refused to pay a British ransom demand of $20,000. Further, because the militia had in fact opposed the landing, Captain Lawrence, the commanding officer of the British light frigate HMS *Fantome*, informed the town leadership that the "village shall now feel the effects of war."[36] By the time the British were finished with the town, there was no doubt that the hard hand of war had come to the Chesapeake Bay.

Cockburn suspected that Lieutenant O'Neill was Irish and sent him on board the HMS *Maidstone* to determine his actual nationality. Worried that the British intended to execute O'Neill as a traitor to the Crown, Maryland militia brigadier general Henry Miller wrote to Warren on 8 May 1813 and demanded O'Neill's release. Miller informed Warren that if "Lieutenant O'Neale" (*sic*) was executed, he would have to "resort to the law of retaliation," and that "two British subjects shall be selected by lot or otherwise, and immediately executed." Warren responded to Miller two days later and told him that the aforementioned "O'Neale" had already been released "upon the application of the magistrates

Admiral Cockburn and British Landing Party Burn and Loot Havre de Grace, Maryland, May 1813, etching by William Charles. Courtesy of the Maryland Historical Society, H151

of Havre de Grace, on parole." However, to appear not to have knuckled under to Miller's threat of retaliation, Warren added that if he had been aware of the prisoner's Irish antecedents, "he certainly would have been detained, to account to his sovereign and country for being in arms against British colors."[37] Both British naval officers refused to countenance the possibility that O'Neill was a naturalized American citizen.

After having sacked Havre de Grace, Maryland, Cockburn sent a small expedition about six miles up the Susquehanna River. There the expedition members burned a warehouse belonging to John Stump near Stafford's Mills, across the river from the town of Port Deposit, Maryland. While Port Deposit was a more lucrative target, the arrival of substantial numbers of militiamen was enough to deter the raiders from making an attempt on the town. Instead, Cockburn sent another barge-borne force up the nearby Northeast River and burned the Principio Iron Works. The ironworks was probably the most militarily significant target in the entire region since it supported one of the few cannon factories in all of the United States. During the attack Cockburn's men destroyed at least forty-six cannon, including twenty-eight 32-pounder cannon then being readied for shipment. Cockburn noted to Warren that the Principio Iron Works "was one of the most valuable Works of [its] kind in America."[38] The British also swept up all the livestock on Spetsutie Island, adjacent to the smoldering town of Havre de Grace. They paid their American owners sixteen dollars a head for cattle and three dollars a head for sheep. Cockburn later reported to Warren that the total haul of guns taken from the battery at Havre de Grace (six guns) and those disabled at the Principio Iron Works amounted to a total of "51 guns and 130 stand of small arms."[39]

After his forces had destroyed the Principio Iron Works, Cockburn returned again to Maryland's Eastern Shore. Since the Sassafras River was the only significant waterway in the upper bay that had not yet been raided, the citizens of the small villages of Georgetown and Fredericktown, lying opposite one another on the river, feared the worst when on 5 May they spotted the HMS *Maidstone* in the company of five other sloops. Cockburn quickly sent another fifteen-barge raid force upriver in company with three small support vessels along with a rocket boat. As happened at Frenchtown, the raid force got lost on its way to the objective. Sending two captured slaves ashore under a white flag with a message that the town would be spared if no resistance was encountered, Cockburn ordered the raid force to immediately move on Fredericktown.

As it turned out, only eighty Cecil County militiamen, many armed with personal fowling pieces, had reported for duty at Fredericktown. These men were under the command of Col. Thomas W. Veazey of the Forty-Ninth Maryland Regiment. Veazey threw up a temporary breastwork. Unfortunately, he had only one 6-pounder cannon and a few rounds of ammunition with which to resist the British amphibious assault. As the British marines pulled within range of Veazey's militiamen, the Marylanders opened a heavy fire on them. The British returned fire from swivel guns and small cannon mounted in the barges and launched Congreve rockets from a rocket boat. About half of Veazey's militia immediately fled the scene. Left with only thirty-five men, Veazey fought the invaders until forced to retreat. Because the colonel had ignored Cockburn's offer to spare the village if the Marylanders did not resist, the admiral ordered the entire town to be burned. He even personally came ashore to supervise part of the town's destruction. British casualties at Fredericktown amounted to only five men wounded.

The Royal Marines burned a few small boats and seized sugar, lumber, and other military stores. Knowing that the nearby village of Georgetown was weakly defended by the Kent County militia, Cockburn savagely looted the farms of the local inhabitants and used only four barge loads of marines to complete the town's destruction.[40]

By "7 AM, the fires from what had once been the ports of Fredericktown and Georgetown could be seen from the decks of the HMS *Maidstone* ten miles away and were so entered in the master's log." A while later, the home of Colonel Veazey was pillaged, but he personally escaped capture. By 4:00 p.m. the British had loaded all the loot they possibly could into their barges, and they were soon on board their larger ships in the river. American newspapers referred to Cockburn and his men as "tiger banditti." A Lexington, Kentucky, newspaper hyperbolically referred to the admiral as "Satan on his cloud when he saw the blood of man from murdered *Abel* first crimson the earth, exulting at the damning deed." A few other upper bay towns, such as Charlestown on the Northeast River, sent deputations to Cockburn to inform him that there would be no further resistance and no militia allowed within the village environs if the towns were spared from plunder. This was exactly the effect Cockburn had hoped for, and he later wrote, "All the places in the upper part of the Chesapeake have adopted similar resolutions . . . as there is now neither public property, vessels, nor warlike stores remaining in this neighborhood."[41] With Cockburn's mission largely accomplished and a rumor that the French were sending a relief fleet to the Chesapeake (as they had in 1781) circulating, Warren ordered Cockburn's squadron to immediately return to Lynnhaven Bay.

In retrospect, with the exception of the reduction of the Principio Iron Works, Cockburn's raids on the northern bay towns did not have much lasting military impact other than making his name anathema to the local citizenry. However, his depredations did ultimately prove that the Americans, fixated as they were on Canada, were woefully unprepared to defend the Chesapeake region against seaborne attacks. Cockburn also liberated about four thousand slaves, primarily from Maryland's Eastern Shore. A number of these freed slaves later joined British West Indian regiments or were formed into colonial marine detachments and used on further raiding expeditions.

As for the town of Baltimore, Cockburn's brief spring appearance in the Patapsco River and his return to the area in August 1813 had certainly changed

Sir George Cockburn is pictured in front of the burning of Washington in an engraving by Charles Turner from 1819. Prints and Photographs Division, Library of Congress, LC-DIG-pga-02909

the situation there. An itinerant journalist named George Douglas, who had been to Baltimore in 1808, described how much the city had changed and said that it literally may be "called a *new town* [emphasis in the original]." Douglas stated that "on entering the state of Maryland, sloth, indolence, & poverty, seem to be the ruling powers." However, "on toping [*sic*] the hill above Baltimore, you are all at once thrust with a full view of this city, lying round the margin of a basin of water, surrounded by hills, forts, camps, numerous country houses, a variety of streams, and a distant prospect of the Chesapeake." Douglas observed, "The people here are hard put to it in the Military way. Besides strong weekly detachments for the fort & different camps, they are obliged to furnish nightly parties, to watch the enemy."[42]

Warren, however, was not ready to return to passive blockade duty before he took a shot at capturing the highly vulnerable seaport of Norfolk, Virginia. Arriving from Bermuda in late May 1813, the 102nd Regiment of Foot, under the command of Colonel Sir Sidney Beckwith—an officer of some renown who had served under the Duke of Wellington, Sir Arthur Wellesley—and more Royal Marines reinforced Warren's growing squadron. Beckwith's second in command was Lieutenant Colonel Charles Napier. Beckwith and Napier also brought with them two infantry companies of Independent Foreigners. These companies soon proved to be more trouble than they were worth.[43]

But truth be told, even the regular troops under Beckwith and Napier, the 102nd Regiment of Foot, also possessed a less-than-stellar prior service history. The 102nd Regiment was originally formed in 1789 as the New South Wales Corps. The unit, as its name implied, garrisoned the British colony of Australia and in fact served as a sort of penal regiment for the entire British army. Soldiers court-martialed in other regiments were frequently sentenced to serve in the New South Wales Corps. Now renamed the 102nd Regiment of Foot, the unit returned to England in 1810 and was briefly stationed on the island of Guernsey. Before leaving Australia, the regiment had been allowed to recruit "150 lads born in the Colony of free birth and good character." Some of these same Australians might still have been with the unit when it was ordered to the Chesapeake Bay in 1813.[44] Thus, by the midsummer of 1813, Warren had well over twenty-four hundred army troops and Royal Marines under his direct command, and he believed he now had the strength to attack and seize the rich prize of Norfolk, Virginia.

4

THE CAMPAIGN TO TAKE
NORFOLK

*W*ith the upper Chesapeake Bay in turmoil, Admiral Warren and Admiral Cockburn, at long last reinforced by the 102nd Regiment of Foot and at least two battalions of Royal Marines, were ready to take a stab at Norfolk, Virginia. To accomplish this task, the British had to first get past the town's considerable defensive network. According to Lieutenant Colonel Napier, Beckwith "divided his force into two brigades, the largest under me; and other under Lieutenant Colonel [Richard] Williams of the Marines. My fear is that my *gents* may be too eager; all young soldiers are dangerous in that way; but ours will be less so than the Americans, for they are young also and without even theory."[1]

It was abundantly clear to Warren and Colonel Beckwith, commander of the landing force, that the key to the American defensive system was Craney Island, located at the mouth of the Elizabeth River. The Port of Norfolk was located a few miles down the Elizabeth River from the island and protected by the fortifications of Fort Nelson, located on the river's west bank, and Fort Norfolk on the east. Their idea was to take out the American defenses on the island, advance ground and supporting naval forces down both banks of the Elizabeth River, attack the forts from their landward sides, and then march into the city.

Fort Nelson was originally known as the "Fort at Portsmouth [Virginia]" and was built on a point of land called Windmill Point or Tucker's Mills (for the family who owned the land during the American Revolution). The original fort had parapets "14 feet high and walls that were 15 feet thick with embrasures for 42 guns." However, since the fort was primarily for seaward defense, its landward side was considerably weaker.[2]

Fort Norfolk had been originally constructed during the Revolution but had long been neglected. By the time of Washington's second administration, both Elizabeth River fortifications were in a considerable state of disrepair until Congress, at the request of President George Washington, ordered that the nation's dilapidated land fortifications be improved. A parsimonious Congress appropriated just $3,000 to repair both forts. Washington appointed the renowned French military engineer Major John Jacob Ulrich Rivardi to temporarily supervise the work and also planned improvements to Baltimore's Fort Whetstone (soon to be renamed Fort McHenry). However, Norfolk's defenses received higher priority because of the city's more immediate vulnerability to seaborne attack.[3]

There was also the important Gosport Navy Yard at Portsmouth, Virginia, to worry about. Located nearby was a small U.S. Marine barracks with about twenty-two Marines assigned to provide local security. Because of Gosport's importance and vulnerability to attacks from the sea, the defenses of the Norfolk region were augmented by no less than twenty-one gunboats. These boats were the product of former president Thomas Jefferson's controversial program to save defense dollars by building coastal naval craft instead of more expensive frigates or ships of the line. Each gunboat was 50 to 75 feet long and could be propelled using sails or oars. The boats usually mounted "a 24 or 32 pounder cannon in the bow or on a pivot amidships and two 12 pounder carronades, one on each side." However, by 1813 the real issue with the gunboats was that they were indifferently manned— mostly by local militiamen who had been forced into such service and usually deserted given their first opportunity.[4] Throughout the summer of 1813, at best the U.S. Navy could fully man only about seven or eight Norfolk-based gunboats at any given time.

A fortuitous and not insignificant addition to the defenses of Norfolk came in the form of the temporarily blockaded frigate USS *Constellation* (forty-four guns). The commanding officer of the *Constellation*, Captain Charles Stewart, was greatly concerned that most of the troops assigned to protect Norfolk and his own ship from attack were from the usually unreliable militia. In fact, the militia's commanding officer, Brigadier General Robert Barraud Taylor, a lawyer from Norfolk, wrote to Virginia governor James Barbour on 11 March 1813 and complained that "the Gun Boats are most wretchedly manned . . . and should they fall into the Enemy's hands, as they must if boarded by night, they will be turned against us." Stewart echoed Taylor's complaints to Secretary of the Navy Jones and stated that he found "the gunboats so weakly manned and so utterly incompetent to protect themselves should the enemy make the attempt to board them in the night, [that] to protect their falling into their hands, I was under the necessity of withdrawing them within the fortifications of Norfolk. . . . Ten of the boats have been sent up to the Navy Yard . . . which rendered them about half-manned."[5] Stewart also lamented that "a strong work has not [yet] been erected on Craney Island, I mean a strong work for eight or ten guns made sufficiently high to prevent an escalade or surprise; the Narrows piered and secured with strong booms and chains; should that have been done, the Gun Boats well manned and stationed above the booms, it appears to me we might bid defiance to their operations by water."[6] The defenses on Craney Island were the responsibility of General Taylor. Initially, Taylor was more concerned about the men he commanded than about fortifications. Thanks to a spring militia draft ordered by the governor, Taylor had nearly fifteen hundred men on hand to defend Norfolk, but few of them were properly equipped, supplied, or, in some cases, even armed.

Taylor's militia arrived unevenly in companies and battalions and under the command of their own officers. Two of the regiments, the Fourth and Fifth, had been recently called up by the governor once the British appeared in force in the Chesapeake Bay in early 1813. Although the forts nearer the city possessed regular Army forces consisting primarily of artillerists, Taylor drew up his more numerous polyglot militia into a more manageable brigade of five infantry regiments. He wisely focused their efforts toward defending the landward approaches to the forts. In reality, Taylor's militia was fairly spread out throughout the southern Virginia tidewater region; hence, he allowed his five subordinate regimental commanders significant initiative to individually defend their various sectors without too much interference from higher headquarters. For example, the Fourth Regiment, under Lieutenant Colonel Henry Beatty, along with some separate artillery units, was eventually sent forward to Craney Island. Beatty was given wide latitude in making the island defensible, but it was clear to one and all that the vulnerable northwest corner of the island needed the most attention, and this was where the militia concentrated its efforts. Beatty remained within supporting distance of reinforcements in and around the forts a few miles to the south. Taylor made up for his logistical and organizational shortfalls by becoming a veritable whirlwind of activity. He visited all of his posted units and made sure the men were kept busy preparing for a potential British amphibious assault that he was sure was not long in coming. He also purposely spread the various county militia companies across his entire brigade in order to avoid the problem of nepotism prevalent in the Virginia militia as a whole.

Virginia militiaman James Jarvis, an orderly sergeant in the Portsmouth Rifles, described this problem very well: "It is a fact that most of the members of the militia companies were blood relations. In some of the companies, the captains would have at least three brothers, one or two uncles, and perhaps ten or fifteen cousins; then in consequence of later marriages, the balance of the company were half brothers, etc., to the brothers, cousins, and uncles. Here was a pretty mess of discipline. It was not unusual for a private to sing out to his captain, 'Nat, what in the devil do you keep us marching all day for?'"[7]

The militia was indeed difficult, but at least the men had largely turned out for duty. General Taylor complained to Governor Barbour about three members of the Religious Society of Friends (Quakers) who had been sent along with the Nansemond County militia draft of March 1813. Because of their religious convictions, these men "refused to do duty, to furnish substitutes, or receive rations." Taylor placed them under guard but wryly admitted to the governor that he did not really know what to do with these men since if he just sent them home without any sort of penalty, "Quakerism should become the predominant religion in our ranks."[8]

By early June, having been ordered by the Secretary of the Navy to take command of the frigate USS *Constitution*, Stewart was temporarily replaced by Master Commandant Joseph Tarbell. Captain John Cassin, now the senior U.S. Navy officer in the region, decided to reposition the gunboats toward the mouth of the Elizabeth River and forward of the line of sunken block ships. They formed a mutually supporting defensive arc of boats that extended from Lambert's Point on the east bank of the river to low-lying Craney Island on the west bank. Further, the War Department finally completed the long-desired field fortifications on the vulnerable northwest corner of the island. Besides Beatty's 450 Virginia militia-men, Taylor later sent forward about 100 of *Constellation*'s sailors, commanded by Lieutenant B. J. Neale, USN, and about 50 U.S. Marines from the ship's detachment, under Lieutenant Henry Breckinridge, USMC, as reinforcements.[9] Neale's sailors provided much-needed expertise for inexperienced militia gun crews and would man and fire the heavier pieces of ordnance. Breckinridge's Marines did the same for the infantry and were also trained to manage light artillery. In sum, Taylor had about 740 men to oppose a British attack on the island—a substantial force with which to face down Warren's regulars and Royal Marines. Militia sergeant James Jarvis noted that all "arrangement thus made to defend the post, we waited the approach of the enemy and felt we were prepared to give them a decent reception for our troops were full of ardor."[10]

However, the real problem with the defense of Craney "Island" was that it was hardly an island at all. Separated from the mainland by a narrow inlet, the island in 1813 was only "900 yards long by 233 yards wide." Not a single structure stood on it. In fact, the narrow inlet, also called the Thoroughfare, near Wise Creek was allegedly fordable "at low or even half tides." By mid-June 1813 Taylor had "2 companies of artillery, Captain Arthur Emmerson's Portsmouth Light Artillery and Captain Richardson's Light Artillery under the overall command of Major James Faulkner of the Virginia State Artillery; Captain Robert's company of riflemen; and 416 infantry [militia], under the command of Lieutenant Colonel Henry Beatty and Major Andrew Waggoner." The Americans clearly saw the forest of masts of Warren's fleet anchored approximately five miles from Craney Island. Shifting what troops that could be spared from the garrison at Fort Norfolk, Taylor ordered thirty regular U.S. Army troops, under the command of Captain Richard Pollard, and an additional thirty militiamen and two officers to reinforce the Craney Island defenses.[11]

By 20 June 1813 it became apparent to the Americans that the British were going to attack Craney Island. Assault troops crowded on the decks of nearby British ships, and they moved several of their frigates closer to the island. Sir Sidney Beckwith's troops made up the bulk of the British assault force. Before his arrival, Beckwith had submitted a questionnaire to Cockburn asking about the American defenses and the best location for making an amphibious assault. Beckwith seemed to be inclined to assault from the west, making an unopposed landing on the east bank of the Nansemond and marching overland to attack Fort Nelson's weakly defended landward side. Cockburn countered this idea and pointed out that unless Beckwith quickly seized the bridge to Gosport, American forces from the Norfolk side of the Elizabeth River could rapidly reinforce threatened positions in and around Fort Nelson. It would be far easier and more direct for the British, after their forces had subdued the Americans on Craney Island, to attack and occupy the Portsmouth side of the Elizabeth and simultaneously threaten the Norfolk side to keep potential reinforcements pinned down. Cockburn also believed that once the west bank of the river was completely in British hands, the Americans would voluntarily decide to abandon Norfolk (since the port would be unusable) and burn or surrender the *Constellation*.

Before the landing of the 102nd Regiment and Royal Marines, Warren advanced the frigate HMS *Junon* (thirty-eight guns) into Hampton Roads near the mouth of the Elizabeth River. The *Junon* was supported by two frigates farther out in Lynnhaven Bay. During the early morning hours of 20 June 1813, Captain Cassin ordered Master Commandant Tarbell to attack this seemingly isolated frigate with his gunboats, which heretofore had been derided by all in Norfolk as next to useless. One newspaper correspondent wrote that everyone was "impatient to know how Mr. Jefferson's *bull dogs* would acquit themselves; and whether the philosopher's system would prove upon trial, a monument of his wisdom or his folly." At approximately 3:30 a.m., Tarbell's gunboats opened up on the *Junon* and initially, because of the surprise factor, did fairly well against their British adversary. Unfortunately for the Americans, a favorable breeze allowed the other two supporting frigates to come up in support, and their combined weight of ordnance was enough to cause the gunboats to withdraw back toward Craney Island. While the Americans later claimed they would have taken the *Junon* if not for the intervention of the other two vessels, British after-action reports did not indicate that the frigate was ever in any real danger. Tarbell's losses were slight as well. However, on gunboat No. 139 a master's mate named Allison was killed when an 18-pound ball "passed through him and lodged in the mast."[12] Nevertheless, while not successful in taking a lone frigate, the gunboats had acquitted themselves well— although they never totally proved the efficacy of Jefferson's decision to build them. The action of twenty-three-year-old gunboat commander William B. Shubrick was especially noteworthy. Shubrick fought his gunboat in close proximity to the *Junon* until he was ordered by Tarbell to break contact in order to tow off another disabled gunboat. He remained on active duty with the U.S. Navy, retiring at the rank of rear admiral in 1859.

Captain Cassin noted in his 21 June after-action report to the Secretary of the Navy that he and Tarbell had used a total of fifteen gunboats in the attack on the *Junon*. These boats were organized into "two divisions," one of which was commanded by Robert Henley II "from the frigate" (the *Constellation*). Cassin believed that the *Junon* was "severely handled" in the engagement and that "had the calm continued one half hour that frigate must have fallen into our hands or been destroyed."[13]

During the early morning hours of 22 June, a nervous American sentry on Craney Island thought he spotted a boat moving through the water near the Thoroughfare and fired an alarm gun. The boat turned out to be river debris, but the entire American garrison was now roused as dawn broke over Hampton Roads. By this time the Americans could clearly see barge loads of red-coated soldiers and Royal Marines landing and assembling at the nearby Wise Farm. The senior American commander on Craney Island, Lieutenant Colonel Henry Beatty, arranged his militia, his few regular U.S. Army and U.S. Marine infantry, and Richardson's artillerymen into a line that faced the Thoroughfare and dominated the northwestern part of the island near where most of the British were seen massing. Militia major James Faulkner had overall command of the island's artillery. His expertly handled guns proved decisive in the coming battle. Originally, three heavy naval guns, an 18-pounder and two 24-pounder guns, were located in an incomplete battery started by Major Thomas Armistead on the southeastern part of the island. Without oxen or horses to haul them to other island positions, it was thought that the guns could not be relocated. Nevertheless, Faulkner managed to transport the heavy ordnance to the threatened part of the island and combine it into a single battery with the crack Portsmouth Light Artillery (four 6-pounder light guns). Manning the heavier guns were sailors from the *Constellation*; Virginia militiamen and a few U.S. Marines worked the 6-pounder weapons.[14]

Beckwith planned to demonstrate in front of the Americans from the Wise Farm area, while another portion of his troops would force a crossing of Wise Creek from the Stringer Farm, located toward the western side of Craney Island. Meanwhile, ship's barges full of soldiers and Royal Marines were to make a direct assault against preselected northwestern beaches. Artilleryman Sergeant William Young saw numerous British boats transporting troops to and from their vessels crowded near Craney Island. Lacking a proper flagstaff, Young noted, the Americans had nailed their flag to a long pole. Young could distinctly see the British forces "marching and countermarching on the beach [on the opposite shore of the Thoroughfare]."[15]

Beckwith's plan was good but required both attacks to be closely coordinated so that the militia could not take advantage of interior lines of communication. If the attack succeeded, the Americans risked total annihilation or capture. However, it was not long before the situation began to go seriously awry for the British. Both Wise Creek and the Thoroughfare proved not fordable at this particular moment, and Beckwith's troops, unable to cross, began stacking up on the Thoroughfare's banks. To draw the attention of the American gunners on the island away from this suddenly lucrative target, Beckwith had his Congreve rocket batteries, located immediately behind a building on Wise Farm, fire their noisy missiles at the Americans. Unfortunately for the British, this attack drew extremely accurate American counterbattery fire, which destroyed the building and caused a number of casualties. Fleeing from the cover of the building and into the open, the British soldiers were then subjected to grapeshot from Faulkner's massed battery. Firing from the American line was so rapid that one of the large 24-pounder guns and a 6-pounder from the Portsmouth Light Artillery jarred their barrels loose from their gun carriages and were temporarily out of action. Nonetheless, Faulkner had five operating guns that continued to hammer the British whenever they came within range.[16]

While this carnage was taking place, the second British assault force of fifteen hundred soldiers and Royal Marines in fifty barges furiously pulled toward the northwestern shore of the island as planned. Led by Admiral Warren's personal barge, the *Centipede* (so called because of its bright green color, numerous oars, and a small brass 3-pounder cannon mounted in the bow), "the British barges began to close on the island at 11AM." The amphibious assault was commanded by Royal Navy captain Samuel G. Pechell of the HMS *San Domingo* (Warren's flag captain). Pechell wanted to time his assault just as Beckwith's troops were completing their own flank attack. Unaware that Beckwith's redcoats had been smashed by Faulkner's artillery and had never landed on the island, Pechell's men doggedly moved toward their assigned landing points. Faulkner's five remaining guns could now focus solely on Pechell's approaching boats. Holding fire until the barges were well within range, Faulkner's gunners unleashed a deadly torrent of solid shot and grape. To make matters worse, most of the barges grounded on unseen mudflats about three hundred yards from the shore and ceased making forward progress. The American gunners poured shot after shot into the stationary targets. Soldiers and Royal Marines who jumped over the sides of their barges to wade ashore found themselves trapped in knee-deep muck. Standing in the *Centipede*, Royal Navy captain J. M. Hanchett tried to rally his men when a shot crashed through the boat's hull and he was severely wounded in the thigh. Hanchett and his men were forced to abandon the *Centipede*. Surviving troops in nearby barges picked up the dying and wounded as best they could and retreated back toward their ships. It was not long before Pechell ordered a general retreat.[17]

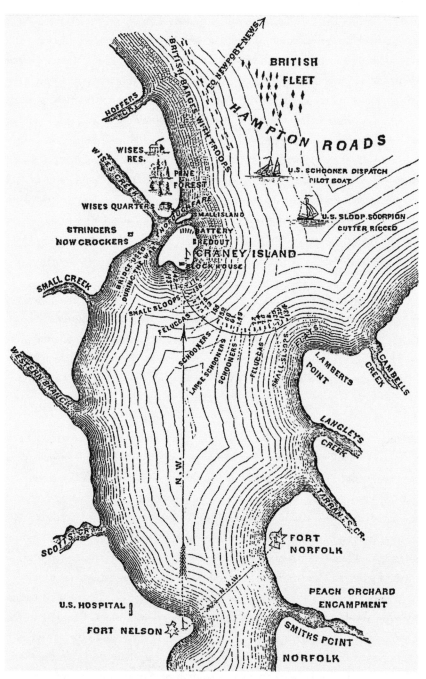

Map 4-1. The British assault on Craney Island at the intersection of the
Hampton Roads, by Benson J. Lossing. *The Pictorial Field Book of the War of 1812*
(New York: Harper & Brothers, 1868), 679.

With the withdrawal of the amphibious assault force, Warren ordered the return of all the troops in the vicinity of Wise Farm to the safety of their ships. It was a tremendous American victory. During the lull General Taylor hurried more militiamen to Lieutenant Colonel Beatty, but he did not need them. Warren had already decided to forsake taking the island by force.

Midshipman Josiah Tatnall, a future commodore in the Confederate Navy, wrote years after the battle that when he and his mates waded out into the mudflats and approached the damaged *Centipede*, they found a number of wounded men in and around the vessel, including a "Frenchman in her with both legs shot off." Tatnall noted that this man was carried ashore in a hammock, but he later died of his wounds. It was reported that at least thirty members of one of the companies of Independent Foreigners deserted to the Americans. Other witnesses believed they had been captured en masse in one of the grounded boats. Nevertheless, when these men did not return to their ships during the general withdrawal, many assumed they had been killed by the Americans in the mudflats. Later muster rolls for the Independent Foreigner companies listed at least forty-two men missing—an indication that at least some must have deserted during the action.[18] Writing to Secretary of the Navy Jones, Cassin was especially commendatory of the *Constellation*'s 18-pounder crew members, who, he said, "fired their [cannon] more like riflemen than Artillerists. I never seen such shooting and seriously believe they saved the Island yesterday." While the Americans did not report any casualties, the British lost at least sixteen men killed and sixty-two missing.[19]

Cassin's official report was later reprinted in the 30 June 1813 edition of the *Baltimore Patriot*. In his report Cassin noted that gunboat No. 67 played an instrumental role dispersing the British at Wise Farm. He wrote, "All day deserters from the army coming in; I have myself taken in 25, and 18 prisoners belonging to the *Centipede*." Ominously, Cassin appended to his letter that "Captain Tarbell has this moment come up, and informs me that the enemy has withdrawn his troops from Craney Island, and landed at Newport-News, and is firing Congreve Rockets."[20]

Clearly dissatisfied with the outcome of the Craney Island affair, Admiral Warren had indeed turned his attention toward the vulnerable town of Hampton, Virginia, opposite Norfolk and across wide Lynnhaven Bay. Hampton was targeted because Warren believed the town "commanded communication between [the] upper country and Norfolk."[21] In reality, Warren wanted revenge for his check at Craney Island. At that moment Hampton was weakly defended by Virginia militia major Stapleton Crutchfield and about 450 militiamen. At Hampton the British had no river forts or gunboats or sunken hulks to contend with, and the numerous nearby undefended landing inlets made the town an especially inviting target.

This time the aggressive Cockburn took personal charge of the operation. He wasted no time positioning his ships off Blackbeard's Point near Newport News. Landing on 25 June a joint force of Royal Marines, under Lieutenant Colonel Richard Williams, and soldiers of the 102nd Regiment of Foot, under Colonel Sir Sidney Beckwith, the British came ashore with nearly two thousand men about two miles west of town. These troops advanced eastward toward Hampton on the Celey Road, while launches and barges from Cockburn's flotilla fired their cannon at the main American militia camp and an artillery battery commanded by militia captain B. W. Pryor, then located at a farm ironically known as Little England. Little England was just southwest of Hampton and divided from the town by a small creek. It was an extremely poor defensive location. Crutchfield later reported that Pryor's battery repelled the British advance "in a manner worthy of veteran troops," but it was not Cockburn's intention to land at Little England just yet. Rather, he hoped to hold Crutchfield's attention long enough for Beckwith's troops to arrive on the Americans' right flank via the Celey Road.

Crutchfield soon received a warning from militia captain R. Servant, commanding a rifle company guarding the road, that the enemy was advancing with a large body of troops from the west. The major immediately marched the bulk of his forces to reinforce Servant and his men. But the British were much closer than Crutchfield had assumed, and his militia was ambushed as it approached some heavy woods that flanked the road. He described the action:

> We advanced in column of platoons, thro' a lane and open cornfield which led from our encampment to the enemy, and to the main and Ceyle [sic] Roads. When in the field within 200 yards of the gate opening into the Ceyley [sic] road and a thicket of pine, we were fired upon by the enemy's musketry from a thick wood at the upper end of a field immediately bordering on the road. Upon this discharge, orders were given to wheel to the left into line and march upon the enemy. In that position we had not marched more than 50 yards when the enemy opened

upon us two six-pound field pieces loaded with grape and canister shot and his machines filled with rockets of a small size.[22]

Heavy and confused fighting took place in the woods that separated the British on Celey Road and the main American militia camp at Little England. It was not long before the Americans were in full flight through the town of Hampton and northward toward Yorktown. The British easily overran Pryor's battery at Little England—but not before his cannoneers spiked their guns—and the Americans swam the creek to avoid capture. They reported losses of only five men killed, thirty-three wounded, and ten missing in action. The Virginia militia losses were slightly higher at seven men killed, twelve wounded, and eleven missing. Most of the townspeople fled toward Yorktown. Many of the surviving militia ended up stopping at Halfway House, a point between Hampton and Yorktown. Other militia from York and James City Counties rushed to defend the town of Williamsburg.[23]

The now mostly deserted town of Hampton was in for a huge surprise as soldiers began breaking into homes—some of them still occupied by residents who were unable to flee or who thought that their private property would be safer if they were present. Many of the homes were occupied by women whose husbands or male relations had been driven off during the fighting. According to a number of contemporary accounts, in revenge for the Americans allegedly firing on their wounded comrades in the mudflats during the Battle of Craney Island, the British troops, and especially the Independent Foreigner companies, looted and burned a substantial part of the town. Much has been written about the destruction of Hampton, Virginia. Officers with the British troops later confirmed a number of crimes their men committed. However, they were nearly unanimous in blaming the green-coated Independent Foreigner companies for the egregious conduct.

At the time the First Company of Foreigners was commanded by British captain Sylvester Smith. Smith had been the First Company commander when it was briefly garrisoned on Bermuda in February 1813. Although his company was on the island for less than four months, unit records revealed that at least one of his men had been shot to death by a firing squad for "endeavoring to incite a mutiny." Nonetheless, following their successful attack on Hampton, the Independent Foreigners were initially commended by Sir Sidney Beckwith, who wrote that "the gallantry of Captain Smith, the officers and men of the two companies [of] Canadian Chasseurs [Independent Foreigners] who led the attack was highly conspicuous and praiseworthy." Interestingly—and perhaps because of the gross behavior that came to light after the fighting had ended—this sentence was crossed out in the official record.[24]

Beckwith later quietly shipped the Independent Foreigners off to bleak Nova Scotia for the rest of the war. They alarmed the citizens of Halifax when a few of them broke into a house in a neighborhood known as Dutch Town. This was the final straw as far as Warren was concerned, and he quickly arranged for the Independent Foreigners to be shipped back to England. During the spring of 1814, the government in London took advantage of Napoleon's brief exile to Elba and repatriated to France all the Independent Foreigner companies with three months' extra pay.[25]

The Americans loudly complained to the British commanders in the tidewater region about the behavior of their troops in Hampton. Allegations of rape and murder were made. An elderly man named Kirby was shot and killed in his sickbed with the ball passing through his body and grazing his wife's hip. The Americans claimed the shooting was intentional, although after the war, Kirby's wife testified that soldiers were attempting to silence Kirby's barking dog and had shot the man by accident.

Colonel Richard Parker of Westmoreland County was appointed to investigate what took place at Hampton and to corroborate the claims of others, like Crutchfield, who alleged that "the unfortunate females of Hampton who could not leave the town were suffered to be abused in the most shameful manner, not only by the venal, savage foe but by the unfortunate and infuriated blacks, who were encouraged in their success." Crutchfield goes on to mention the death of Kirby, the killing of his dog, and the wounding of his wife as well. Parker corroborated the killing of Kirby, but he believed that the British merely hastened the gravely ill man's ultimate demise. He also interviewed one woman who claimed she had been "seized by five or six ruffians, some of them *dressed in red* and *speaking correctly the English language* [emphasis in the original], and stripped naked. . . . She at one time made her escape and ran into a creek hard by, followed by a young daughter, whence she was dragged by monsters in human shape to experience new and aggravated suffering." Several other women testified that they had been sexually molested by soldiers "*who were in green* [emphasis in the original]." An old man named Hope was allegedly stripped of all his clothes, "even his shoes and his shirt." The church was looted, as was a general store. Parker thundered in this letter, "Men of Virginia! Will you permit all this?" He concluded his investigation by urging readers of his letter to avenge what happened at Hampton.[26]

Not to be outdone in hyperbole, General Taylor complained in writing directly to Admiral Warren. Sir Sidney Beckwith replied for Warren and countered that during the previous engagement at Craney Island, "several Americans, I assure you most solemnly, waded off from the Island and, in presence of all engaged, fired upon and shot these poor fellows" (that is, the trapped Independent Foreigner companies in the mudflats). Beckwith believed that this alleged incident caused the Independent Foreigners to get out of hand at Hampton. Taylor responded that "worthless is the laurel steeped in female tears, and joyless the conquest which has inflicted needless woe on the peaceful and unresisting." Nevertheless, Taylor appointed a board of inquiry to determine if there was any validity to Beckwith's allegation. Not surprisingly, Taylor believed that the British claims were unfounded and that Americans waded into the mudflats to secure damaged and sinking British boats and to rescue the wounded and dying. He admitted that one surrendered soldier was purposely shot at but only after he tried to escape. Eventually Beckwith ceased answering the numerous complaint letters coming from the American camp. The truth as to what took place at the Craney Island mudflats and Hampton likely lies somewhere between the British rationalization of the conduct of the Independent Foreigners and the claims of the American camp. The fact that Hampton had been largely abandoned gave the former French POWs the idea that they had carte blanche to do what they wanted. Moreover, the type of fighting they were used to in Spain was more brutal than what had heretofore occurred in the North American theater. Once the rules of war were loosened, it was difficult to control even the most disciplined soldiers. Lieutenant Colonel Charles Napier of the 102nd Regiment later wrote that his own men "nearly mutinied at my preventing them joining in the sack of that unfortunate town." Napier also wished that Sir Sidney had "hanged several villains at Little Hampton; had he done so the Americans would not have complained: but every horror was committed with impunity, rape, murder, pillage: and not a man was punished!" Napier later confessed he was uncomfortable making war against the Americans and called the conflict a "bastard rebellion."[27]

Sergeant James Jarvis, whose company had been stationed near the ropewalk located in the rear of the city of Norfolk, was sent forward to Craney Island following the British retreat. Jarvis noted, owing to the three hundred yards of mudflats that he saw, "the enemy was never enabled to approach near enough for the riflemen and infantry to make a display of their gallantry." Hence, he believed that Beckwith's charge was "wholly groundless."[28]

As expected, the American newspapers were especially condemnatory of the alleged British behavior at Hampton. The 24 July 1813 edition of the *Norfolk Herald* began with the headline "The Monsters of Hampton." Story after story of various alleged and salacious "outrages," especially against women, were printed in all the area papers. Most of these stories were pure propaganda, but their sheer volume indicates that at the very least some sort of egregious conduct on the part of the British troops, and especially the Independent Foreigner companies, certainly took place.[29]

Following the battle at Hampton, Warren detached Cockburn and a few ships and had him raid North Carolina's Outer Banks. By doing so, Warren hoped to interdict the backdoor intercoastal trade that Norfolk had resorted to since the British began their blockade on the Chesapeake Bay. Cockburn's foray was not all that fruitful. However, once again he employed his favorite and most effective naval commando, Lieutenant George Westphal, in a cutting-out operation. Westphal's aggressive activity netted the British two very fine letter-of-marque schooners, the eighteen-gun *Anaconda* and the thirteen-gun *Atlas* (which was immediately reflagged by Cockburn as the HMS *St. Lawrence*). Westphal later sailed the *Anaconda* to Halifax, Nova Scotia, where it was condemned as a legal prize and reflagged under the same name. In recognition of his excellent service, Lieutenant Westphal was given personal command of the reflagged HMS *Anaconda*, and the ship later played a central role in the New Orleans campaign. The HMS *St. Lawrence* would briefly become the scourge of the Chesapeake Bay during the 1814 campaign only to later fall prey to Thomas Boyle's privateer *Chasseur* (nicknamed the *Pride of Baltimore*).

While Cockburn was away raiding North Carolina's Outer Banks, Warren ordered Captain William H. Shirreff, commanding officer of the HMS *Barrossa*, to take his vessel and four other shallow-draught boats—the *Mohawk, Conflict, Laurestinus,* and *Highflyer*—along with six hundred troops composed of Royal Marines and elements of the 102nd Regiment farther up the Potomac to test

Washington's defenses and take soundings of the river channel in anticipation of future operations there. However, Washington's fortifications were much less robust than those of Norfolk or even Annapolis, Maryland. Many believed that the city's best defense was its largely inaccessible geographic location and the fact that other than the Navy Yard and its political value as America's new national capital, Washington, D.C., remained a swamp-ridden, sleepy, backwater town of little real military importance. Shirreff made a landing near the "cliffs of Nomini" in Westmoreland County, Virginia, and skirmished with the militia, which, according to the *Baltimore Whig*, killed four British soldiers while losing seven of its own.[30]

Warren hoped that directly threatening the American national capital would force the Madison administration to detach at least some of its regular Army troops then stationed on the Canadian border. While the approaching British riverine force did cause large numbers of Maryland and Virginia militia to be mobilized, the American regulars stayed put on the Canadian border. Secretary of War John Armstrong did direct two regular units, the newly formed and very raw 36th and 38th Infantry Regiments, to assemble at Fort Washington. The British vessels never got closer than forty miles below the city. Having run up on the treacherous Kettle Bottom shoals and not having a reliable pilot on board, Captain Shirreff decided to take soundings of the shoals and move his boats back toward the mouth of the river. Before leaving the area, Shirreff briefly engaged the gunboat *Scorpion* and the schooner *Asp* off Yeocomico River—a tributary of the Potomac River. These vessels had been trying for months to break out of the Potomac and come to the defense of more vulnerable Baltimore. British boarders drove off the *Scorpion* and temporarily captured the *Asp*, but since the *Asp* was on fire, they quickly left it to burn.[31] American newspapers reported that the British had murdered the *Asp*'s commander, Lieutenant James Sigourney, after he had surrendered, along with another man who had asked for quarter. A midshipman named McClintock, along with several other sailors, jumped overboard and swam ashore. Once the British had abandoned the burning *Asp*, the Americans returned, put out the flames, and recovered Sigourney's body. The valuable *Asp* lived to fight another day for the Americans.[32]

If Shirreff had continued up the river, he would have had to pass at least one river fort. Originally named Fort Warburton (and quickly designated Fort Washington because of its proximity to George Washington's Mount Vernon home), the fort was described by its chief engineer, Captain George Bomford, as "an enclosed work of masonry comprehending a semi-elliptical face with a circular flank on the side next to the Potomac." Fort Washington possessed some serious deficiencies. The fort's original shape and size were based on a standardized plan that was used to build Fort Madison, at Annapolis, Maryland. However, this plan made the footprint of the fort too large for its tiny four-acre Digges Point site. The fort's engineer had no choice but to scale it back and thereby reduce the number of guns it could mount to just fifteen. To be effective, the fort should have had double this number of guns. To make matters worse, the site did not allow enough space to house troops for its landward defenses. Thus, the militia was given this mission for most of the War of 1812. The only regular soldiers in the fort were artillerymen assigned to man the guns. Captain Bomford lamented that "Fort Washington was really an attempt to adopt a standardized plan to an unsuitable site. It violated a fundamental rule in the art of fortification—the fort must suit its site."[33]

Most of the locals suspected that the fort was inadequate for the task. In May 1813 a deputation of citizens from Georgetown, Maryland; the District of Columbia; and Alexandria urged the federal government to do something about improving Fort Washington. Secretary Armstrong sent U.S. Army colonel Decius Wadsworth to investigate the situation. Wadsworth was the Army's chief ordnance officer, and his word regarding fortifications carried much weight. Wadsworth soon returned from the site and, incredibly, claimed that no further reinforcement of heavy guns was necessary at Fort Washington. He believed the difficulty of navigating a large naval force up the shallow, muddy Potomac was in and of itself enough protection for the national capital. Nevertheless, Major General James Wilkinson was not convinced. He later remarked that Fort Washington was nothing more than a water battery and one that "could easily be knocked out either by the guns of a frigate or taken by force at night from the back." Writing to Secretary of the Navy Jones on 13 April, Lieutenant Edmund Kennedy, the commanding officer of the Potomac flotilla, noted that while he had been ordered to cooperate with the fort, "I really do not calculate on receiving any aid from that Quarter, the Platform being very badly constructed & in miserable Order—one Gun Boat well mann'd might attack it in the present Situation with certain Success."[34]

By this time Cockburn had returned from his Outer Banks foray. Landing about 400 troops on Blakiston (St. Clements) Island, near St. Mary's City, Maryland, he put them to work digging wells to provide his nearby ships with a convenient source of freshwater—always a problem for a blockading force. Moreover, having been in the bay area since February, Warren's ships and embarked soldiers and marines also needed fresh provisions. Hearing of yet another British incursion into southern Maryland, Secretary of State James Monroe personally rode south from Washington to reconnoiter their activity in St. Mary's County. He requested that Secretary of War Armstrong send at least 350 regular soldiers south to drive them off. Armstrong refused but did send a small detachment of soldiers to at least make a show of force.

The actual defense for much of the region continued to reside in the Maryland militia. And while the state had earlier organized its militia into twelve brigades of three thousand men each, most of these units never came close to mustering that number of men. For example, the defense of southern Maryland had been assigned to the Fifth Maryland Brigade. Because of a lack of men, this single brigade was made responsible for local defense from Baltimore County all the way to the tip of Point Lookout in St. Mary's County. This part of Maryland was honeycombed with bays, creeks, and inlets, making it nearly impossible to defend against a superior seaborne force. Moreover, most of the Maryland militia was poorly armed and lacked combat experience. In sum, southern Maryland had been essentially abandoned by both federal and state military authorities. A committee of citizens from St. Mary's petitioned the state and the federal government for a regular infantry regiment to be sent there, pleading "in the name of justice, we solicit [both governments] to rescue and save us. In the name of God we crave it for the sake of suffering humanity." Nevertheless, Annapolis and Washington did not respond to their pleas. However, one bright spot for American military fortune during this long hot summer of 1813 came courtesy, once again, of the Virginia militia. When Cockburn decided to send foraging parties up Mattox and Rosier Creeks on the Virginia side of the Potomac, they were driven off by a light infantry company under Captain John P. Hungerford. Nevertheless, by late July the British, having cleaned out most of southern Maryland to the greatest extent possible, evacuated their base near Point Lookout and sailed their fleet once again up the bay toward Annapolis and Baltimore.[35]

Portrait of Commodore Joshua Barney, commander of the Chesapeake Bay flotilla, by Rembrandt Peale. Courtesy of the Maryland Historical Society, CA682

During the summer of 1813, with the British raiding the length and breadth of the Chesapeake at will, Commodore Joshua Barney, a native of Baltimore, took it upon himself to write to Secretary of the Navy Jones and propose a plan for defending the region against further British seaborne depredations. Earlier that year, Major General Samuel Smith had tried to convince the Maryland legislature to resurrect the Maryland Barge Act, which would have essentially resurrected a state navy in 1813 along the lines of that which had existed during the American Revolution. Unfortunately, the antiwar Federalist Party dominated the Maryland House of Delegates and the Barge Act was easily voted down. However, with the British eviscerating southern Maryland and the Americans having no other options, Commodore Barney elegantly laid out the problem of defending the Chesapeake Bay from the American perspective. Estimating that the British had on hand eleven ships of the line, thirty-three frigates, thirty-eight sloops of war, and numerous smaller craft and were capable of landing a total of eight thousand men for any given operation, he wrote,

> The question is, how to meet this force with a probability of success. *Our* ships (two frigates) cannot act, our *old* gunboats will not answer, they are too heavy to Row, and too clumsy to sail, and are only fit to lay *moor'd*, to protect a pass, or Assist a Fort. I am therefore of the opinion the only defence we have in our power, is a Kind of *Barge* or *Row-Galley*, so constructed, as to draw a small draft of water, to carry *Oars*, light sails, and *One heavy long gun*, these vessels may be built in a short time, (say three weeks) [and] Men may be had, the City of Baltimore could furnish Officers & men for *twenty Barges* [emphasis in the original].[36]

Barney proposed to create a large oar-driven flying squadron of barges to operate against Warren's deeper-draught fleet. He also recommended that four or five light sailing vessels be fitted out as fire ships (something the Americans had astonishingly not tried against Warren's ships). Barney noted that the cost for constructing his entire row galley flotilla of barges was approximately one half of what it cost to build a single frigate. He also recommended that the men used to furnish sailors and marines for the barges not compete with the recruiting efforts of the U.S. Navy or Marine Corps but be selected from the merchant sailing community of Baltimore and other bay towns and that "this *Marine* force would be *separate from*, and unconnected with the *Navy*, and could be so organized, as to have *One Regiment of troops*, annexed to it, the whole under the command of an able, active Naval officer, and *one Colonel*, with powers to correspond, not only with the General Government, but with the *Governors of Virginia & Maryland*, and to act in concert whenever circumstances required [emphasis in the original]."[37]

Barney was fairly sure that if his new proposal was approved, he would be named the "able, active Naval officer" to command the force, although he did have his detractors, such as Lemuel Taylor of Baltimore (likely the same man who endeavored to save a number of Federalists during the Baltimore riots of 1812). Taylor wrote a letter to Secretary Jones on 20 August 1813 stating his

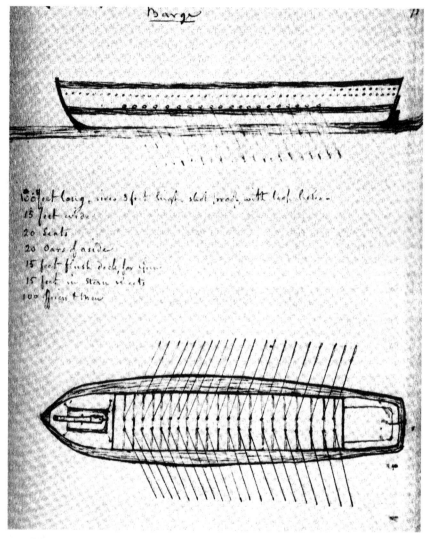

Barney's proposal sketch for the defense of the Chesapeake Bay using shallow-water barges. National Archives and Records Administration, RG45, Area File 11, Roll No. 405

incredulity over Barney's appointment to command the flotilla. Taylor believed Barney was "a most abandoned rascal, both as to politics and morals; and that he is despised by nine-tenths of all who have taken an active part in the defence of Baltimore." Taylor had his letter published in Alexander C. Hanson's notorious *Federal Republican* newspaper (the same paper that had touched off the 1812 Baltimore riots). Both Taylor's letter and Jones' response to it were published in the 14 September 1813 edition of the *Eastern Shore General Advertiser* (Easton, Maryland). Secretary Jones' response was equally as sharp, and he refuted Taylor's accusations by invoking the high esteem Barney was held in by no other than President George Washington. According to Jones, Taylor, through the offices of "a friend," had challenged the secretary to a duel, but Jones deftly parried this gambit by stating that "as every man of honor and common sense in my situation would have done, I declined the invitation."[38]

Perhaps ironically, on the same day that Lemuel Taylor wrote his scathing letter against Barney, Secretary Jones positively responded to Barney's 4 July letter and told him that the president of the United States had agreed with his plan and that he had been appointed as commanding officer of the special command (as Jones called the flotilla force then under construction). So as to not offend officers of the naval service who were senior to him, Barney was given the rank of "Acting Master Commandant, in the Navy of the U. States" and was "entitled" to the "pay, rations, and emoluments of a Master Commandant." According to Jones, the flotillamen were to "be shipped for twelve months, for the special service of the Flotilla, and not liable to be draughted for any other service." A few days later, Jones ordered James Beatty, Esq., the Navy agent in Baltimore supervising the construction of eight galleys "for the defence of the Chesapeake and its waters, four of which are to be 75 feet long, and 4 of 50 feet long," to begin assisting Barney in getting his new special command into the water and ready for action. Jones ordered Beatty to turn over to Barney a "number of 24 Pounders, belonging to the Navy Department, and immediately transported to Baltimore; four of which you will appropriate to the four largest Galleys, in addition to which, they will have a 42 pd. Carronade, . . . [or] you will substitute four of the 32 pd. Carronades in Baltimore." The smaller galleys received long 18 pounders and 32- or 24-pounder carronades. Jones reminded Barney that when he was last in Washington, he had inspected the row galley *Black Snake*, then under construction at the Navy Yard, and that this was exactly the type of vessel that he (Jones) had in mind for Barney's new flotilla. He informed Barney that the *Black Snake* drew only twenty-one inches of water and that its construction was done precisely "in order to serve as an exact guide for those built elsewhere."[39]

Barney was certainly appreciative of Jones' help. On 31 August 1813 he informed Jones that he was not entirely happy with the Baltimore barge building effort and lamented that the contracted barges were going to likely take longer than the originally projected three weeks. Barney wrote that the "contractors appear to me, either not to understand what they are about or will not understand." He closed with an appeal to the secretary "for gods-sake send me the *Black Snake* [to be used as a template], or I must come again to Washington, to see her, and make these thick-skuls here do their duty."[40]

Since 8 August 1813 the British had had fifteen of their ships anchored just outside the mouth of the Patapsco River. Samuel Smith ordered the Baltimore County Brigade of militia to move to a narrow point of land on Patapsco Neck. But as it was in the spring, the appearance of the British turned out to be a false alarm because they soon weighed anchor and headed south to threaten Annapolis, Maryland. They quickly decided Annapolis was too strongly defended for an attack at that moment, and Warren opted instead to once again raid the nearly defenseless Eastern Shore of Maryland. This time he established a temporary base on Kent Island, located across the bay from Annapolis and close to the Eastern Shore, on 9 August 1813. The island positioned Warren's fleet and forces to simultaneously threaten both Baltimore and Annapolis, and since scurvy had broken out among his men, landing on Kent Island allowed them to gather fresh provisions from nearby farms and towns. A number of companies from the 102nd Regiment and some Royal Marines were landed, and the tiny local island militia was easily driven off. The British proceeded to build huts for themselves in the woods, as they intended to stay for several weeks. They also erected a battery at the Narrows, which seemed to indicate they planned to stay on the island for some time.[41]

Owing to a rumor that the Americans had armed vessels in the Miles River but more likely because this prosperous little town had thus far escaped the ravages of war, the British planned to raid St. Michaels, Maryland, on 10 August. Embarking about three hundred troops in cutters and barges on the evening of 9 August 1813, Cockburn planned a surprise predawn attack so that the Maryland militia, under the overall command of Brigadier General Perry Benson, might be caught by surprise. The primary American fortification guarding the town was a four-gun position located at nearby Parrot's Point and commanded by Maryland militia lieutenant William Dodson. Lieutenant John Graham commanded a small two-gun battery positioned directly on one of the town wharves. Another two guns (the Easton artillery) were emplaced on Mill Point and commanded by Captain Clement Vickers.

While the Americans thought they were fairly well prepared to defend the town, the British decided to land on Parrot's Point just as dawn was about to break and take out the largest of the American defensive works. They were able to get within thirty yards of Dodson's guns before their presence was discovered. Dodson fired at least one of his guns, and this single volley supposedly caused at least a few casualties, but the British troops quickly overran the American position, and Dodson's men fled toward the town. As it was now dawn, the surging British were immediately fired on by Captain Vickers' Easton artillery. Having destroyed the Parrot's Point battery and seeing no boats in the harbor, the British decided to return to their barges. Small-caliber guns from British barges in the river fired into the town but had little effect. General Benson noted that a few St. Michaels houses had been perforated by cannonballs. By 1:00 p.m. the British were on their way back to Kent Island. While the Americans claimed they had inflicted twenty-nine casualties on the British assault force, the commanding officer of the sloop *Conflict*, Commander Henry L. Baker, reported to Warren only two seamen wounded. The Americans themselves reported no losses.[42] For years afterward, a local St. Michaels town legend held that the British attacked Parrot's Point, rather than the town itself, because of a deception effort by the local inhabitants, who tricked the British into thinking that the Parrot's Point woods was the actual location of the town. They allegedly did this by hanging lanterns in the trees. However, no contemporary account mentioned any such deception plan, and the British likely attacked Parrot's Point because they knew that Dodson's battery was the primary American defensive position in the area.

A few days later, Cockburn decided to go after slightly larger prey. The Queen Anne County militia (the Thirty-Eighth Maryland Regiment) was known to be loitering near Queenstown, Maryland, located a few miles across the Kent Island Narrows. At the time the understrength regiment of approximately 244 militiamen was commanded by Major William H. Nicholson. A small cavalry unit (a hundred men), under the command of Major Thomas Emory, and a company of artillery (thirty-five men) and two 6 pounders, commanded by Captain Gustavus Wright, were attached to Nicholson's command.

In the early morning hours of 13 August 1813, Major Nicholson was aroused by a cavalry scout and informed that a large body of troops had crossed the Narrows and was headed down the main road toward Queenstown. These troops turned out to be elements of Sir Sidney Beckwith's 102nd Infantry along with a large number of Royal Marines. Beckwith had hoped to surprise the American piquet guard but was thwarted when a nervous British officer ordered the advance guard to fire at the Americans. Now fully alerted, Nicholson immediately ordered his entire force paraded and told his men to prepare to resist the enemy's advance. Having earlier placed two companies of infantry into the neck of land that separated his camp from the Narrows, Nicholson was concerned that his advanced guard, under Captain James Massey, would be captured or annihilated. Riding forward, he heard heavy firing to his front and assumed that all his men forward of his position had been killed or captured by the advancing British. At about 4:00 a.m., another scout informed Nicholson that a large number of barges carrying three hundred Royal Marines had entered Queen Anne's Creek and were coming ashore at the Bowlingly plantation house. Fortunately for Nicholson, the British amphibious force had been delayed in arriving at the house. Earlier, their barges had mistakenly landed at Blakeford (the home of Governor Robert Wright), across Queen Anne's Creek, instead of at their intended objective (Bowlingly), located on the immediate outskirts of Queenstown. This navigational error took some time to correct and enabled the Maryland militiamen to easily escape the trap the British had laid for them. Nicholson ordered a silent retreat of his entire force toward Centreville, Maryland.

However, once the British had established themselves at Bowlingly, they were able to seize Queenstown without any further resistance. According to witnesses, while the British did not burn Bowlingly, they damaged its interior and furnishings, seemingly out of sheer spite. The only real fighting that took place between the British and the Maryland militia occurred on the road from the Narrows to Queenstown. At a defile on the main road at a place called Slippery Hill, James Massey's piquet guard shot and killed two British soldiers along with Beckwith's horse. After they had looted a few more homes in and around Queenstown, the British pulled back to Kent Island with little to show for their exertions.[43] They had completely withdrawn from the island by 24 August 1813.

With hurricane season approaching and swarms of Chesapeake Bay mosquitoes causing hundreds of his largely ship-bound soldiers, sailors, and marines to become sick with various fevers and ailments, and after another brief swipe at St. Michaels on 26 August, Warren ordered all his ships to fall back down the bay toward Norfolk and Cape Henry. The admiral had decided to bring the campaign to a close. However, he did direct that a small naval base be established on Tangier

Island—mainly to train the growing number of runaway slaves whom his forces had liberated or who had fled to his troops for safety and to incorporate them into a unit called "colonial marines." In fact, Lieutenant Colonel Napier of the 102nd Regiment had earlier proposed forming a corps of liberated slaves. By doing so, he believed, he could bring the war to a swift end and abolish the odious institution of slavery in America at the same time. It appears Warren had decided to take Napier up on the idea.

By September 1813 Warren had decided largely to quit the Chesapeake Bay, and he sailed with the majority of his fleet to Halifax, Canada. Cockburn took a few ships to Bermuda. Both officers were happy to escape to a cooler, less-insect-prone climate for the winter. Warren ordered Captain Robert Barrie in his seventy-four-gun HMS *Dragon*, along with several frigates, brigs, and schooners, to remain behind on blockade duty. Meanwhile, in Baltimore Acting Master Commandant Joshua Barney used the departure of the British from the upper bay to recruit men for his Chesapeake Bay flotilla. Fearful that the British intended to return to the bay in the spring of 1814, Secretary Jones ordered Barney to construct ten more barges (to be built at St. Michaels, Maryland) and to continue to recruit seamen and marines to man them. To assist him in this endeavor, Barney requested and received the services of Solomon Frazier, a highly popular state senator from Maryland's Eastern Shore. Barney hoped that Frazier's popularity would translate into even more recruits.

The Americans possessed one advantage in having the USS *Constellation* blockaded in Norfolk and the corvette USS *Adams* getting ready for sea at the Washington Navy Yard. Until Barney's flotilla was operational, these vessels represented the only remaining and credible naval threat in the entire region. A few other U.S. naval combatants were under construction in the Baltimore and Washington yards, but they would not be ready until sometime in 1814. Just having the *Constellation* at Norfolk required Warren to detach a sizable number of his vessels and position them on semistationary blockade duty in Hampton Roads. This gave the Americans an opportunity to experiment with creating a poor man's navy—that is, using semisubmersible mines (then called torpedoes).

During the summer of 1813, the soon-to-be new commanding officer of the Norfolk-based USS *Constellation* was Maryland-born Captain Charles Gordon. Before his September 1813 *Constellation* posting, Gordon had been assigned to direct Baltimore's naval defenses, and in this capacity he became familiar with an inventor named Elijah Mix. Mix had originally developed a floating mine to be used against British ships lingering in the Patapsco River during the summer of 1813. When Warren and Cockburn withdrew their vessels to the vicinity of Kent Island, Gordon asked Mix to consider using his revolutionary weapon against British shipping in Hampton Roads. However, what Mix needed for this weapon to succeed was a stationary target. As luck would have it, Warren had ordered the seventy-four-gun HMS *Plantagenet* to anchor on blockade duty near the Cape Henry light. This was the opportunity Mix and Gordon had been looking for all summer.

While Mix had originally envisioned ten torpedoes for the defense of Baltimore, the city fathers had refused to appropriate any money for boats to deliver the weapons (the politicians, rightly, assumed that the vessels would be destroyed in any subsequent torpedo explosions). Nevertheless, Mix was able to produce at least one prototype weapon by the summer of 1813. On the evening of 18 July 1813, using an open boat named *Chesapeake's Revenge*, Mix and two volunteers decided to attack the anchored HMS *Plantagenet* with a single torpedo. Mix rowed the *Chesapeake's Revenge* under muffled oars to within eighty yards of the stationary British seventy-four and quietly dumped the weapon over the side. At the moment they unleashed the weapon, they were discovered by an alert lookout on board one of the *Plantagenet's* guard boats. This caused Mix and company to quickly reel in the torpedo and flee the scene.

Two nights later, Mix tried again. This time he got the *Chesapeake's Revenge* to within twelve yards of the *Plantagenet*, just under the jibboom of the man-of-war. It was point-blank range; the torpedo could not possibly miss. As Mix and his two volunteers prepared the weapon for deployment, they were once again spotted by a lookout, and the alarm was immediately sounded. The light from rockets fired into the air revealed Mix's vessel, and the British rapidly prepared to lower boats in response. Once again, the *Chesapeake's Revenge* was forced to flee before Mix could fully deploy his torpedo.[44]

Mix had slightly better luck on the evening of 24 July, and although he was farther away this time, he was able to deploy his weapon without being spotted. As the torpedo was carried by the current toward the side of the *Plantagenet*, it suddenly detonated prematurely, just yards away from its target. The resultant explosion sent volumes of seawater cascading onto the *Plantagenet's* deck and swamped a nearby ship's boat but did remarkably little damage to the vessel's hull. Mix and Gordon's naval innovation had failed once again, but barely. Later in the war, torpedoes were fixed to floating logs at Newport, Rhode Island, by Stephen Decatur, and Gordon himself tried the same tactic to supplement the defenses of the Gosport Navy Yard in 1814. As for the British, they noted the use of torpedoes by the Americans but did not seem overly concerned about them—especially since they remained an unproven and unsuccessful concept.[45]

Gordon was an innovator and risk taker but also exceptionally unlucky for a naval officer. At first glance he appeared to be on his way to a bright future in the new U.S. Navy. However, in 1807 Gordon had the misfortune of being the flag captain of the ill-fated USS *Chesapeake* when the ship was precipitously attacked by the HMS *Leopard*. Gordon's immediate superior, Commodore James Barron, received most of the blame for this ignominious incident in U.S. naval history, but during the aftermath of the *Chesapeake* affair, Gordon testified against Barron. Although Gordon was also found guilty of negligence and received a private reprimand, Secretary of the Navy Robert Smith allowed him to temporarily remain in command of the *Chesapeake*. Barron, in contrast, was suspended from further service—his naval career all but ruined. Owing to his role in convicting Barron, Gordon found himself fighting a series of duels in an era when dueling, especially among officers of the naval service, was especially common and often a means for resolving what would today be considered exceptionally trivial arguments. Nevertheless, in the early years of the U.S. Navy, an officer who was allegedly insulted or directly challenged could not allow such slights to go unanswered. In fact, just three months after the *Chesapeake* affair, Gordon fought a duel with a Norfolk doctor named Stark, who had taken it on himself to avenge the reputation of James Barron. During the duel Stark was shot in the arm by Gordon's second, Lieutenant William Crane, because the doctor allegedly fired his pistol before being given the command to do so. As a result, Gordon fought yet another duel against Stark's second and was slightly wounded in this particular scrape.[46] There seemed to be no end to this nonsense.

Just eighteen months later, the incendiary Federalist newspaper editor Alexander C. Hanson wrote a disparaging article about Gordon's role in the *Chesapeake* incident. While honor even at that time did not require Gordon to respond to Hanson since the editor was renowned for casting wild aspersions against nearly everyone who did not agree with him, Gordon decided to challenge Hanson to a duel anyway. The affair took place on 10 January 1810 on the historic dueling

"The Yankey Torpedo," a political cartoon of American explosive machinery and cannon. Etching by Thomas Tegg. British Cartoon Prints Collection, Prints and Photographs Division, Library of Congress, LC-USZC2-604

grounds of Bladensburg, Maryland, just outside the District of Columbia line (since dueling was unlawful inside the district). Hanson, no stranger to dueling and a crack shot, accurately fired his weapon and hit Gordon in the lower abdomen. At the time, a shot to just about anywhere in the body was considered a mortal wound, and most expected Gordon to quickly expire. But Gordon asked to be taken to the residence of Albert Gallatin, the secretary of the treasury. Mrs. Gallatin, who was Gordon's aunt, discovered that the bullet wound, while serious, had not hit any vital organs, and she was able to slowly nurse the young naval officer back to a reasonable level of health (although the wound would plague him for the remaining six years of his life).

After a short stint again in command of the hard-luck USS *Chesapeake*, then in ordinary in Boston, the still-recovering Gordon requested that the Secretary of the Navy return him to his native Maryland. Jones acceded to this request and placed Gordon in charge of Baltimore's sea defenses and its sole remaining gunboat. In September 1813 Gordon was given command of the U.S. frigate *Constellation*. Although challenged to a single ship duel by the British (as they had done to nearly all other U.S. frigate commanders), this time Gordon refused the offer. Despite his best intentions to break out into the open sea, where *Constellation* might have a better effect on the war's outcome, a series of bad breaks and contrary weather prevented Gordon from escaping the confines of Norfolk before the war ended.[47]

The results of the Chesapeake campaign of 1813 cannot be interpreted by historians as anything other than an unmitigated disaster for the American war effort. With the notable exception of the successful defense of Norfolk, Virginia, and Elkton, Maryland, Warren's amphibious task force was unstoppable. Dozens of valuable schooners, merchant ships, and privateers fell into British hands without too much effort on their part. Raiding ashore at widely scattered locations throughout the bay area, the British liberated at least four thousand slaves from the Maryland and Virginia Eastern Shore; seized tons of food, tobacco, and other military stores; and made off with a significant amount of cattle, sheep, and poultry. Cockburn himself personally destroyed a number of Maryland towns such as Havre de Grace, Frenchtown, Fredericktown, and Georgetown—all before he had knowledge of the American destruction of York, Canada. He seized and looted numerous bay islands, such as Kent, Spetsutie, Poplar, Sharps, Smith, and Tangier. The British raided southern Maryland, and especially St. Mary's County, at will and simultaneously threatened three major towns (Baltimore, Annapolis, and Norfolk) and the national capital (Washington, D.C.). The town of Hampton, Virginia, remained devastated.

As for the Americans, it was readily apparent, again with the exception of Norfolk, that they had not given much thought to defensive preparations for the Chesapeake Bay. The large, prosperous Port of Baltimore was initially guarded by a single gunboat and a single land fortification (Fort McHenry). The defensive arrangements for Washington, D.C., were even worse. Its sole land fortification, Fort Washington, was an ill-conceived disaster in waiting unable to adequately defend against river-based or landward assaults. Having no real military deterrent in the region, the federal government was forced to cast its hopes on Barney's untested flotilla. It remained to be seen whether the new, hastily built galleys would be up to the task come spring. The Maryland militia had proved less reliable largely because of the ability of Cockburn's seaborne forces to strike rapidly at various points up and down the bay. Whenever and wherever Cockburn decided to strike, the militia was nearly always at a disadvantage. Regular U.S. Army troops for the region were still few and far between. While the War Department had finally raised two brand-new regiments, the 36th and 38th Infantry Regiments, the vast majority of their officers and men had no combat experience. Despite all this, the president of the United States and his secretary of war, John Armstrong, remained fixated on what was going on at the Canadian border.

Yet not all was in the negative column for the Americans. The arrival of the British in the upper bay alerted Maryland officials, such as Major General Samuel Smith, to increase future readiness for an attack. Long after the war, Smith wrote, "The preparations made in 1813 [were] the cause of [Baltimore's] preservation in 1814." Twice during the spring and summer of 1813, British ships appeared without warning in the Patapsco River. Smith recognized that the superior seaborne mobility of the Royal Navy made it possible for them to potentially bypass Fort McHenry, Baltimore's primary defensive bulwark. This caused him to rethink his defensive arrangements for the vulnerable eastern side of the city and for Patapsco Neck. This also led him to order supporting fortifications (Battery Babcock and Fort Covington) to be built to protect the landward side of Fort McHenry from barges and sloops that might attempt to use the western Ferry Branch. The British arrival in the Patapsco in April 1813 also galvanized the U.S. Navy into action, and Captain Charles Gordon urged the Secretary of the Navy to contract with four privately owned privateers to act as a viable sea-based harbor defense. Soon Captain Gordon commanded four fine schooners—the *Revenge*, the *Patapsco*, the small *Wasp*, and the *Comet*—thus making the famous privateer Thomas Boyle, if only for a short period, an officer in the U.S. Navy. Cockburn made the mistake of allowing Smith and Gordon to observe his vessels taking soundings of the river, making it clear to them that he intended, at least at some point, to return. Once the British departed the Patapsco, Gordon used gunboat No. 138 to locate and destroy all the channel markers left behind by the British from the harbor entrance of Baltimore to Kent Island.[48]

5

THE BRITISH RETURN—1814

$\mathcal{T}$he spring of 1814 was ominous for the United States. Following his defeat by coalition forces at Leipzig in October 1813, on 6 April 1814 Napoleon was sent into exile (temporarily as it turned out) on the island of Elba. The British were now free to focus on the war in North America. Before Leipzig the British had had more than 75,000 troops on the continent of Europe and just 20,000 soldiers in all of North America. Now that their Napoleon problem had been resolved, the British doubled down on their troop commitment to North America and promised to wage war on the very doorsteps of every major American city on the Eastern Seaboard.

Deciding that Vice Admiral Warren had been too cautious the year before, the Crown relieved him of command. In his place, a more aggressive vice admiral, Sir Alexander Cochrane, was appointed. This move was welcomed by the fiery Rear Admiral George Cockburn, who bridled under Warren's command. While Cockburn remained the second senior naval officer in the Chesapeake theater, he believed he now had a commanding officer who understood his strong desire not only to defeat the Americans on the field of battle but also to punish them.

Cochrane possessed one major advantage over his predecessor. He had significant prior service in North America. During the American Revolution he had supported General William Howe's successful campaign to take the American capital of Philadelphia. He became a post captain in 1782 and was in command of the Leeward Islands station by 1805. He served there until 1810. He was appointed military governor of Guadeloupe following its seizure from the French and was in this position when war with the Americans was declared in 1812.[1]

Even before the war began, Cochrane had given the potential outbreak of hostilities with America some thought. He was convinced the United States

Portrait of Vice Admiral Sir Alexander Cochrane by Charles Turner, after Sir William Beechey. Courtesy of the National Portrait Gallery, Greenwich, London, #BHC2615

remained most vulnerable in two locations: the Chesapeake Bay and New Orleans. Because the Americans lacked a viable navy to defend the Chesapeake, he believed the interior of the region, "even Washington . . . [was] not free from a surprise." He argued that the Chesapeake's slave population was another opportunity that should not be overlooked. Cochrane believed that the slave population remained "British in their hearts, and might be of great use if war should be prosecuted with vigor." As for New Orleans, this prized location at the mouth of the Mississippi River represented the linchpin to future American growth. Cochrane thought that "self interest being the ruling principle with the Americans, those in the interior will join the party that pays for their produce." Once the British possessed New Orleans, the only market in the region for the planters in the interior territories would be the British West Indies. Cochrane stated that he had "not a doubt they [the American interior territories] would separate from the Atlantic states."[2]

By late February 1814 Cockburn had once again resumed his seaborne raids throughout the bay, and as during the 1813 campaign, there was little the Americans could or would do about it. However, because the British were now clearly increasing their troop strength in North America, the American government finally raised more regular regiments. Nevertheless, despite clear evidence that the British navy had returned to the Chesapeake, the War Department still earmarked most of the newly raised regiments for service on the Canadian border.

With the exception of the corvette USS *Adams*, which managed to slip past the reduced British winter blockade in early 1814, American naval forces remained too weak to take on a ship larger than a frigate. Moreover, the most powerful American vessel in the region, the USS *Constellation*, remained blockaded at Norfolk. Thus, the most credible American military force in the region was Acting Master Commandant Joshua Barney's Chesapeake flotilla. The British focused their initial efforts for the upcoming 1814 campaign on this command. Their thinking was that once Barney's flotilla was eliminated or made ineffective, then Cochrane's forces were free to either continue large-scale raids or possibly sack the wealthy bay towns of Baltimore or Annapolis, Maryland, with reinforcements that had been promised by the home government.

On 18 February 1814 Secretary of the Navy William Jones enthusiastically embraced the flotilla concept and bombarded Barney with myriad directives and questions:

> It will be of importance to have a very fast sailing pilot boat attached to the Flotilla as a Despatch or look out Boat, and a single carronade on a pivot. . . . I am of the opinion that the Barges now building at St. Michael's had better be armed with a long 12 pr. instead of a heavy 18 and a 32 pd. Carronade instead of a 24—they will be equally formidable, the two Guns will balance each other and the Barges will row lighter.—We have beautiful long 12 prs. at the Navy Yard and abundance of Ammunition.—What progress is making with the Barges at St.

Baltimore from Federal Hill, 1830, by W. J. Bennett. Prints and Photographs Division, Library of Congress, LC-DIG-pga-00193

Michael's.—are they to be brought over to be armed, or is their armament to be transported to them? It is time to be moving, we shall have warm work.—How comes recruiting?[3]

Several weeks later, Barney was able to inform the secretary that he thought he could purchase and outfit a pilot boat he had his eye on for the sum of $500. He asked Jones for orders on this issue "as I am to give an immediate answer." Barney described other issues and mentioned that the intended flotilla flagship, the former Jefferson-era gunboat *Scorpion,* was outfitting at the Baltimore Lazaretto (the quarantine station located directly across the northwest branch of the harbor from Fort McHenry). He lamented that *Scorpion's* "brass 42 lb. Howitzer [had] been taken out of her, for the *Adams.*" Because his flotillamen—and not government contractors—did most of the "heaving out" work, Barney believed that the cost of reconditioning *Scorpion* would "cost but a trifle." As for recruiting, Barney noted that Baltimore's maritime-oriented harbor militia force, the U.S. Sea Fencibles, might be inclined to join his flotilla. He believed that these "men are very dissatisfied, and wish to join us, I could easily manage the matter if it was not, that the officers are mostly Landsmen."[4]

By May 1814 Barney combined the heretofore ineffective Potomac flotilla with his Baltimore boats and made the Jefferson-era gunboat *Scorpion* his flagship. Meanwhile, back in Baltimore, the town's blockaded shipyards were in the process of building two new sloops of war, *Erie* and *Ontario*. But these ships were no help since it was clear the British blockade effectively strangled the shipping and commerce of the entire region. Barney's new opponent, Cochrane, wasted no time in informing the commander in chief and governor of Canada, Sir George Prevost, of his intentions:

> I hope to be able to make a very considerable diversion in the Chesapeake Bay, to draw off in part the Enemy's Efforts against Canada—It is my intention to fortify one of the Islands in the Chesapeake, to facilitate the desertion of the Negroes, and their Families, who are to have their choice of either entering into His Majesty's Service, or to be Settled with their Families at Trinidad or in the British American Provinces—Recruiting Parties are to be Sent from all the West India Regiments to Bermuda, and those who may choose to enlist, are to have their Wives and Families Provided for in the same manner, as those permitted to attend the Regiments abroad, by which it is hoped in a certain time the Regiments will furnish their own Recruits.[5]

Cochrane decided to wage both a kinetic and economic war against Maryland and Virginia plantation societies. He published a proclamation that promised slaves "their choice of either entering into His Majesty's sea or land forces, or of being sent as free settlers to the British possessions in North America or the West Indies, where they will meet with all due encouragement."[6] The proclamation was a subtle shift in policy from just the previous year, when Lord Bathurst warned Sir Sidney Beckwith "on no account give encouragement to any disposition by the Negroes to rise against their Masters." Beckwith was authorized to enlist volunteers "in any of the Black Corps . . . but you must distinctly understand that you are in no case to take slaves away as Slaves, but as free persons whom the public become bound to maintain."[7] Concerned that the Americans would logically claim that the slaves had merely traded one master for another (in the West Indies), the British wanted their ground commanders to fully understand that those slaves who made their way to British lines were going to be free men (and women) thereafter. Bathurst was not fully or financially prepared to initiate a full program in 1813. However, just a year later, he granted Cochrane much more leeway.

Cochrane's plans included the creation of a formation of former slaves called colonial marines. Promising freedom to slaves also had a political benefit for the British. It certainly gave them the moral high ground, at least in Great Britain. A wide variety of British wartime pundits noted how "perfect freedom—that freedom that the vaunted 'Land of Liberty' denied [slaves]—was guaranteed" if they made it to the British lines.[8] Moreover, despite a barrage of American entreaties both during and after the war, British commanders steadfastly refused to return runaway slaves to their owners. This policy enabled the British to portray themselves as liberators. However, after the war the Americans accused the British of selling runaways slaves in the West Indies (where slavery was still tolerated by the British government). Cochrane and others went to great lengths to formally refute these charges. Nonetheless, the inconsistent British policy of being antislavery at home while allowing slavery to continue in the West Indian colonies partially undermined the British troops' status as true liberators.

In 1814 these issues made little difference to Alexander Cochrane. From his perspective as a commander in chief, liberating slaves made eminent military sense. He incorporated a slave liberation policy as a matter of military expediency. He felt that it was vitally important to establish that if the former slaves decided to fight for the British cause (and their own), they did so voluntarily, without any hint of coercion. He made sure that his policy was seen by both the slaves and the whites in the Chesapeake as advocating liberation vice servile insurrection. By doing so, he negated the potential use of the issue by the Americans as a means of boosting white militia recruitment in the way that William Henry Harrison and others had done in the Ohio country when confronted by Tecumseh's pan-Indian confederacy.

The base Cochrane had in mind for the encouragement of runaway slaves and their families was the previously established camp on Tangier Island in the lower Chesapeake Bay. Tangier was closer to the larger British blockade ships lingering in Hampton Roads. These ships could easily reinforce the base, whereas locations farther up the bay were considered too vulnerable to raids by Barney's Baltimore-based flotilla. Cochrane's choice of Tangier, which had good timber and water, was excellent. Hundreds throughout the tidewater region responded to his proclamation, and at least three hundred men signed on to become red-coated colonial marines.

On Tangier Island the British built a defensive work they named Fort Albion. The fort came with a hospital, church, and barracks for troops. The island was geographically located in the heart of Virginia planter country and just a dozen miles offshore of the state's lightly defended Eastern Shore. The island's seaward location was thought to be more conducive to keeping the region's swarms of malaria-carrying mosquitoes in check than other upper bay locations such as Kent, Poplar, or Sharps Islands.

On Tangier, when runaway slaves arrived (either on their own or via British naval vessels), the adult males were given the option of signing on as colonial marines, joining the regular British West Indian regiment, or awaiting further available transportation to another West Indian location such as Jamaica or Trinidad. Since the Americans had long propagandized about the "true" intent of the British in sending the escaped slaves to such places, many preferred to remain in the Chesapeake region, and thus it was not too difficult to enlist the men (and some of the women) as marines. While the British home government initially wanted to place the former slaves in their all-black West Indian regiment, the army recruiting officer, Lieutenant Thomas Brown, did not get to the region until July 1814. By this time Cockburn had already organized the escaped slaves into colonial marine companies, which meant they fell under Royal Navy control. In the end Brown's late arrival did not matter, since no former slaves seemed willing to enlist in the West Indian regiment in the first place owing to its notorious reputation. The escapee women and children were called supernumeraries, and many women performed duty as guides or river pilots for long upriver raids. Those men who enlisted received monthly pay, an enlistment bounty, and most important, a suit of clothes including the famous British red coat. Having previously been clothed in rags, a liberated colonial marine returning to his former neighborhood must have been a major inducement for others waiting to take their chances with the British.[9] Actual pay, better food, and most important, decent clothes were as strong a recruiting incentive as could be found at the time. The Americans, of course, only offered the status quo—continued enslavement.

During the spring and summer months of 1814, colonial marines formed the bulk of raiding parties launched against Virginia's Eastern Shore. On 29 May colonial marines landed in Accomack County and took out a militia battery with the loss of Michael Harding—the first recorded colonial marine casualty. Colonial marines participated in Captain Robert Barrie's HMS *Dragon* Patuxent River campaign and in an attack on Barney's flotilla on 1 June. They also landed at Chesaconessex, again in Accomack County, and went after a second militia battery. Captain Barrie reported that he was "highly pleased with the conduct of the Colonial Marines, under Ensign Hammond, every individual of which Evinced the greatest eagerness, to come to Action with their former masters."[10]

The British even experimented with a completely integrated unit called the Third Battalion of Royal and Colonial Marines. This unit of approximately five hundred men had two hundred white Royal Marines and three hundred black colonial marines. It was rare that the British went ashore without at least some colonial marines as part of the landing party. The colonial marines were attached to the Twenty-First Regiment of Foot and entered Washington, D.C., on the night of 24 August 1814. They often provided British commanders with excellent local intelligence owing to their intimate knowledge of the waterways and plantations being raided at any given time. As a result, the British were able to raid much farther inland than anyone in Virginia or Maryland at the time imagined. Moreover, the planters lived in mortal fear of servile insurrection. Mere rumors of a nearby body of armed former slaves were enough to freeze large portions of the local militia in place.

There can be no doubt that the return of the British and the announcement of Cochrane's proclamation were greeted largely with enthusiasm by the slaves of the Chesapeake region. In late 1813 Captain Robert Barrie of the HMS *Dragon* noted,

> The Slaves continue to come off by every opportunity and I have now upwards of 120 men, women, and Children on board. I shall send about 50 of them to Bermuda in the [HMS] *Conflict*. Among the Slaves are several very intelligent fellows who are willing to act as local guides should their Services be required in that way, and if their assertions be true, there is no doubt but the Blacks of Virginia & Maryland would cheerfully take up Arms & join us against the Americans. Several Flags of Truce have been off to make application for their Slaves [meaning their owners were trying to recover them] . . . but not a single black would return to his former owner.[11]

It is estimated that approximately thirty-four hundred slaves were able to self-liberate from a Virginia or Maryland plantation during the War of 1812. One 1814 raid on a Lancaster County, Virginia, plantation known as Corotoman saw sixty-nine slaves, angered at their harsh treatment there, make their way to the British lines. Another slave who ran off that year was a man named Bartlet Shanklyn, a highly trained blacksmith. After the war he took up residence in Nova Scotia. In 1820, when it was clear that he would reside in Canada for the rest of his life, he took the time to write his former master in America, a man named Abraham Hooe, to let him know how he was doing as a free man:

> Sir, I take this opportunity of writing these lines to inform you how I am situated hear. I have [a] Shop & Set of Tools of my own and am doing very well when I was with you [you] treated me very ill and for that reason i take the liberty of informing you that i am doing as well as you if not better. When i was with you I worked very hard and you neither g[ave] me money nor any satisfaction but sin[ce] I have been able to make Gold and Silver as well as you. . . . So I Remain, Bartlet Shanklyn P.S. My love to all my friends, I hope they are doing well.[12]

The arrival of the Royal Navy in the Chesapeake represented a number of things related to both the British and American war efforts. First and foremost, the wooden world of British naval vessels was the best opportunity in a very long time for thousands of enslaved men, women, and children to become free. At least twenty-five hundred like Bartlet Shanklyn, made their way to Nova Scotia either during or immediately after the war—some coming from Bermuda, others from Cumberland Island, Georgia, and New Orleans. At least 19 percent of the runaway male slaves signed on to become colonial marines—a fairly high percentage.[13]

Despite the enthusiastic support of the new colonial marines, Cockburn had been dissatisfied with the performance of the British land forces in the previous year's campaign. He was especially disgusted at the British failure to take Norfolk and blamed much of the debacle on Sir Sidney Beckwith and his 102nd Regiment of Foot. Cockburn hoped the Crown would send a better man for the coming 1814 campaign. On the bright side, Cockburn's experience in the region was unsurpassed. Thus, he often possessed remarkable intelligence on the defenses of the Chesapeake region, and his opinions carried the day during counsels of war held by Cochrane. For example, he pointed out to Cochrane that "there is not a Fort, from Norfolk to Baltimore that has a Bombproof Casemate in it or Splinter proof—there is not a Fort or Battery within the same extent while a Line of Battle Ships or even a frigate drawing upwards of three Fathoms can approach within battering distance.... The whole of these Shores are as usual in a wretched state of Defence and excepting Norfolk, I do not think there are any Regulars doing Duty."[14] His estimate of the Chesapeake's defensive arrangements was more accurate than even he realized at the time.

Meanwhile, the last best hope of the Chesapeake Bay, Joshua Barney, struggled with manning his newly established flotilla. Once it was obvious that the now completed sloop *Ontario* (eighteen guns) was trapped in the Port of Baltimore, Secretary of the Navy Jones ordered many of *Ontario*'s idle sailors to join Barney's flotilla. So Barney got his men, but forty of them arrived "drunk" and had to be immediately placed in irons. In desperation Barney advertised in Baltimore newspapers for men to fill out his flotilla, "where an honorable and comfortable situation offers to men out of employ during the Embargo; where Seamen and Landsmen, will receive two months pay advanced, and their wives to receive half-pay monthly, and single men can provide for aged parents, and widows for helpless children in the same manner; with the advantage of being near their families, and not to be drafted into the militia, or turned over to any other service."[15] Barney got the state of Maryland to appropriate $30,000 as a further encouragement for potential recruits. But even these extraordinarily attractive terms were not enough to fully man the flotilla. In fact, the maritime community saw the flotilla service as the absolute worst sea duty that anyone could sign up for because the likelihood of these particular ships earning prize money for captured vessels was highly remote.

By late April 1814 Barney had about fifteen vessels under his command—the gunboat *Scorpion* (formerly of the Potomac flotilla), gunboats No. 137 and No. 138, and twelve row galleys. More galleys were being built at Fells Point and St. Michaels. However, the first time Barney put his galleys into the water, he discovered that they neither sailed nor rowed very well. The galleys drew too much water, and the gunboats were too heavy to row and did not sail very well. After Barney had escorted the recovered sloop *Asp*, which he decided to use to transport stores owing to the vessel's poor sailing qualities, to Baltimore, he complained to Secretary Jones that provisions placed on board the gunboats had been lost because their hulls were leaky. Barney complained, "I found a great quantity [of bread] has been *wet* by leaks in [No. 137's] deck, which Obliges me to take everything out and to have her caulked, before she can serve again; indeed Sir, she and No. 138 are both such miserable tools I do not know what to do with them [emphasis in the original]." Barney even had trouble with his new, smaller (fifty-foot) row galleys, noting that he had to remove most of their cannon shot because their low freeboard caused them to "take on great quantities of Water." To keep the water out, Barney wrote, he was "required to have *Wash-boards* put round them about 8 Inches high, which will keep out the water and make them more safe, I am Obliged to do this as the men are very unwilling to remain in them in their present state [emphasis in the original]."[16]

Once Barney had made the necessary repairs to his flotilla, he again moved down the bay. On 1 June 1814 he was anchored just north of the Potomac River's mouth. His intention was to push farther down the bay and possibly raid the British naval base on Tangier Island. Nearly simultaneously, fearing further British raids against long-suffering southern Maryland, Colonel Henry Carbery, commanding officer of the U.S. 36th Infantry Regiment, sent a detachment of soldiers to St. Mary's County, Maryland. When the regular soldiers arrived, many citizens assumed the government was finally taking a stand in southern Maryland. But events soon proved otherwise. As Barney edged his flotilla southward, a lookout spotted the British schooner *St. Lawrence* (thirteen guns); the HMS *Dragon*'s tender, *Catch-Up a Little*; and a number of barges reconnoitering nearby St. Jerome's Creek. Barney moved in for the kill. The *St. Lawrence* and the other boats immediately fled southward. Barney continued the chase until he in turn spotted the large seventy-four-gun HMS *Dragon* coming up the bay. Now it was Barney's turn to retreat. As he rounded Cedar Point (the southern edge of the Patuxent River mouth), contrary winds forced Barney to flee up shallow St. Leonard's Creek—a tributary of the larger Patuxent River.

Barney and his flotilla were trapped, and there was little he could do about it unless he could devise a bold and daring plan of escape—a plan that certainly would require the assistance of land forces. Unfortunately for Barney, Lieutenant Colonel Michael Taney (Thirty-First Maryland Regiment—Calvert County), who commanded the local Maryland militia in the area, proved to be of little help.

Moreover, Barney remained suspicious that Taney was possibly trading with the enemy since his large plantation was repeatedly bypassed by British raiding parties that had burned all the others in the same neighborhood.[17]

While Barney pondered his next move, on the evening of 9 June 1814, the British attacked his flotilla with twenty barges of their own, another rocket boat, and two schooners in support. Captain Barrie of the HMS *Dragon* planned the attack. Barrie hoped that his barges would lure or drive Barney's boats within range of the *St. Lawrence* (thirteen guns), the razee *Loire* (thirty-eight guns), and the sloop of war *Jaseur* (eighteen guns), then lurking near the mouth of St. Leonard's Creek. The razee was a former frigate that had had its spar deck razed, or taken off, to make it lighter and faster than a standard frigate. Unfortunately for Barrie, the creek was too shallow for even the razee. Moreover, Barney had cleverly cut down the masts of his own boats so that they could anchor along the creek bank and blend into the tree line, making his vessels harder to identify and target. He had also taken the precaution of securing a line of retreat farther up the creek and established two gun batteries on opposite sides of the creek bank just below St. Leonard's Town. With piles driven into the creek bed, the forts were supported by a defensive boom that would halt (at least temporarily) any boats attempting to ascend the creek. Maryland militia guarded the approaches to St. Leonard's Town as best they could. As additional support, Secretary Jones sent 110 U.S. Marines, under the command of Captain Samuel Miller, from the Marine barracks in Washington, D.C., along with three light 12-pounder cannon.

On the morning of 10 June 1814, Barney decided to counterattack the British at the mouth of the creek. Around 2:00 p.m. his flotilla collided with Barrie's own Royal Navy barge force at the confluence of St. Leonard's and Johns Creeks. Initially, Barney's flotilla drove the British barges back toward the creek entrance. But as Barrie had hoped, this allowed him to bring his larger, more powerful brigs and schooners into play. Yet even the lighter-draught *St. Lawrence* found itself aground, and it became the principal target of Barney's cannon fire and was heavily damaged. Once Barrie landed Royal Marines on the high ground on the east bank of the creek, Barney was forced back to the tenuous safety of his own fortifications and supporting Maryland militia near St. Leonard's Town. During the engagement, the Americans did not lose a man.

The first battle of St. Leonard's Creek was a tactical draw, and both sides largely remained where they had started at the beginning of the day. Barney's

Action in St. Leonard's Creek, June 6, 1814, by Irwin John Bevan. Courtesy of the Mariner's Museum, Newport News, Virginia

attempt at a breakout had been foiled by the Royal Marines and Barrie's larger ships. If Barney was going to escape from St. Leonard's Creek, he needed to keep the Royal Marines from landing on his flank and at the same time drive Barrie's larger ships away from their blockade stations. Before the American could give these issues any thought, Secretary Jones sent Barney an extraordinary order for him to prepare to beach his galleys and transport them overland. Barney was aghast at receiving this order and told the secretary that if he tried to conduct this risky move, the British would likely respond by shelling the operation with their rocket barges. Instead, he proposed a joint flotilla–U.S. Army operation to temporarily drive the British away from the mouth of the creek so that his flotilla could make its escape. Accordingly, Secretary of War John Armstrong sent Colonel Henry Carbery's entire 36th Infantry Regiment back into the area. Armstrong also reinforced the 36th Infantry with a battalion of infantry from the 38th Infantry Regiment. Colonel Decius Wadsworth, the U.S. Army's commissary general of ordnance, proposed that the 36th Infantry (reinforced) support the establishment of land batteries on the west bank of St. Leonard's Creek near its confluence with the Patuxent River. Wadsworth immediately sent a few large-caliber cannon toward St. Leonard's Creek in support of the operation. A second battalion from the 38th Infantry was ordered to the area from Baltimore. The

Secretary of the Navy ordered Captain Samuel Miller's U.S. Marine company to support the operation as well. Wadsworth commanded the U.S. Army and militia land forces, and Barney remained in command of the flotillamen and all the U.S. Marines.

However, the acerbic Barney was not especially pleased with the 36th Infantry's commanding officer and believed that Colonel Carbery "finds much fault publickly to the Inhabitants about my coming into this creek, [and] he seems to have no disposition to give me [any] *real* assistance [emphasis in the original]." What had really upset Barney was Carbery's unilateral decision to pull back from a strong defensible position near the mouth of the creek. This move defeated the purpose of the entire operation. Barney bitterly complained that he could "expect no support from [Carbery], Major Steuart [Alexander Stuart] or the men, the fact is, there is no order or discipline in that Corps, the men under no controle, ranging the country, committing their depredations, on the persons & property of the Inhabitants, leaving their Camp when they please, such sir is my situation at present and loudly calls for relief."[18] Nevertheless, Barney's flotilla was better off now that the 36th Infantry had arrived. Major Stuart erected a small battery near Johns Creek and deployed soldiers along the St. Leonard's Creek banks to snipe at any British barges that might venture toward the defensive boom. This activity denied the British critical intelligence on the exact whereabouts of Barney's flotilla.

Following the first battle of St. Leonard's Creek, Captain Barrie contented himself with blockading the flotilla with just a few ships. This was all he needed. Purposely avoiding further engagement with Barney, Barrie sent barges of Royal Marines and bluejackets to raid farms and plantations throughout the lower Patuxent River region. On 11 June 1814 elements of the Forty-Fifth Maryland Regiment fired on British raiders in barges at a plantation near Hallowing Point in Calvert County, Maryland. In keeping with Admiral Cockburn's standing orders to severely punish any location that demonstrated resistance, Barrie immediately deployed 140 Royal Marines and 30 black colonial marines sent up from Tangier Island and burned the farm of Captain John Broome of the Thirty-First Maryland Regiment. Cockburn sent Barrie a reinforcement in the form of the frigate HMS *Narcissus* (thirty-two guns) and thirty-one more colonial marines. On 15 June 1814 Barrie raided the Patuxent River town of Benedict, Maryland, and proceeded the following day farther upriver to Lower Marlboro, causing the Maryland militia to flee without offering any resistance. The British were able to burn more than twenty-five hundred hogsheads of tobacco "valued at more than $125,000." It was said that the pungent smell of tobacco smoke lingered in the area for weeks afterward. The plundering was fairly widespread.[19] On 18 June 1814 Colonel Carbery informed Barney that he was taking his regular infantry upriver in an alleged effort to stop the raids. In reality, Carbery seemed more content to merely shadow the activities of the British; he never directly engaged them.

The British remained in the area of Benedict, Maryland, and appeared off the town of Nottingham farther up the river. Finally goaded into action, on 19 June 1814 Secretary of War Armstrong sent approximately 280 men, under the command of District of Columbia militia major George Peter; 6 fieldpieces of the Georgetown Artillery; an infantry company and some dragoons, also from Georgetown; and another rifle company from Alexandria to march immediately for Nottingham. Riding ahead, the dragoons believed the town had been burned to the ground. However, before their arrival the fortuitous presence of a small detachment of the U.S. 36th Infantry and several 18-pounder guns under the command of Lieutenant Thomas Harrison had deterred the British from making an actual sortie against the town. The following day, elements of George Peter's force surprised a British raiding party near Benedict, Maryland, and took some prisoners following a particularly vicious fight with a Royal Marine sergeant named Mathieu, who refused to surrender and was shot to death after he had nearly done in several senior militia officers. A rumor later spread among the Royal Marines that Sergeant Mathieu had been killed after he had surrendered.[20]

Despite this activity Barrie kept Barney and his flotilla firmly blockaded up St. Leonard's Creek. Barney continued to purchase drays, block and tackle, and large wheels so that the option to move the flotilla overland remained viable. However, on 20 June 1814, like a thunderbolt from the blue, Barney received an order from Secretary Jones to haul off what military matériel he could salvage and destroy the flotilla. In his letter to Barney, Jones reasoned that the loss of the flotilla (after the removal of all military stores) would not exceed $25,000 or the equivalent, in his words, "of a single Baltimore schooner."[21]

Barney was absolutely crestfallen by his new orders since it meant that his plans for a daring escape were now over. He dutifully began dismantling at least six of his smaller galleys, the two gunboats, and even his flagship, the *Scorpion*. But before he could proceed any further, Colonel Wadsworth convinced the secretary

Portrait of Secretary of War John Armstrong Jr. by Rembrandt Peale.
Courtesy of the Independence National Park, National Park Services

to countermand his original destruction order and suggested that he (Wadsworth) be allowed to use the artillery he had brought south from Washington, D.C., to drive the British away from the mouth of St. Leonard's Creek. Jones agreed to rescind his order to Barney.

On 24 June 1814 Barney held a council of war with Colonel Wadsworth and Captain Samuel Miller of the U.S. Marines. As previously planned, later that evening Wadsworth would erect an earthen fort on the bluff on the west bank of St. Leonard's Creek and emplace his 2 powerful 18 pounders there. Plans were also made for a furnace to heat shot, which was secretly erected under the cover of darkness. Wadsworth's men rapidly shoveled up embrasures for his cannon, and the earth fort on the west bank of the creek was soon a reality. During the

Portrait of Secretary of the Navy William Jones by Gilbert Stuart.
Courtesy of the Naval History and Heritage Command, #NH-54764-KN

construction, 260 more regular soldiers from the 38th Infantry, under the command of Major George Keyser, arrived. These men were placed under Colonel Carbery and were deployed in support formation immediately behind Wadsworth's gun battery. Wadsworth was in overall command of all the land forces except the Marines, who remained under Barney's control but who had been ordered to cooperate with Wadsworth. Miller's Marines manned and supported their own 3 12-pounder fieldpieces while 20 sailors from the flotilla, under the command of Sailing Master John Geoghegan, supplied skilled gunners for Wadsworth's heavy guns. Once all gun preparations were completed, Wadsworth, after having coordinated with Barney, was to open fire on the British blockade force while Barney's flotilla simultaneously attacked from the water.[22]

By 3:00 a.m. on 26 June 1814, the fort was considered as complete as it was going to be. Geoghegan had placed Wadsworth's cannon on the brow of a high hill near the creek mouth. However, when Wadsworth arrived at the position, he was not happy with the emplacement and ordered Geoghegan to move his cannon to the reverse slope of the hill. With some amount of grumbling, Geoghegan made preparations to reemplace the cannon on the reverse slope. At the same time Wadsworth informed Barney that the cannon emplacement was not ready. Thus, Barney remained idle farther up the creek and awaited word on the preparations ashore. Just before dawn Barney was surprised to hear Wadsworth's and Miller's artillery open fire on the British ships at the mouth of the creek. His flotilla force was not where it was supposed to be and had a fatiguing forty-five-minute row to close with the British ships at the mouth of the creek. Nonetheless, the British had been caught by surprise. In command because of Captain Barrie's temporary absence was Captain Thomas Brown in the razee *Loire*. Wadsworth's cannonballs and Miller's lighter solid shot arced toward Brown's ships. Brown fired at least six hundred rounds at the land batteries in response but found that he could not dislodge them. He then sent some barges loaded with Royal Marines along with a rocket boat up the Patuxent River to flank the right of the American position on the creek bluffs. Brown, however, was not especially concerned about the land batteries. Each time Wadsworth's heavy guns fired, they had a tendency to roll farther down the sandy hill, and his gun crews had to move them back into position after each discharge. The work was slow and time consuming. If Wadsworth's barrage was ineffective, so was that of the British as their return fire tended to sail well past Wadsworth's guns. Brown ordered his sailors to reduce their charges, but even this tactic did not allow his shot to properly target the hill's reverse slope. Still, the Americans suffered a few casualties. Geoghegan's second in command, Lieutenant William Carter, lost an arm while loading a heated shot that caused his gun to fire prematurely.[23]

During this fighting Barney's flotilla finally reached the scene, and the commodore was able to open fire on Brown's ships at close range. Because Barney was late and the British ships were no longer concerned about Wadsworth's ineffectual land batteries, Brown was able to focus his guns entirely on Barney's flotilla. Nonetheless, Barney's men kept up a heavy fire, hit the razee *Loire* at least fifteen times, and heavily damaged the small frigate *Narcissus* as well. Grapeshot and canister flew back and forth between the flotilla and Brown's ships, which had dropped slightly downriver to more effectively fire their broadsides at Barney's swarming galleys. The British ship's stout bulwarks provided better protection than Barney's low-slung row galleys, and "three of the barges under Sailing Masters Worthington, Kidall, and Sellers suffered heavily." But the British ships were largely stationary, whereas the vessels in Barney's flotilla were more maneuverable and swarmed around like angry bees. After some time at close-quarters fighting, Barney needed to assess the damage to his ships and temporarily retired three-quarters of a mile up St. Leonard's Creek. At that particular moment, unknown to Barney, Brown made a similar decision and dropped down to Point Patience, south of the mouth of St. Leonard's Creek, to make immediate repairs to his own vessels. As he did, Barney's sailors noticed a number of the British ships working their pumps heavily to keep their vessels afloat. As soon as Brown reached his new position, the wind fortuitously died, and the way was now clear for Barney and his flotilla to escape St. Leonard's Creek. Brown soon observed a sloop (most likely the *Scorpion*) and eighteen barges calmly and steadily rowing up the Patuxent River toward Benedict, Maryland. For the time being the British were out of business in the Patuxent River valley. In order not to be slowed down, as he had been by the decrepit gunboats a few weeks earlier, Barney ordered No. 137 and No. 138 scuttled near the head of the creek. In a letter to his brother, Louis, in Baltimore, he wrote, "Thanks to hot & cold shot the blockade has been raised."[24] But this was only partially true. Barney had indeed escaped St. Leonard's Creek, but he was still blockaded up the larger Patuxent River.

The American after-action report on the fighting (or lack thereof) ashore in and around Wadsworth's battery was far less positive. As previously noted, soon after the British had been engaged by Wadsworth's battery on the western shore of the creek, Brown ordered a number of his own row galleys, along with a reinforced detachment of Royal Marines, to maneuver around the right flank of the American gun line in an attempt to enfilade their position. Carbery and his men had been positioned behind Wadsworth's guns in the first place to counter this exact maneuver. Not long after the large naval guns had opened fire, Captain Miller, on Wadsworth's right, notified Wadsworth that he believed British barges were going to land marines to the right and rear of the American position on the bluff. Nearly simultaneous to the receipt of this information, a 32-pounder cannonball hit in midflight an 18-pounder ball fired by Geoghegan's guns; sparks fell on an ammunition supply in one of the gun positions, causing an explosion that wounded a number of the gunners, including Geoghegan himself. Geoghegan's wound, while painful, was not serious, and he remained in command of the guns. Meanwhile, Miller's 12 pounders had run out of round shot, and the Marine observed three other 12-pounder guns, under Lieutenant Thomas Harrison across the field, not being used at all. Wadsworth had left the fort to investigate what was going on behind him, and as a precaution he had ordered a detachment of infantry toward the Patuxent River shoreline to deal with the possible landing of marines in the rear of his position.

While Wadsworth made his investigation, Miller informed Geoghegan that he was out of the proper ammunition to fire at the British ships, and unless Geoghegan wanted Miller to stay, Miller was going to reposition his guns to deal with the possible flank attack from the British barges. Moreover, Miller believed that "as our canister up the hill could be of no earthly service, to take the ground to our right in the open plain, the more effectually to act upon the barges." In essence, Miller was out of antiship ammunition and wished to reposition his guns so they could be of some use if the British landed marines to his right. Geoghegan, in temporary command of the "great guns," did not object. Miller found "the small frigate [most likely the HMS *Narcissus*] had brought her guns to bear upon the plain to rake it, and the barges under the cover of a high bluff at the point were firing in perfect safety, with grape and 32-pounder carronades, their guns being considerably elevated and they entirely unseen from any upon the plain. Thus situated I found it necessary once more." Although Geoghegan's flotillamen had been assigned to work Colonel Wadsworth's cannon and the U.S. Marines were there to service and defend their own organic 12-pounder cannon, Captain Miller believed that he was not under the direct control of senior Army commander Colonel Wadsworth and that his chain of command ashore ran via Geoghegan to Barney himself in the flotilla force.[25]

Once repositioned facing the Patuxent River, Miller observed the 36th and 38th Infantry in full retreat. He noted that his change in position may have inadvertently caused the 36th and 38th Infantry Regiments to "leave the field." The departure of the detachment that Wadsworth had ordered to watch the riverbank caused the green Army troops to think that a general retreat had been ordered, and so they all started back up the peninsula. Miller noted, "Every description of troops was leaving the field and the battery [Wadsworth's] was abandoned." In fairness, the 38th Infantry had been directed to follow the 36th wherever it went, and although the battery had been damaged, it was not entirely out of action.

Since at that moment the 36th Infantry was retreating, in conformance to its orders, the 38th did so as well. Many of the soldiers in both regiments believed that they were merely being repositioned to repel an assault by the British barges seen earlier in the river. Miller, seeing the infantry marching back toward St. Leonard's Town, also assumed that Wadsworth had ordered a general retreat and ordered his men and his light artillery to follow. With barely enough sailors from the flotilla left unwounded to man a single 18 pounder in the forward gun position, Wadsworth ordered his guns spiked, and he rode to the rear to try to stop his men from going any farther.[26]

Wadsworth was certainly disgusted with the performance of his troops and especially that of the 36th Infantry and the light artillery. In his report he wrote, "The fact is, the infantry and light artillery decided upon a retreat without my orders before they lost a single man killed or wounded." However, he continued, "In justice to the infantry, [I] acknowledge that they did not take to flight, but quitted the ground in perfect order." Wadsworth stated that after a while he was able to bring his forces back, but by this time Brown had decided to retire down the river and had already recalled the barge force. Volunteers, led by Captain Thomas Carbery, gallantly retrieved Wadsworth's abandoned guns, equipment, and even a few wounded men left behind during the precipitous retreat.

Wadsworth also wrote a "disparaging letter" to Secretary Jones concerning Miller's behavior. Jones immediately ordered a court of inquiry to ascertain the facts of the matter. Both the indispensable Geoghegan and even Barney himself were called to Washington to testify at Miller's inquiry, although Barney avoided a personal appearance because he was needed in the field. In the end, Barney's absence did not matter, and after much delay and recrimination, Miller was fully acquitted of any wrongdoing.[27] Nevertheless, according to contemporary historian Gary J. Ohls, the cloud of suspicion about Miller's behavior at St. Leonard's Creek may have been a motivating factor in his later stalwart performance during the Battle of Bladensburg. There was no way Miller would let anyone accuse him of leaving the field of battle without orders ever again.

In early July 1814 Barney was ordered to Washington to confer with Secretary Jones about what to do next in the region. They decided to keep his flotilla on the Patuxent River. Barney selected the town of Nottingham, Maryland, as the place to station the galleys. He retained the *Scorpion* as his flagship. However, the citizens of Nottingham were less than thrilled to see him there. When Major George Peter's District of Columbia militia departed for home, many believed that the government was once again abandoning the region. Most of the staunchly anti-government locals forcefully argued that if the government or even their own local militia detachments were not willing to put up a fight, then having Barney and his flotilla in the vicinity only invited trouble for them. Writing to his brother in Washington, D.C., Calvert County resident Thomas E. King said, "If he [Barney] had never of come in the Patuxent the British would never have thought nor had any idea that they could come as high as Lower Marlboro in the world." He believed that the only reason Barney had shown up in southern Maryland in the first place was he knew "Calvert, St. Mary's, Charles, and Prince Georges Counties were all Federalist," and by means of his flotilla, he would certainly "make them all advocates of old Jim Madison, but [instead] it has enraged them so that a great many that were in favor of him now are abusing him every day, but I think when I tell you the mischief the British have done it will be enough to make you and every man abuse Jim Madison and old Barney in Hell if you could."[28]

Now that the flotilla had escaped St. Leonard's Creek, St. Leonard's Town was left uncovered. Sailing Master Geoghegan was sent back to the town to recover and remove any military stores that remained. He had hoped to recover some material from the previously scuttled gunboats, No. 137 and No. 138. To his chagrin he found that the local inhabitants had largely beaten him to it. But as it turned out, he did not have much time anyway. A new local British commander, Captain Joseph Nourse, had arrived in the HMS *Severn* (fifty-six guns). He was soon joined by the sloop *St. Lawrence*, recently returned from Tangier Island. On 2 July Nourse sent a number of barges and two schooners under the command of Captain Thomas Brown to land a reinforced detachment of marines and raid St. Leonard's Town. Geoghegan had been warned by scouts that the British were coming, and he positioned his small detachment near the creek bank. As soon as the lead British barge came within musket range, he let loose a volley upon them. The British responded with a heavy barrage of grapeshot from their barge cannon and drove Geoghegan's men back from the creek bank. They immediately landed, and again following Cockburn's standing protocol, they laid waste to the entire town, sparing only the local doctor's house, where some wounded were being cared for. They even tried to detonate the scuttled gunboats. Near nightfall, loaded with hogsheads of tobacco and other plunder, they retreated back down the creek to the safety of their larger ships anchored in the Patuxent River.

6

THE PATUXENT RIVER AND BLADENSBURG

On 4 July 1814 Rear Admiral George Cockburn, in his new flagship, HMS *Albion* (seventy-four guns), arrived off St. Jerome's Creek. Following now-standard operating procedure, Cockburn immediately sent several cutters ashore with Royal Marines to raid the local St. Mary's County plantations once again for food, livestock, and slaves who could be transported to Tangier Island. Finally—in large part because the British were clearly planning to stay in the Chesapeake for yet another summer season—the American government had decided to address the confusing military administration of the bay area. Moreover, American spies in England and France informed President Madison that a large invasion force was preparing to set sail for the North American theater of war. Many believed that the Chesapeake was its likely target. While those in Britain greatly preferred that Sir Arthur Wellesley, the Duke of Wellington, lead this expedition, instead—and perhaps because the British had low regard for American military prowess—the command was given to the relatively junior Major General Robert Ross.

Underestimating Ross—notwithstanding his relative youth—and discounting his military skill would be a serious mistake. Born in Dublin, Ireland, he later came into a sum of inheritance that allowed him to purchase an estate in Northern Ireland, known then and now as Rostrevor, on the Ards Peninsula. Choosing a military career, a path that befitted a second son of minor gentry in those days, Ross experienced a considerable amount of combat as an army officer. He was severely wounded in fighting as part of the Anglo-Russian army in Holland. He fought as part of the Twentieth Regiment of Foot in Egypt and Italy, where he commanded a battalion. During a battle against the French at Maida, Ross and his regiment turned the tide. He, along with other senior officers, was awarded a gold medal, and his gallantry was mentioned in dispatches back home. Eventually

135

Portrait of Major General Robert Ross, commander of the British forces at Bladensburg, by an unidentified artist. Courtesy of Stephen Campbell

sent to fight in Portugal and Spain, Ross received a second medal for gallantry during the retreat to Corunna. Sent to Ireland to recruit more men to make up for losses incurred by battle and especially disease, Ross returned to Spain in 1812, again received a medal for combat performance, and was noticed by Wellington himself at Vittoria, Pamplona, Roncesvalles, and Sorauren. On 27 February 1814, at the Battle of Orthez, Ross was seriously wounded in the face and neck. With war against Napoleon essentially over, Ross, who had been promoted to major general in June 1814, and his Iberian Peninsula veterans were ordered to America. By the time he arrived in the Chesapeake Bay in mid-August 1814, he had not yet totally recovered from his neck wound. While both Cochrane and Cockburn heard rumors that between 10,000 and 20,000 troops were coming with Ross, only 3,000 red-coated infantry were actually on board the transports. Although this force was double the size of the one that had come under Sir Sidney Beckwith the previous year, both admirals decided to place another 1,000 Royal Marines at Ross' disposal. The British invasion force of 1814 never exceeded these 4,000 available men on any given day.[1]

To prepare for the coming onslaught in the Chesapeake, Madison created the Tenth Military District by disestablishing the old Fifth District, which had heretofore been ineffective. The new district comprised Virginia territory as far south as the Rappahannock River and extended northward to the Potomac, the District of Columbia, and the entire state of Maryland. Over the objection of Secretary of War Armstrong, Madison appointed Brigadier General William H. Winder to command the new district. Winder had been captured at an earlier American-Canadian frontier battle, Stony Creek, in June 1813. Even so, he was one of the few higher-ranking American officers to turn in an adequate performance during the ill-fated 1813 campaign along the St. Lawrence River. Further, Winder had been only recently exchanged. Madison had selected him for command for what might be described as purely political reasons. General Winder was the nephew of the sitting Federalist Party governor of Maryland, Levin Winder. Madison hoped that given the militia's past unsatisfactory performance, neither the brigadier general nor the governor would hesitate to fully engage the alleged military potential of Maryland's forces.

General Winder gratefully accepted the command but immediately found what Cockburn had discovered during his raids of the previous summer and spring—the region remained woefully unprepared to contest an invasion. On 9 July 1814, writing to Secretary of War Armstrong, Winder lamented that at best he could muster around a thousand regulars (mostly the heretofore untested U.S. 36th and 38th Infantry Regiments) for the defense of the entire district, to include garrisoning a number of forts around Washington, D.C., Annapolis, and Baltimore. He reminded the secretary that the British had been in the region on a regular basis for over a year and had conducted raids and made soundings in

Portrait of Maryland governor Levin Winder, Brigadier General William Winder's uncle. Courtesy of the Maryland State Archives. Reproduced with permission.

every major river. In sum, Winder recognized two salient features of his command: a British invasion force could appear nearly anywhere in the bay with little to no warning, and there was little that he or anyone else could do about it. In addition, as was the case during the 1813 campaign, Winder recognized that the actual defense of the region rested almost entirely on the unsteady shoulders of the Virginia and Maryland militia establishments.

Throughout the hot summer weeks of July 1814, Cockburn once again raided southern Maryland at will. Although Barney had miraculously escaped St. Leonard's Creek, he was still trapped up the larger Patuxent River and could do little about Cockburn's powerful squadron, which daily seemed to be increasing in size. Recently arrived were the seventy-four-gun *Asia*; three troops ships, the *Regulus*, *Melpomene*, and *Brune*, which had on board another battalion of Royal Marines and an artillery company; another sloop of war, the *Manley* (twelve guns); and most important, a powerful bomb ship, the *Aetna* (eight guns). The *Aetna* was a specialized ship that could fire shells at a high angle and penetrate enemy shore emplacements and magazines with weak overhead cover. In essence, this ship was designed to flatten cities and forts near the sea.

However, as late as 17 July 1814, Vice Admiral Cochrane was still unsure of where the Crown expected him to use his promised army reinforcements. In a rambling letter to the first lord of the Admiralty, Dundas Melville, Cochrane debated attacking locations all along the American Eastern Seaboard, including the cities of Boston, New York, Newport, Philadelphia, Baltimore, and Norfolk, and towns as far south as the Carolinas. He also mentioned the Gulf Coast cities of Mobile and New Orleans. In a separate letter to his subordinate Cockburn, Cochrane revealed the Crown's indecisiveness in selecting a target city for the upcoming summer campaign. In response, Cockburn unabashedly recommended that the Chesapeake region remain the principal target and specifically pointed out the advantages of landing an invasion army at the town of Benedict, Maryland, where such a force could simultaneously threaten Washington, D.C., Annapolis, or Baltimore. The location, Cockburn noted in a "secret" message to Cochrane, was "only 44 or 45 miles from Washington [the town is in fact much closer], and there is a high road between the two places which tho hilly is good. It passes through Piscataway no near[er] to Fort Washington than four miles, which fortification is sixteen miles below the city of Washington, and is the only one the Army would have to pass."[2]

Cockburn believed that landing a sizable task force at Benedict would mystify the newly appointed Winder and freeze the American militia in place, as neither would know whether Washington, Annapolis, or Baltimore was the true British objective. Cockburn was confident that British regulars could deal with the rest of the American defense in the region, such as it was, and he laid out reasons why the national capital must be taken before Annapolis and Baltimore. Not only would the fall of Washington be a "great blow to the Government of a country, as well on account of the resources as of the documents and records the invading army is almost sure to obtain," but Annapolis and Baltimore would surely fall like dominoes after the capital had been overrun. Cockburn pointed out to Cochrane, perhaps in memory of the previous year's debacle at Craney Island, that "Annapolis is tolerably well fortified. . . . It is natural to suppose precautions have been taken to frustrate and impede our advance in that direction." He went on to write that because Ross could expect no support from the Royal Navy owing to the

> shallowness of the water, it is possible and probable the occupation of it might cost us some little time, which would of course be taken advantage of by the enemy to draw together all the force at his command for the defence of Washington, and at all events enable the Heads of Departments there to remove whatever they wish. Baltimore is likewise difficult of access to us from the sea, we cannot in ships drawing above sixteen feet, approach nearer than even to the mouth of the Patapsco than 7 or 8 miles and Baltimore is situated 12 miles up, it having an extensive population, mostly armed, and a fort for its protection about a mile advanced from it on a projecting point where the River is so narrow as to admit of people conversing across it.[3]

Cockburn was convinced that both Annapolis and Baltimore should "be taken without difficulty from the land side; that is coming down upon them from the Washington Road." He also recommended sending a small detachment once again to the upper bay to occupy the militia there. If Philadelphia was selected as a target, he advised landing a force much in the same fashion as the Howe brothers had done during the American Revolution—landing somewhere near Elkton, Maryland, and marching overland while the Royal Navy sailed up Delaware Bay in support. He also recommended that another diversionary force ascend the Potomac River to "amuse Fort Washington if it does not reduce it." Cockburn believed that if the British landed in largely Federalist southern Maryland, "American guides will not be difficult to obtain in this country when we have the force to protect them and money to pay them." He concluded his letter by reminding his commander in chief that "Norfolk seems to be the only place where the Americans expect a serious attack" but advised against going there again since he believed "that place has been considerably strengthened of late."[4]

In fact, throughout the summer of 1814, especially in the Patuxent Valley, Cockburn had received a high level of cooperation from the locals. He noted in a letter to Captain Barrie of the HMS *Dragon*, "One of them on the left bank of the river (about 40 miles from Washington) sent to me to beg I would give him permission to go from his property for a few days to visit relatives ten miles distant." Incredibly, Cockburn said that another resident asked "leave to send a few of his young geese to another of his houses where part of his family resided." Cockburn observed, "In short it is quite ridiculous the perfect dominion we have from the entrance of the river to Benedict. Mr. Madison must certainly be either in confident expectation of immediate peace or preparing to abdicate the chair."[5]

Although revenge may have been on his mind, it should be noted that nowhere in his lengthy letter does Cockburn mention sacking Washington to avenge the Americans' burning of Little York the previous year. Moreover, his three-pronged strategy was ultimately adopted by Cochrane. Cockburn was more concerned about embarrassing the Madison administration and seizing records than anything else, and so he designed a lightning strike against Washington and then a quick turn to the more lucrative targets of Annapolis and especially Republican-minded Baltimore.

Meanwhile, Cochrane had more immediate activity in mind for his second in command, and this time revenge was indeed a motive for action that followed. In direct response to an American raid on Dover, Canada, during which homes and mills had been burned—similar to Cockburn's raids in the upper Chesapeake in 1813—Cochrane ordered an immediate retaliation against American towns that were accessible to his men. But before his forces moved forward, Cochrane decided to inform American secretary of state James Monroe on 18 August 1814 as to the British intentions: "Having been called upon by the Governor General of Canada to aid him in carrying into effect, measures of retaliation against the inhabitants of the United States for the wanton destruction committed by their army in Upper Canada, it has become imperiously my duty . . . [to] order to destroy and lay waste such towns and districts upon the coast as may be found assailable."[6]

Cochrane pointed out that "the Executive of the United States" could avoid the coming storm if he would make "reparations to the suffering inhabitants of Upper Canada." Secretary Monroe responded along predictable lines, arguing in a 4 September 1814 letter to Cochrane that the British were to blame for the increased brutality against civilians and, "without dwelling on the deplorable cruelties committed by the savages in the British ranks, and in British pay, on

American prisoners at the *river* Raisin, which to this day have never been disavowed or atoned," describing in detail the demise of Havre de Grace and Georgetown, Maryland, and the damaging plunder raids up and down the Chesapeake Bay. Monroe believed that this more than justified an American response in Upper Canada. However, the secretary took it a step further and provided an official explanation for other burnings in Canada, such as that of Newark. He said that the destruction of this town had been unavoidable because Newark was built right next to Fort George. Nevertheless, the American government had disavowed the decision of the officer in charge to set fire to the town. Monroe noted that the torching of Dover, Long Point, and St. David's were the illegal acts of "stragglers" and that the American government never intended such activity. Interestingly, Monroe's letter entirely ignores American incendiary activities at Little York.[7]

Admiral Cockburn, however, was quick to respond to Cochrane's orders because they comported with the way he believed the Chesapeake campaign should be fought. Dividing his force into two squadrons, he directed Captain Nourse in the *Severn* to maintain watch over Barney's force in the Patuxent. He also sent the *Loire* and *St. Lawrence* up the bay toward Baltimore. Meanwhile, he took his own ship, the *Albion*, and a number of other smaller draught vessels to the Potomac. Thus, by appearing in three major thoroughfares at the same time, Cockburn hoped to mystify Winder as to exactly where the British invasion force might land and what water route they would likely come by.

As in 1813, Cockburn's brilliant use of the bay and its tributaries set the stage for later British success in the region. Meanwhile, Nourse was sent to attack the area around the former village of Calverton via the lower Patuxent River, and his force burned the farms entirely to the ground. Interestingly, the nearby home of local militia commander Michael Taney was left unscathed, perhaps lending credence to Barney's earlier suspicions about Taney's true loyalties. On 17 July 1814 Nourse's men burned a large warehouse in the village of Hunting Town. The flames from the warehouse set the rest of the small town ablaze as well. Two days later, Nourse raided Prince Frederick, the county seat of Calvert County, and burned the courthouse and jail. The local militia, as they had on nearly all other occasions, ran off without putting up much of a fight. On their way back down the river, just north of the destroyed former village of Calverton, Nourse's marines attacked and burned the large estate of Dr. John Gray because evidence that the militia had been there had been found. That evidence turned out to be a single military canteen, but it was enough to have Gray's home turned into ashes.

Black and white print of James Monroe based on a portrait by Gilbert Stuart.
Library of Congress, LC-USZ62-104958

Cockburn even made raids against Virginia's heretofore undamaged Northern Neck. In mid-July he went after Nomini Landing and burned Nomini Hall
Church. According to Lieutenant James J. Willes, adjutant of the Third Battalion
of Royal and Colonial Marines, on 20 July 1814 "poison being found at Nominy
[*sic*] in some spirits—induced the Admiral [Cockburn] to destroy by fire every
house on both sides [of] the River going back." On 23 July Willes noted that
British forces brought out four schooners from Clements Bay and "burned a house
returning from which a boat had been fired on going up." Three days later, on
Machodoc Creek in King George County, Virginia, six more schooners were
destroyed, and Willes mentioned that the British "brought off about 100 head of

Cattle." At Chaptico they took "70 Hogsheads of Tobacco, Forage &c." On 3 August Cockburn sent approximately twenty barge loads of Royal Marines up the Yeocomico River. As they were landing, they were attacked by elements of the Forty-Seventh Virginia Regiment, under the immediate command of Captain William Henderson. Running out of ammunition, Henderson and his militia retreated. The British found out where Henderson's local plantation was located and tore it apart. They proceeded to burn and loot farms and plantations in the area with a renewed fervor that the Virginians had not seen even at Hampton the previous year.[8]

For slaves, all this activity in Virginia's Northern Neck had a positive outcome. According to Brigadier General John P. Hungerford, commanding officer of the Virginia militia, large numbers of slaves flocked to the British, and many took advantage of the turmoil to find freedom. Slaves in southern Maryland took similar advantage. Liberation of slaves had been made a legitimate military objective, and Cochrane had publicly announced this objective once he took command. Free Marylander and soon-to-be member of Joshua Barney's flotilla Charles Ball described what took place during the 1813 raids in the slaveholding Chesapeake region:

> In the spring of 1813, the British fleet came into the bay, and from this Time, the origin of the troubles and distresses of the people of the Western Shore, may be dated. I had been employed at a fishery, near the mouth of the Patuxent, from early in March, until the latter part of May, when a British vessel of war came off the mouth of the river, and sent her boats to drive us away from our fishing ground. There was but little property at the fishery that could be destroyed; but the enemy cut the seines to pieces, and burned the sheds belonging to the place. They then marched up two miles into the country, burned the house of a planter, and brought away with them several cattle, that were found in his fields. They also carried off more than twenty slaves, which were never again restored to their owner; although, on the following day, he went aboard the ship, with a flag of truce, and offered a large ransom for these slaves.[9]

Although slaves used the arrival of the British to gain their freedom, liberation was not specific Crown policy, at least during the summer of 1813. To avoid a charge of hypocrisy levied against them by the Americans (a charge they had suffered during the Revolution, when many liberated slaves were either reenslaved in the British Caribbean or sent to bleak Nova Scotia), Lord Bathurst told Colonel Sir Sidney Beckwith that he was to take only those slaves who "in the course of your operations have given you assistance, which may expose them to the vengeance of their Masters after your retreat." Beckwith was allowed to enlist freed slaves "into any of the Black Corps if they are willing to enlist; but you must distinctly understand that you are in no case to take slaves as Slaves, but as free persons whom the public become bound to maintain."[10]

Throughout the war in the Chesapeake, local American newspapers held to the false hope that most of the runaway slaves had been forced to leave their plantations by the British army. In reality, many more left on their own accord. Moreover, white planters had lived in mortal fear of servile insurrection for more than a hundred years and most recently had endured a scare in 1800 around Richmond, Virginia, known as Gabriel's Rebellion. The prospect of freedom outweighed any loyalty the slaves may have felt for a Maryland or Virginia tobacco farm.

Most likely because he was a free man, Charles Ball was asked by local planters to help repatriate around a hundred slaves who had fled the southern Maryland plantation of a Mrs. Wilson in a single night. He was told to masquerade as a servant to one of the white men in the deputation and then mingle among the escapees. The slaves had been able to make their incredible escape because, the day before the breakout, two or three of Mrs. Wilson's slaves had paddled a canoe out to a British man-of-war and informed its crew that a large number were willing to desert the Wilson plantation. The British told the slaves to return and to be prepared to be picked up in barges on the shore the following evening—and this is exactly what happened, although how many may have been coerced by either more motivated slaves or the British is difficult to ascertain. Ball noted in his journal that this "was the greatest disaster that had befallen any individual in our neighborhood, in the course of the war." Once on board the man-of-war, he found the newly freed men and women "lounging about on the main deck, or leaning against the sides of the ship's bulwarks." Ball attempted to persuade them to return to Mrs. Wilson, who had allegedly "never treated them with great severity." But he could not change their minds once they had reached the relative safety of the British vessel and "found that their heads were full of notions of liberty and happiness in some of the West Indian islands." In the meantime the

British prepared to set sail for Tangier Island and even invited Ball to go with them. He was told the ultimate destination of the now former slaves was the island of Trinidad in the Caribbean, "where they were to be free." Ball declined the invitation and finally revealed to the British that he was a free man.[11]

Soon, the British laid waste to the village of Kinsale in Virginia's Northern Neck. They chased Brigadier General John P. Hungerford's Virginia militia into the interior, where they could no longer protect the riverside plantations. On 6 August Cockburn pushed up Virginia's heretofore "unvisited" Coan River. Rowing marines up to the head of the river, the raiders once again burned farms, confiscated supplies, and seized three schooners, although the Lancaster County militia put up a stout fight over the vessels before being driven off. "In all, nine raids were made in 25 days."[12] A newspaper report noted, "Mr. Henderson's Store and all his houses within five miles of Farnham church are in ashes. . . . We are all here in the utmost confusion; houses and farms deserted, women and children living in tents in the woods." The report said that Colonel Richard Parker had had a close call with a British foraging party and was wounded in the hand and thigh when he tried to jump his horse over a fence.[13] As he had the previous year, Cockburn seemed to be everywhere at once.

According to the American newspapers, whose information and commentary were certainly not unbiased, the behavior of Cockburn's raiders was getting worse and worse. Allegedly, graves were robbed, town wells were ruined, homes were burned seemingly out of spite, and according to one salacious story, women had been strip-searched in front of a gaggle of leering British officers. It was clear that by 1814 the fighting in the Chesapeake region was brutal and remorseless. Each side legitimately believed that it was avenging atrocities committed by the other.

Because the *Loire* and *St. Lawrence* were spotted moving toward the upper bay, General Winder was convinced that Annapolis was the next British target. Accordingly, he ordered the 36th and 38th Infantry Regiments to leave Nottingham and establish a new camp on the South River, nearer Annapolis. He ordered General Stephen West's Prince Georges County militia to stand ready to replace them. There were rumors of the enemy landing in a wide variety of locations, but Winder remained convinced that Annapolis was the next British target. At one point he ordered Fort Madison, one of two primary forts that guarded Maryland's capital, dismantled because of his concern that if this fort was taken, its guns would be used against the other bastion, nearby Fort Severn. A week later, he countermanded his own order. While Winder was indeed a whirlwind of activity, he seemed to focus entirely on military minutiae vice the big picture of defending the region against a major invasion. He incessantly worried about supplies, horses, and equipment, but rarely did he consider what he might do if the British made a major incursion into his district. Militia units were activated and sent on wild goose chases, while the two regular infantry regiments were frozen in place near Annapolis. Winder also had a habit of riding miles over the Maryland country-side, and he frequently showed up in person at various locations throughout south-ern Maryland when sending an aide or a subordinate might have been more effective. His confused behavior was exactly what Cockburn had hoped to achieve and was a reprise of his strategy from the previous summer, when he had raided numerous upper bay towns and rivers from midbay Kent Island to the Elk River at the top of the Chesapeake. Thanks to the rapidity of Cockburn's attacks and the great range over which he conducted them, local militia commanders and the gov-ernor could rarely muster enough force to oppose even minor incursions. Most of the bay towns demanded that their local militia stay home. Moreover, the British operational strategy of making nearly simultaneous attacks over a wide area made the effective employment of the regular regiments problematic.

On 14 August 1814 Vice Admiral Cochrane and his massive flagship, HMS *Tonnant* (eighty guns), rendezvoused with Cockburn's advance squadron at the mouth of the Potomac River. Two days later, Ross and the main invasion force transports arrived. In addition to the Royal Marines and about a hundred colonial marines and field artillery, Ross brought with him four large veteran regiments, the Fourth, Twenty-First, Forty-Fourth, and Eighty-Fifth Regiments of Foot. Three of the four regiments had significant combat experience in the Napoleonic wars. The sight must have been absolutely impressive. Lieutenant George Robert Gleig of the Eighty-Fifth Regiment of Foot wrote, "The sight was . . . as grand and imposing as any I ever beheld; because one could not help remembering that this powerful fleet was sailing in an enemy's bay, and was filled with troops for the invasion of that enemy's country. Thus like a snow-ball, we had gathered as we went on, and from a mere handful of soldiers, were now become an army formi-dable from its numbers as well as discipline."[14]

Much to Cockburn's initial disappointment, neither Cochrane nor Ross believed that Washington, D.C., should be the focus of their upcoming invasion. Ross and his staff believed that the city was too far away from the proposed

Benedict, Maryland, landing point and that their force too small to last for long that deep into enemy country. Moreover, Ross lacked a cavalry force for scouting purposes and only possessed a few pieces of light, mobile artillery. Cochrane seemed inclined to agree with his land force commander. However, at least according to Cockburn and his aide, it was Cockburn's insistence on Washington, D.C., as a primary target of any landing that eventually won the day. Pointing out that time and again, small forces of Royal and colonial marines had easily dispersed the Maryland militia, Cockburn convinced the other senior leaders that they had little to fear from the Americans. As a compromise, they decided to deal first with the sole credible military threat in the region: Barney's flotilla at Nottingham, Maryland. They would clear any viable bodies of militia from the banks of the Patuxent River, and once these objectives had been accomplished, decide at that point, if the way was largely clear, to attack Washington, D.C.

At 2:00 a.m. on 19 August 1814, lead elements of Ross' invasion force landed unopposed at Benedict, Maryland. The last troops did not get ashore until the following day. Ross took his time getting his men on the road toward Barney's flotilla at Nottingham, and they did not reach this location until late on 21 August 1814. Cockburn used his ship's boats and barges to parallel the right of Ross' advance from the river. It did not matter, though, because Barney had already moved his flotilla farther north a mile or so above a bend in the river known as Pig Point. This was about as far north as Barney could possibly get on the increasingly narrow and shallow waters of the upper Patuxent River. Barney knew that if the British moved up the west bank of the Patuxent toward Queen Anne's Town and Upper Marlboro, his flotilla would be doomed. As soon as he had been made aware that the enemy had landed at Benedict, Maryland, Barney immediately marched with his flotillamen to Washington, D.C., to join forces being slowly gathered there under Winder. He left behind Lieutenant Solomon Frazier and five men per barge with orders to burn the boats if the British suddenly showed up. Barney also ordered Captain Samuel Miller's U.S. Marines along with their three light 12-pounder cannon to meet him on the road from Upper Marlboro so as to unite the Marines with his flotilla force. If Lieutenant Frazier had to burn the flotilla, he would then join Barney as soon as he could.

On the morning of 22 August 1814, as Ross' men headed toward Pig Point, Cockburn's screening riverine force rounded Pig Point and spotted Barney's flotilla. Cockburn wrote,

On approaching Pig Point (where the enemy's flotilla was said to be), I landed the marines under Captain Robyns on the left bank of the river, and directed him to march round and attack, on the land side, the town situated on the point. . . . I plainly discovered Commodore Barney's broad pendant in the headmost vessel, a large sloop [the *Scorpion*], and the remainder of the flotilla extending in a line astern of her. Our boats now advanced towards them as rapidly as possible; but on nearing them, we observed the sloop bearing the broad pendant to be on fire, and she soon afterwards blew up. I now saw clearly that they were all abandoned, and on fire, with trains to their magazines; out of the seventeen vessels which composed this formidable and much vaunted flotilla, sixteen were in quick succession blown to atoms, and the seventeenth (in which the fire had not been taken) we captured.[15]

On this same day Secretary of the Navy Jones notified Master Commandant John O. Creighton, whom he had appointed to command Washington's ersatz river defenses, that six British ships had made their way past Kettle Bottom shoals and been spotted "ascending the Potomac." Admiral Cochrane had ordered these ships up the Potomac as a diversionary tactic to keep the Americans from solely focusing on Ross and Cockburn's main body at Benedict, Maryland. The squadron was led by Captain James A. Gordon in the HMS *Seahorse*. In addition to three bomb ships—the *Devastation*, *Aetna*, and *Meteor*—and a Congreve rocket ship—the *Erebus*—Gordon also brought along a second frigate, the HMS *Euryalus*. The British rightly believed that this force was more than enough to flatten poorly constructed Fort Washington since the corvette USS *Adams* had broken through the blockade earlier in the year. The few sloops and gunboats the Americans still possessed in the Potomac were far inferior to Gordon's squadron. Gordon's biggest concern was Fort Washington; hence, he had brought along the bomb ships. At the Washington Navy Yard, the Americans were in the process of completing the light frigate USS *Columbia* (thirty-two guns), but the vessel was unable to assist in the defense of Washington before Gordon made his ascent up the river.[16]

By the afternoon of 22 August, General Ross and his red-coated infantry and Royal Marines were in full possession of Upper Marlboro, Maryland, in Prince George's County. Winder had ordered all his forces to fall back from the vicinity and gather at a place called Long Old Fields (near present-day Andrews Air Force

Base), about eight miles from Washington, D.C., and directly on the road that led from Upper Marlboro. At the time Cochrane sent a message to Cockburn congratulating him on the destruction of Barney's flotilla—an objective that Cochrane apparently believed was the primary goal of Ross' landing force, since he wrote that he thought "the matter is ended, [and] the sooner the Army get[s] back [to Benedict, Maryland] the better." Having received this note, Cockburn then proceeded to join Ross at Upper Marlboro. He had heard from some of the more aggressive staff members that Ross was waffling on whether he should proceed to Washington, D.C., or return to Benedict, Maryland. Whether this was true is difficult to determine since Ross was anything but indecisive in operations against Napoleon's forces. Cockburn was apparently persuasive, and after some minor delays, Ross agreed to go after the American national capital. Cockburn informed Cochrane that he now found "Ross determined (in consequence of the Information he has received & what he has Observed of the Enemy), to push on towards Washington, which I have confident Hopes he will give a good account of. I shall accompany him & of course afford him every Assistance in my Power." In reality, Cockburn probably wanted to accompany Ross not to ensure that he did not change his mind but more likely to be in on the kill once the British engaged the Americans in battle.[17]

Meanwhile, at Long Old Fields General Winder attempted to build up as much military strength as he could. As early as 4 July 1814, Secretary of War Armstrong had issued a general call-up of 93,000 militiamen. Of this number, the states of Virginia, Maryland, and Pennsylvania were expected to respectively provide 12,000, 6,000, and 14,000 men. However, Winder did not have any control over these men unless there was imminent danger of invasion of the Tenth Military District. To make matters worse, the state of Pennsylvania was in the process of reorganizing its state forces and as a result not a single Pennsylvania militiaman was available (at that moment) to augment Winder's forces in Maryland. Winder had about 330 regulars of the U.S. 36th and 38th Infantry Regiments, under the overall command of Lieutenant Colonel William Scott, available for duty as well as 400 of Barney's now-dispossessed flotillamen and a 103-man U.S. Marine company under the command of Captain Miller. To his credit, Secretary of the Navy Jones did all he could to assist Winder in the defense of the national capital. The secretary ordered naval forces under Commodore John Rodgers from as far away as Delaware Bay to come to the immediate aid of the capital, but none of these men got any farther than Baltimore before the British launched their attack. Jones also ordered Captain David Porter and Captain Oliver Hazard Perry, then on temporary duty in the capital, to prepare available naval detachments in the city to assist in the defense of Fort Washington.[18]

The District of Columbia provided 2 brigades of militia under the overall command of Major General John P. Van Ness. The first and larger brigade was commanded by Brigadier General Walter Smith and included 2 companies of light artillery and two rifle companies. This brigade numbered 1,070 men in all. A second brigade of approximately 500 men from the Alexandria militia (Alexandria was then part of the District of Columbia), under Brigadier General Robert Young, crossed the Potomac and were located near Piscataway, Maryland, where they could support Fort Washington or threaten the rear of the enemy if they marched on Bladensburg. However, owing to James Gordon's feint up the Potomac River, which coincided with Ross' advance on Washington, Young's men did next to nothing in the coming battle either at Bladensburg or Fort Washington and did not move from their established location.

Owing to the British military buildup in southern Maryland, on 20 August 1814 General Samuel Smith at Fort McHenry directed Brigadier General Tobias Stansbury to march his thirteen-hundred-man, Baltimore-based brigade to assist Winder. Comprising mostly Baltimore City men, elements of Stansbury's brigade arrived at a campsite near Bladensburg, Maryland, two days later, as the British were entering Upper Marlboro. The following day, the Fifth Maryland Regiment, under Lieutenant Colonel Joseph Sterett, and another militia rifle battalion, under former U.S. attorney general Major William Pinkney, along with some light artillery units, reached Bladensburg as well. Other various militia detachments and volunteers from Maryland, the District of Columbia, and Virginia arrived in the next twenty-four hours, including one large eight-hundred-man unit commanded by Colonel William D. Beall from Annapolis, Maryland. The Sixtieth Virginia Regiment, under Colonel George Minor, arrived from Falls Church, Virginia. However, the militiamen had left Falls Church in such a hurry that many of them were without powder or flints for their weapons, and until these critical items were issued, their service could not be immediately counted on. Instead of preparing for battle, Minor's Virginians spent the evening of 23 August sleeping on the floor of the House of Representatives. Winder informed Minor that Colonel Henry Carbery, formerly in command of the hard-luck U.S. 36th Infantry, would provide him with the necessary military accoutrements.

One youthful member of the United Company of the Fifth Baltimore Light Dragoons (the Baltimore Fifth) was eighteen-year-old private John Pendleton Kennedy. In his journal Kennedy vividly described the grand march of his regiment toward the battlefield near Washington: "What a scene it was, and what a proud actor I was in it! I was in the ecstasy of a vision of glory, stuffed with any quality of romance. This was a real army marching to a real war. The enemy, we knew, was in full career and we had the certainty of meeting him in a few days." But it was not long before the hot march on sandy roads softened Kennedy's vision of martial glory. He wrote on 22 August 1814, "We were in winter cloth uniform, with a most absurd helmet of thick jacked leather and covered with plumes." Kennedy was weighted down by a great coat he had been issued in August, a thick wool blanket, and several changes of clothing. Interestingly, he noted, "Among these articles I had also put a pair of [dancing] pumps which I had provided with the idea that, after we had beaten the British army and saved Washington, Mr. Madison would very likely invite us to a ball at the President's House, and I wanted to be ready for it." Kennedy estimated that his knapsack weighed ten pounds and that his "Harpers Ferry" musket—so named because it was produced by the U.S. Arsenal at Harpers Ferry, Virginia—was at least fourteen pounds. Nonetheless, he concluded that his company of volunteers bore its situation fairly well.[19]

More militiamen from Alexandria, under the command of Colonel William A. Daingerfield, were sent to reinforce Fort Washington. Late on 22 August 1814, Winder ordered elements of the District of Columbia militia under Major Peter to reconnoiter the British camp at Upper Marlboro in order to discover Ross' direction of march. The rest of the district's militia—including the 330-man regular infantry unit under Lieutenant Colonel Scott, primarily made up of most of the U.S. 36th Infantry Regiment, detachments from the 38th Infantry, and an 80-man company from the U.S. 12th Infantry Regiment—would move toward the Wood Yard on the road to Upper Marlboro, closer to Ross' army. Winder also ordered Stansbury's and Sterrett's troops to prepare to move up from Bladensburg.

The morning of 23 August 1814 found the British still resting on their arms at Upper Marlboro. Early that same day, President James Madison arrived at Long Old Fields and decided that he would review the army with members of his cabinet. Secretary of War Armstrong remained convinced that at most the British would make a "Cossack hurrah"—or a quick hit-and-run raid against the national capital. He convinced the president that since the British possessed no cavalry or artillery (he was wrong on the latter point), they were in no condition to take the city by storm. Both Armstrong and Winder firmly believed that Annapolis was still the most likely target of the British expedition.[20]

However, by 2:00 p.m. on the twenty-third, Ross had finally decided to remove all doubt about his next objective. After he had left behind a heavy rear guard of Royal Marines at Upper Marlboro, he placed his regiments in a column on the road toward Washington. Ross' advance guard easily brushed aside George Peter's District of Columbia militia and light artillery, and the British rapidly advanced on the Wood Yard after they had conducted some countermarching to confuse the Americans about their true axis of advance. Peter's men fell back to Long Old Fields, and Winder ordered all his forward-based troops to fall back to this position as well. Secretary of State James Monroe, who had heretofore ridden all over the countryside and fancied himself more of a military man than a diplomat during these intense weeks, wrote a hasty note to Madison: "The enemy are advanced six miles on the road to the Wood Yard, and our troops are retiring. Our troops were on the march to meet them, but in too small a body to engage. General Winder proposes to retire till he can collect them in a body. The enemy are in full march to Washington. Have the materials prepared to destroy the bridges. P.S.— You had better remove the records."[21]

Just before nightfall Winder ordered all his forces at Long Old Fields to retreat back across the Eastern Branch. Most of the men made a fatiguing forced march, crossed over the branch via the two lower bridges, and collapsed in several fields near the Navy Yard. Countermanding his earlier orders to Stansbury and Sterett to move forward, Winder now told them to begin forming a defensive line on the other side of the small bridge that spanned the Eastern Branch at Bladensburg. Stansbury, however, began to fall back toward the city. Only after Winder had insisted he return did he finally begin to dig in opposite the town of Bladensburg and directly in front of the small bridge that spanned the branch. All this movement caused the American forces at Bladensburg to be even more unprepared when the British finally arrived in their vicinity.

If Winder possessed one advantage, it was that once Ross committed to advancing on Washington, he was limited as to the number of routes he could take to cross the Eastern Branch of the Potomac River (known today as the Anacostia River). From Bladensburg southwest to the mouth of the branch, where it enters the Potomac River, there were only three bridges. The lowest bridge crossed the river near the Washington Navy Yard. The next higher span allowed access to the area of Washington east of Capitol Hill. The branch was too broad at both of the lower sites, and if the bridges were destroyed, it would be impossible for the British to cross directly into Washington. However, the far upper span was located at the small town of Bladensburg. Here the branch was quite narrow and, if required, could be easily forded. Moreover, an army advancing from Upper Marlboro would not likely risk going any farther to the northeast to minimize the chance of being attacked from the rear by forces coming from Baltimore. So Winder was fairly certain that if the British persisted in their march to Washington, they had just three options for crossing the branch and were most likely to cross at Bladensburg.

By the evening of 23 August, Ross' army had encamped at a place called Melwood, not far from Long Old Fields and about ten miles from the city. Ross was amazed that, other than the brief skirmish with Major Peter's District of Columbia militia, the Americans had done little to impede his route of march. In fact, he was astounded at the lack of American military activity. Inside the city of Washington, however, a sense of panic had begun to build. Wagons and teams of horses were at a premium, and government officials from the Washington Navy Yard to the Treasury and State Departments had been empowered to impress them into service if they could not directly hire vehicles to cart away their handwritten records. Winder wandered off to see if, according to his orders, the two lower bridges had been prepared for destruction. To his shock and horror, he found that they had not. The East Capitol Bridge, or Stoddert's Bridge, as it was called, was not even properly guarded.

Winder finally ordered the Washington Navy Yard commandant, Captain Thomas Tingey, to supply some boats and powder for destroying the lower Navy Yard span. Because Joshua Barney was camped nearby, the defense of the Navy Yard Bridge had fallen by default to him, his stalwart flotillamen, and his U.S. Marines, whose barracks at Eighth and I Streets in Washington, D.C., was just up the road. Winder ordered the East Capitol Bridge to be immediately burned. By 3:30 a.m. Stansbury and his men at Bladensburg saw the flames from Stoddert's Bridge lighting up the night sky. But that same evening Ross and Cockburn received an order from Cochrane to proceed no farther and return to Benedict, Maryland. Nonetheless, in the early predawn hours of 24 August 1814, Cockburn forcefully convinced Ross that turning back now would bring "a stain upon our arms." Assuring Ross that the militia would never stand against disciplined British regulars, Cockburn emphatically stated, "We must go on." While it is still not clear if Ross actually needed any convincing, perhaps worn down by the debate, he agreed to press on, and by 5:00 a.m. on 24 August, his army headed directly for the American positions across the branch from Bladensburg.[22]

Meanwhile, Winder was nearly a nervous wreck. Conflicting reports had come in from a number of scouts as to the whereabouts of Ross' army. Not exactly sure where to place his main defensive line and increasingly self-victimized by the sum of all his fears, Winder wrote a note to Secretary of War Armstrong that he "should be glad of assistance of counsel from yourself and the government. If more convenient, I should make an exertion to go to you at the first opportunity." The note was mistakenly sent to the president, who then brought it immediately to Armstrong's attention. Armstrong, despite his considerable military experience, seemed determined to stay completely out of Winder's way. Madison and other members of his cabinet rode out to Winder's headquarters, then near the lower bridge and the Navy Yard. A crowd soon developed, and shortly the scene reached near total chaos as everyone tried to offer the general their "expert" point of view. Conspicuously missing from the crowd was Secretary Armstrong. Even as late as 9:00 a.m. on 24 August, Winder seemed mystified as to the true target of Ross' advance. Finally, by 11:00 a.m., Winder had decided that the British intended to cross the river at Bladensburg. This was not hard to surmise since his scouts were now telling him that Ross' main body was headed right for the bridge there.

Finally issuing orders for Scott's regulars, the District of Columbia militia, and a 140-man company of U.S. dragoons, under the command of Lieutenant Colonel Jacint Laval, to move immediately to Bladensburg, Winder made his way to Stansbury's defensive position on the outskirts of the town. This was his first close look at the American preparations there. Amazingly, he either forgot about Barney's men, now sitting idle at the unthreatened lower bridge, or did not believe they were under his immediate command authority. Not wishing to miss the upcoming fight, Barney appealed directly to a nearby President Madison and asked to be allowed to take his flotillamen and Captain Miller's Marines and light artillery to Bladensburg. Madison consented to Barney's request and decided that he too would go to Bladensburg. The president (along with a sizable entourage of aides and cabinet members) arrived at Bladensburg at about the same time as the British and nearly rode straight into enemy lines. Fortunately, some observant

American officers redirected the president and his men to a nearby orchard to await events. Since Stansbury's militiamen were the only troops who had been on the ground for very long, Winder had little time to sort out units as they arrived from the vicinity of the Navy Yard or other camp locations in Maryland or Virginia. He himself had arrived at the field barely an hour ahead of the British. Thus, the American defense at Bladensburg took on the appearance of a slapdash affair.[23]

Records confirm that Winder arrived at the Bladensburg Bridge around noon. Citizen volunteers had built an artillery emplacement on some elevated ground about 350 yards from the bridge. In hindsight this artillery position was less than effective. Most of the cannon fire on the bridge tended to plunge upon the structure rather than sweep it, which would have cost the British higher casualties as they attempted to cross the span. To partially make up for this weakness, the U.S. Army commissary general of ordnance, Colonel Decius Wadsworth, placed an additional two guns nearby. Stansbury's men, along with Sterett's unit, occupied the ground behind the bridge, covering the roads that forked beyond them—the northern road led to Georgetown while the southern road led directly to Capitol Hill in Washington, D.C. Pinkney's rifle battalion was moved forward nearly to the bridge itself, along with some companies of district militia. Laval's regular dragoons took up a position behind and to the left of Sterett's Fifth Maryland Regiment. They were placed there by Secretary of State Monroe, who suggested that the dragoons occupy a deep ravine. However, the ravine was so deep that Laval could not see anything, and his trained men were of little use to anyone throughout the battle. Incredibly, while Stansbury was organizing the emplacement of his Baltimore light artillery, Secretary of State Monroe, without consulting either Stansbury or Winder, ordered two of Stansbury's other regiments, under Colonel Jonathan Shutz and Colonel John Ragan, five hundred yards to the rear of their original positions. Now too far away from the first line to be of help to anyone, the Baltimore artillery and Pinkney's riflemen were left greatly exposed and largely on their own to face any British attack directly crossing the bridge.

Before Stansbury could do anything about it, the van of the British column appeared outside of town. While members of the president's cabinet were busy confusing matters near the bridge, Winder hurriedly formed a third defensive line. Fortunately, here he encountered less outside interference. Forming this line on a hill behind a ravine crossing called Tournecliffe's Bridge, Winder positioned some district militia to command the bridge crossing. He formed Scott's regulars on the left of the third line and provided several militia rifle companies as support. Walter Smith's D.C. militia, along with George Peter's light artillery, was to Scott's right. Barney's tough flotillamen and heavier artillery commanded the main Washington Post Road, along with Miller's light artillery and Marines, forming to the right of the flotillamen and their guns. Finally, the newly arrived but exhausted Annapolis brigade posted itself on a slight hill to the right of the Marines. The brigade's commanding officer, Colonel Beall, was apparently never told what was expected of him or his men during the battle, and he received no orders from either Winder or any other senior-ranking officer. In sum, the third line comprised Winder's best troops. By high noon the thrown-together American Army was about as large as it was going to get, and Winder had about seven thousand men (mostly militia) on the field to face approximately three thousand British regulars and marines. While the numeric odds seemed to be in Winder's favor, it quickly became apparent that the ill-disciplined, combat-inexperienced, and poorly led American soldiers were in trouble.

Across the branch came the vaunted British army. Earlier, to make better marching time, Ross had organized the regiments into three brigades. His lead unit, comprising the veterans of the Eighty-Fifth Regiment of Foot (and also the light companies of the other regiments in the expedition and a colonial marine company), was a light brigade. These men carried lighter marching gear and thus could make better time on the dust-choked Maryland roads. They arrived a little in advance of the rest of Ross' column and saw the Americans drawn up in battle formation on the other side of the branch at Bladensburg. Ross had to decide to either immediately attack with the light troops he had on hand or wait for the other regiments to catch up. Urged on by the aggressive commanding officer of the Eighty-Fifth Regiment, Colonel William Thornton, Ross ordered his troops not to wait for the Second or Third Brigades; they were to immediately storm the bridge crossing and attack the Americans on the other side. Ross and Cockburn were surprised that the Americans had not turned some of the stout brick buildings in the town of Bladensburg into strongpoints. Looking across the branch, Lieutenant George Gleig of the Eighty-Fifth Regiment of Foot observed that the Americans "were on a bare hill, their battle line very awkward in appearance, drawn three ranks deep." He thought they looked "more like a crowd of spectators" than like soldiers but noted "they were sufficiently armed but wretchedly equipped."[24]

It was now getting close to 1:00 p.m. At about this time the Americans near the bridge noticed elements of the Eighty-Fifth Regiment of Foot preparing to attack. Two 6-pounder cannon, along with Wadsworth's artillery, began to fire into the British brigade, which took a few casualties. Thornton had his men form up behind the cover of nearby Lowndes Hill as the Americans cheered at the temporary withdrawal of his lead echelon. But it was not long before the reformed Eighty-Fifth Regiment began to relentlessly advance on the bridge. At the same time Ross had a Royal Marine rocket battery fire at the American first line.

Thornton now had his men advance at the double-quick, and mounted on his horse waving his sword, he personally led them across the bridge. While he lost a number of men to American artillery fire, he himself emerged miraculously unscathed. Soon elements of his regiment were fanning out left and right of the bridgehead and began to drive Pinkney's riflemen and some of the recently arrived D.C. militia companies from the riverbanks. Re-forming, Thornton's redcoats immediately advanced on what was left of Stansbury's first and second lines. They quickly overran the artillery position as well. Private Henry Fulford, a Baltimore militiaman, observed the British advance with some degree of awe: "Their men moved like clock-work; the instant a part of a platoon was cut down it was filled up by the men in the rear without the least noise and confusion whatever, so as to present always a solid column to the mouths of our cannon."[25] Pinkney himself was wounded trying to rally his fleeing men. Now Thornton's men were reinforced by Ross' Second Brigade (the Fourth and Forty-Fourth Regiments of Foot), led by Colonel Arthur Brooke. These men began to flank what was left of Stansbury's line and fairly soon the Americans began to totally collapse.

When he had first observed the initial British attack pull back behind Lowndes Hill, Winder had ordered Sterett's Fifth Maryland Regiment forward to add further support to the artillery. This particular unit was probably the best of Winder's militia regiments. As Sterett's men moved up, a renewed barrage of rockets struck Ragan's and Shutz's Maryland militia regiments. These men immediately broke and ran for the rear, thus uncovering the right flank of the now halted Fifth Maryland Regiment. At this time Sterett's men began to take some casualties from unseen British musket fire coming from an orchard and a nearby tobacco barn. Winder, fearful that Sterett's men were being flanked, ordered them to fall back toward his third line across the ravine. He immediately countermanded that order but then once again ordered them to fall back. The conflicting orders confused Sterett and his men, and their orderly retreat quickly devolved into a rout. Now Winder's entire first and second lines, along with their surviving associated artillery (Winder's army had a total of twenty-three pieces available that day), came tumbling back toward the third line or fled up the northern road toward Georgetown. Venturing out of the ravine to see what was going on, the retreating militia passed through Lieutenant Colonel Laval's U.S. dragoons. An out-of-control artillery caisson crashed against Laval and nearly broke his leg. A number of his own troops fled along with the militia, leaving him with only fifty-five men. Recognizing at this point that they were of little value, Laval and his men also withdrew along the road toward Georgetown. Farther to the rear, the president and his cabinet witnessed the unfolding debacle, and by 2:00 p.m. they began to sullenly make their way back to Washington to prepare critical elements of the government for evacuation toward Montgomery County Court House (modern-day Rockville, Maryland) or across the Potomac into Virginia. The energetic but misguided James Monroe, however, stayed behind and attempted to rally the fleeing militia.[26]

Now Winder's third line faced the British onslaught. Both Ross and Cockburn were on the field of battle and urged the infantry forward. A musket ball cut the stirrup of Cockburn's saddle. When a nearby Royal Marine moved up to repair it, he was killed by a musket ball and died inches away from his fiery commanding officer. After they had brushed aside the D.C. militia unit guarding Tournecliffe's Bridge on the southern road, Ross' men soon came face to face with Barney's flotillamen. Barney had placed two large 18-pounder cannon in the middle of the road. Miller's Marines were firing their lighter pieces and muskets off to Barney's right and into the approaching British line. Colonel Thornton ordered his men to charge Barney's guns, but repeated blasts of grapeshot temporarily stunned the British attack. Attempting to flank around to the right of Barney's cannon, Thornton ran into Miller's Marines, who shot his horse and severely wounded him in the thigh. Barney ordered Miller to launch a local counterattack, and the Marines, joined by a number of flotillamen armed with cutlasses and pistols, ran at their foes allegedly yelling, "Board 'em, board 'em," as if they were afloat on one of Barney's gunboats. Barney's stalwart Marines and flotillamen briefly drove some of Thornton's redcoats across a field and into the ravine, but there were not enough of them to make much of a dent against the surging British tide, and they too retreated back to their starting positions.[27]

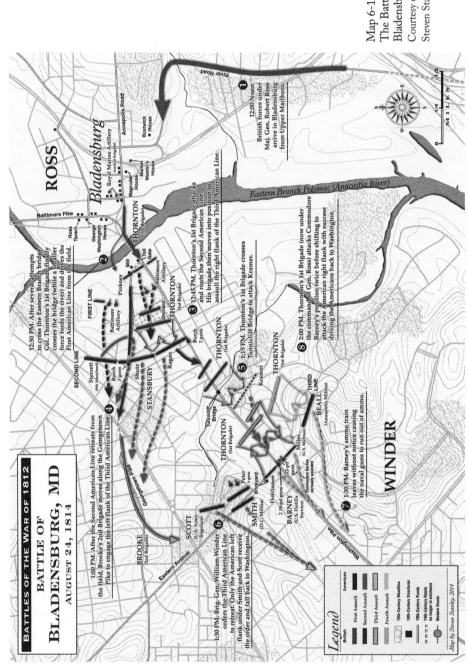

Map 6-1.
The Battle of
Bladensburg.
Courtesy of
Steven Stanley

BATTLES OF THE WAR OF 1812

BATTLE OF
BLADENSBURG, MD

AUGUST 24, 1814

1 12:00 Noon
British forces under
Maj. Gen. Robert Ross
arrive in Bladensburg
from Upper Marlboro

2 12:30 P.M. After several attempts
to cross the Eastern Branch bridge,
Col. Thornton's 1st Brigade finally
crosses the bridge (while a smaller
force fords the river) and drives the
First American Line from the field.

3 12:45 P.M. Thornton's 1st Brigade attacks
and routs the Second American Line.
His brigade then moves into position to
assault the right flank of the Third American Line.

4 1:00 P.M. After the Second American Line retreats from
the field, Brooke's 2nd Brigade moves along the Georgetown
Pike to engage the left flank of the Third American Line.

5 1:15 P.M. Thornton's 1st Brigade crosses
Tunnicliff Bridge to attack Kramer.

6 1:30 P.M. Brig. Gen. William Winder
orders the Third American Line
to retreat. Only the American left
flank under Smith and Scott receive
the order and fall back to Washington.

7 1:30 P.M. Barney's ammo train
leaves without notice causing
the naval guns to run out of ammo.

8 2:00 P.M. Thornton's 1st Brigade (now under
the command of Gen. Ross) attacks Commodore
Barney's position twice before shifting to
attack the American right flank with success
driving the Americans back to Washington.

ROSS

Bladensburg

River Road

Annapolis Road

Bostwick
House

Magruder
House
Market
Master's
House

Royal Marine Artillery
(rocket brigade)

Baltimore Pike

George
Washington
House

Ross
Tavern

THORNTON
(1st Brigade)

Eastern Branch Potomac (Anacostia River)

FIRST LINE

Troll
Gate

Pinkney

Mill

Baltimore
Artillery

THORNTON
(1st Brigade)

SECOND LINE

Baltimore
Artillery

Sterrett
(5th Maryland)

Burch
3 guns

Shutz

Orchard
Artillery

Burch
2 guns

THORNTON
(1st Brigade)

STANSBURY

Ragan

THORNTON
(1st Brigade)

Kramer

Tunnicliff
Bridge

THORNTON
(1st Brigade)

THIRD
LINE

BEALL
(Annapolis Militia)

BROOKE
(2nd Brigade)

SCOTT
(U.S. Army
Regulars)

Peter
6 guns

Brickyard

SMITH
(D.C. Militia)

Flotillamen
2 18-pdr guns

Miller
(U.S. Marines)

3 12-pdr
guns

BARNEY
(U.S. Flotilla
Service)

Commodore Barney
seriously wounded

Georgetown Pike

Eastern Avenue

Washington Pike

WINDER

Map by Steven Stanley, 2014

Legend

British		American
▬ First Assault		▬ American
▬ Second Assault		
▬ Third Assault		
▬ Fourth Assault		▬ 19th-Century Woodline
		▬ 19th-Century Structures
		▬ 19th-Century Roads
■		▬ 19th-Century Roads no longer in existence
═ ═ ═		▬ Modern Roads

MILES

N S E W

It was not long before British light troops lapped around each flank of Barney's formation. Beall's eight-hundred-man militia regiment allegedly fired a single volley at the oncoming British and fled. Other information indicated that Beall was ordered to retreat by a thoroughly panicked Winder, who sent his aide, Lieutenant John Howard, over to Beall to deliver the order in person. By the time Howard had arrived at this position with the order, many of Beall's men had already taken to their heels. Knowing full well that a large part of his army had already given way, Winder ordered the U.S. Army regulars and Smith's district militia to begin a retreat before they fired a shot at the enemy. Believing that it was not appropriate for him to issue orders to naval forces, Winder said nothing to Barney; thus the commodore and his men fought on alone and were largely unaware that their support to the left and the right was leaving the field. During this time frame, Captain Miller's arm was shattered by a musket ball. Barney's horse was shot dead, and Barney himself was severely wounded in the thigh. Civilians contracted to drive the commodore's ammunition wagons drove off in a panic, taking all of the flotilla's reserve ammunition with them. With both flanks collapsed and out of ammunition, Barney ordered his men to spike their guns and retreat as best they could toward Washington, along with the rest of Winder's army. However, because of their wounds, both Barney and Miller (among others) were captured and later paroled by the British. In all the British inflicted approximately a hundred casualties on the Americans. However, largely thanks to Ross' decision to attack the Americans without waiting for his two follow-on brigades, the British incurred close to three hundred total casualties—with losses among junior officers being especially high.

One participant with the U.S. Marines was Captain Samuel Bacon, who had accompanied Miller's company to Bladensburg in his role as corps quartermaster. Bacon had been asked to do so at the last minute by the Secretary of the Navy. He impressed a horse from a nearby civilian named George Weaver and gave him a handwritten certificate for it. Bacon complained that Winder had neglected to order Tobias Stansbury (whom Bacon refers to as Stansburg) and his Maryland militia, which had been "on the ground of the Battle five or six days & could have made their fortification impregnable," to make military defensive improvements around the bridge at Bladensburg. Bacon went on to describe Winder as an "incompetent wretch" for failing to burn the eastern branch bridge and wasting time and men guarding something he should not have worried about. He extolled the valor of Barney's flotillamen and Marines in action, calling the leathernecks "dead shots." By the time Beall's Annapolis militia was driven off, Bacon stated, Winder and his staff had long fled the field. Winder retreated for several days before he realized that the British had already returned to Benedict, Maryland. Not one to mince words, Bacon concluded, "Wi[nder] ought to be hung & would b[e in] any other country." Because Barney, Miller, and Captain Alexander Sevier (Miller's second in command) were wounded, Bacon, as senior surviving officer, took command of the U.S. Marine company and led it from the field through the now "deserted" city of Washington. Following the battle, Bacon—ever the quartermaster—wrote the Secretary of the Navy that during the battle someone had made off with George Weaver's horse. He wanted it on record that the animal was lost during the battle so that he was not liable to its original owner for it. Bacon and the remainder of Miller's Bladensburg company arrived at Baltimore on 28 August 1814 "much fatigued and destitute of clothing, tho'n fine spirits and anxious to meeting the enemy again."[28]

Historian Walter Lord wrote that the debacle of Bladensburg, later known derisively by the British as the "Bladensburg Races," belonged to an entire "catalogue of failures." These failures began with Madison and Secretary of War Armstrong's erroneous assumption that Washington, D.C., was never the true target of Cockburn and Ross' invasion force. Owing to this assumption, no serious effort was made to prepare the capital for an attack. This mistake was quickly followed by a series of tactical errors committed by a mostly inept General Winder, who arrived at the place of battle too late to do much about the amateurish defensive dispositions of his first-line commanders or to put a stop to the well-intended but ultimately destructive interference of the secretary of state and ersatz armchair general James Monroe. In fairness to Winder, he had been forced to defend Washington on short notice with a largely pickup force of disassociated militia units, which could not have been expected to stand against the disciplined firepower of Ross' regulars. However—not forgetting the gallantry of Pinkney's riflemen and the Baltimore artillery at the bridge or of Sterett's Fifth Maryland Regiment—in the one instance when veteran American troops (Barney's men) directly faced Ross' onrushing redcoats, the flotillamen and Marines more than held their own against the British, making one wonder whether Winder might have performed better had the government had the foresight to provide him with more regular Army troops. Nonetheless, the lion's share of the blame must reside with both Madison and Secretary of War Armstrong, who, after having finally realized the seriousness of the threat to the national capital, were still quite willing to risk all on the outcome of a single engagement just beyond the boundaries of the city itself. Moreover, both men had continued to neglect the defenses of the Chesapeake region following the devastation inflicted by Cockburn the previous year.

With the defeat of the American Army at Bladensburg, the way was now completely open for Ross to advance into the city of Washington itself. Most of what was left of Winder's army made its way to Montgomery County Court House while the president and a small remnant of his shattered government fled initially to Falls Church, Virginia, and ultimately to Montgomery County Court House as well. Stansbury's men grimly straggled their way back to Baltimore, arriving there by the late evening of 27 August 1814. As for Ross, he allowed his exhausted but victorious troops a few hours rest, and toward dusk on 24 August, he and his army entered the city via Capitol Hill. A few hours earlier, Secretary of War Armstrong, James Monroe, and William Winder had debated whether to make a final stand on Capitol Hill. Armstrong seemed to believe that the separated wings and stout limestone walls of the Capitol made the place an ideal strongpoint, but Monroe and especially Winder believed that the now greatly reduced American force was too small to make much of a defense. Rather than risk being captured, Winder argued, another retreat should be ordered to the heights beyond Georgetown. The general had previously ordered the heretofore unused and late-arriving Virginia militia under Colonel Minor forward to cover the retreat of his demoralized army, but the Virginians too seemed to have melted away in the confusion that reigned in the city following the defeat of American forces at Bladensburg. Waiting until nearly the last minute, the indomitable First Lady, Dolly Madison, was finally convinced that the time had come to abandon the White House. Taking what she could in a wagon, including the famous portrait of George Washington by the artist Gilbert Stuart, she left the White House half an hour before her husband and some of his key aides arrived on the scene. He too soon departed for Virginia.

With the departure of the last American troops from Capitol Hill, all semblance of order in the city seemed to disappear. It was nearly sunset when the House of Representatives, the Senate, and the Library of Congress were set ablaze by British soldiers, but not before a small group of American diehards tried to assassinate Ross. Firing a volley from a nearby darkened house, once occupied by Secretary of the Treasury Albert Gallatin, they succeeded only in killing Ross' horse and causing the death of another nearby soldier. Not finding the perpetrators, Ross had his soldiers burn the house to the ground; few private residences in Washington suffered a similar fate.

During this time, former British subject and now U.S. Navy captain and Washington Navy Yard superintendent Thomas Tingey prepared to blow up his command in order to keep its valuable stores and machinery from falling into British hands. Tingey also experienced the unfortunate necessity of burning the nearly complete frigate USS *Columbia* and the sloop of war USS *Argus*. To his credit, he delayed the destruction of the yard for as long as he possibly could. When Secretary of the Navy Jones visited the Navy Yard on the evening of 22 August 1814, he found the facility nearly bereft of all available men. He was primarily concerned with evacuating the large store of gunpowder. Tingey suggested that the powder barrels be loaded up and taken to the farm of his son-in-law, Daniel Dulany, in Falls Church, Virginia. Jones agreed and authorized Tingey to requisition the necessary transportation. However, getting the wagons necessary for such a task at this late date was nearly impossible—largely because all the other federal departments in town were in the process of evacuating records as well. Tingey recognized that besides the vessels, which would have to be burned, he would be unable to save the canvas, lumber, cordage, and barrels of salt pork and whiskey that most navy yards possessed on any given date.[29]

Tingey sent his capable clerk, Mordecai Booth, into town to find teams and wagons, and there Booth discovered that both wagons and reliable drivers were in short supply. Nevertheless, after he had engaged one man in a heated argument in an attempt to requisition his wagon, Booth remarked that the man "made use of such language as was degrading to gentlemen" and rode away. Booth was eventually able to scrape up at least seven large wagons. The following day, after a harrowing experience getting the powder across the Long Bridge, Booth's wagon train stopped at the Wren Tavern, about a mile from Dulany's farm, named Oak Hill. Booth had been working around the clock getting the powder out of town and was greatly worried about the safety of his family back in town. To his great joy, he discovered that Tingey had taken the time to send Booth's family to him in Falls Church under a Navy Yard escort.[30]

Booth turned the powder over to Sergeant Major Forrest of the U.S. Marines and a troop of Fairfax dragoons, commanded by Captain George Graham, that had arrived to help guard it. However, to Booth's chagrin, a deputation of local citizens also showed up at the Wren Tavern and loudly demanded that the powder be removed to "a more remote place." Ever the departmental clerk, Booth would consent to the proposed move only if senior personnel present, including Captain Graham, signed a document recommending such action. The document was promptly prepared and signed. Nevertheless, on 27 August the powder still remained at Oak Hill. Sergeant Major Forrest and Captain Graham had not located a suitable alternate site. When apprised of this situation by Booth, Tingey told his clerk to leave the powder where it was since a British squadron had just that day taken Alexandria. By 6 September Tingey had ordered the restoration of the powder to the nearly wrecked Washington Navy Yard.[31]

Booth returned to Washington on the afternoon of 24 August. With rumors of a catastrophic American defeat filtering back into the city, he volunteered to find out firsthand what had happened at Bladensburg. After having crested Capitol Hill, Booth beheld a view of "the commons" and the "turnpike gate," which led to the hills toward Bladensburg. Here he realized the extent of the American defeat. He wrote, "I saw not the Appearance of an Englishman—But Oh! my Country—And I blush Sir! to tell you—I saw the Commons Covered with the fugitive Soldiery of our Army—run[n]ing, hob[b]ling, Creaping, & apparently pannick struck."[32]

As the British entered the city of Washington on the evening of 24 August 1814, the remarkable Mordecai Booth was there to observe their progress. Toward evening Tingey had sent Booth out a second time to bring back definite intelligence on the location of the main body of Ross' army. He had not ridden far up Capitol Hill before he was able to view the turnpike (he had passed a Colonel Tatum of the militia going in the other direction). Joined by a butcher from Georgetown named Thomas Miller, who was furiously whipping his horse and rapidly riding down the hill, Booth stopped him and asked if he had seen the British. Miller replied that he had and offered to show him. Riding a short distance, the erstwhile scouts soon spotted soldiers in both blue and red coats about three hundred yards away. Booth was not convinced they were British troops and suggested they get a little closer. They did and promptly came under musket fire from a British flanking party.

Booth was now convinced, and he and Miller rode across a meadow toward the Casinave Plantation, located at the head of Tiber Creek and the base of Capitol Hill. Riding over to the Navy Yard, Booth found Captain Tingey conversing with another captain, Nathaniel Haraden, at the yard gate and informed them of the nearness of the enemy. As it was now almost dark, Booth thought he should also relay this information to anyone who might still be at the White House. Reaching New Jersey Avenue, Booth came upon Walter Cox, a militia cavalry cornet, and both men agreed to proceed to the President's House. Upon arrival, Booth and Cox were challenged by a lone sentry with a cocked pistol pointed at them. It was Colonel Tatum, the same soldier Booth had seen on his earlier reconnaissance. Cox asked if anyone was still inside whereupon Tatum "pulled the bell several times, knocked at the door, and called 'John!' But all was silent as the grave. . . . Then, and not until then, was my mind fully impressed that the Matropelis [sic] of our Country was abandoned to its horrid fate." Returning to the Navy Yard, Booth picked up a few more companions, including Commodore John Creighton, and this time they ran into British troops, who fired on them at a range of forty yards as they rode toward the House of Representatives on Capitol Hill. Creighton and Booth returned to the Navy Yard, and Tingey ordered Creighton to blow up the nearby bridge over the Eastern Branch. Booth saw the results and noted that bridge timbers were blown "into Splintery fragments, in the Air."[33]

Because Booth had reported during his afternoon reconnaissance of Capitol Hill that he saw no redcoats, Tingey had delayed his planned destruction of the yard. However, Booth's second report at 8:20 p.m. on 24 August made clear that British troops had finally reached Capitol Hill. The Navy Yard was located only a half mile away. Tingey made the decision to destroy what military stores were left and proceeded to set fire to the two largest vessels, the nearly complete *Columbia* and the *Argus*. The hulls of the *New York*, *Boston*, and *General Greene* also went up in flames. At the last moment Tingey decided to not burn the small sloop *Lynx*. Amazingly, the *Lynx* was still there the following morning, when Tingey snuck back to inspect the yard even though the British were still in the city. Left standing were the Tripoli Monument (later relocated to the U.S. Naval Academy in Annapolis), the sloop *Lynx*, and the superintendent's home—and nothing else. To his chagrin, Tingey saw that the neighborhood denizens had broken into the house and ransacked his personal belongings. Returning the day following the British departure from town, he struggled to keep looters from carrying off what had not been already lost or destroyed. Tingey later estimated that after he had recovered what was salvageable, the Navy Yard loss to the government amounted to approximately $500,000.[34] As for the Navy Department clerk Mordecai Booth, his actions before, during, and after the attack on Washington, D.C., were nothing short of incredible for a civilian employee of the federal government. He had more than done his duty on a borrowed horse.

Late in the evening of 24 August 1814 and into the early morning hours of 25 August, Cockburn and Ross proceeded up Pennsylvania Avenue and had the White House and nearby Treasury Building looted and burned. Their method of destruction was simple. Much as they had torched the Capitol and Library of Congress, British troops gathered up all the furniture and combustible material that they could find, piled it all in the center of a room, liberally sprinkled the pile with powder from a Congreve rocket, and set the whole thing on fire. It was not long before the buildings were fully engulfed in flames, although a hard rain that fell later that night did much to limit the damage. Their objective accomplished and with no more organized American military resistance by the evening of 25 August, the British imposed a strict 8:00 p.m. curfew on the citizens of the town and silently began their return march to Upper Marlboro and ultimately to their temporary naval base at Benedict, Maryland. British troops had been in the national capital for less than twenty-five hours.

Other elements of the British invasion were not entirely ready to quit the Washington, D.C., area. On the day after Ross and his men had returned to Upper Marlboro, Captain James Gordon's diversionary Potomac River squadron finally arrived opposite Fort Washington. Two days after the White House had been burned, Gordon's squadron, having struggled mightily to get up the shoal-laden river, passed within view of George Washington's Mount Vernon home. Gordon gallantly dipped his squadron's topmast sails in salute as they passed. As it grew dark, his ships were drawn up in front of Fort Washington just out of cannon range. This fort was considered the primary impediment to Gordon's ascent. It possessed at least two 32-pounder guns, eight 24-pounder guns, a battery built on the riverbank containing at least five 18-pounder guns, and at least six guns of various calibers guarding the landward approaches to the fort. The fort also had a two-story octagonal brick and masonry martello tower, designed principally as protection for supporting infantry and not likely to withstand bombardment by any artillery larger than a 12-pounder naval gun. Gordon's squadron of course possessed the requisite heavier naval artillery with his bomb ships and even some of his larger frigates. Gordon maneuvered his powerful bomb ships into position for a dawn attack on 27 August.[35]

As soon as it became light, Gordon had his powerful bomb ships throw ranging shells at the fort. Earlier, Winder had ordered the fort's commandant, Captain Samuel T. Dyson, to blow up the fort and retreat if he were attacked from its weak landward side. Dyson, however, did not wait for troops to land nearby. Once the first shells began to fall, without firing a gun he destroyed the fort and fled along with his sixty-man garrison. British commanders were astounded at this turn of events. Both Gordon and his second in command, Captain Charles Napier, thought that taking Fort Washington would cost them at least fifty men. Soon after the explosion, Gordon sent bluejackets and Royal Marines ashore to complete the destruction of Fort Washington.

Dyson was later tried by a court-martial and cashiered from further service. At his trial Dyson alleged he was strictly following his orders. He believed the British landing at Benedict was close enough to Fort Washington to qualify as troops threatening the landward approach to the fort, even though these troops at the time were over ten miles away in Upper Marlboro. Nevertheless, Dyson believed Ross intended to cooperate with Gordon's Potomac River squadron. The court did not see it Dyson's way.[36] With the fort now gone, there was nothing to stop the British from invading Washington once again—this time from its vulnerable riverfront. But the still smoldering and already looted city was not Gordon's actual objective. Rather, he was after the fully stocked warehouses of Alexandria.

The storm that struck Washington, D.C., in the early morning hours of 25 August also affected Gordon's squadron. Gordon's command frigate, the *Sea Horse*, had "sprung her mizzen-mast." Captain Napier, on board the thirty-six-gun frigate *Euryalus*, prepared his vessel for the storm in the nick of time. Even so, he noted the heads of all three topmasts had been lost and the vessel's bowsprit had been cracked in two. The bomb ship *Meteor* had been blown upon a riverbank but was quickly recovered.[37] Nevertheless, with Fort Washington destroyed, Gordon decided to proceed to Alexandria. Even before his ships arrived, a deputation of Alexandrians was more than ready to surrender the town in return for Gordon's assurance that he would spare the group's businesses from the torch. In its defense, the Alexandria militia had previously been ordered forward in support of Winder's Bladensburg campaign. Following the Bladensburg disaster, no one remained to defend the town from anything. Gordon stayed in Alexandria for almost five full days, during which time he loaded up his vessels from the town's warehouses and ample naval stores. It was a rich haul and one that Cockburn likely missed in government-centric Washington, D.C.

Even so, Gordon's little squadron was seriously exposed. He still had to get his now heavily laden squadron back down the river. Before the war, it had taken the USS *President*, which had put in to the Washington Navy Yard for some refitting work, more than forty days to travel down the river, and in that time it had to off-load all of its forty-four guns to clear the numerous river shoals. On 7 September 1814 Captain David Porter, in Washington, D.C., at that time to explain the loss of his ship, the USS *Essex*, to the British near Valparaíso, Chile, linked his small command of sailors and Marines up with Brigadier General John Hungerford's Virginia militia. Hungerford positioned his militiamen on the Virginia riverbank, and they constantly sniped at Gordon's ships as they struggled to move back down the river.

Meanwhile, Porter built a reinforced battery several miles below Mount Vernon at a place coincidentally also named the White House and sometimes known as Washington's Reach. At this location the river bluffs were nearly sixty feet high, and it was thought that the British could not elevate their guns high enough to hit the position with counterbattery fire. Porter also brought along several furnaces for heated shot. However, with the wind in his favor, Gordon opened a tremendous concentrated fire on Porter's guns, firing solid shot and rockets at the White House. Getting the proper elevation did not prove to be a problem. The cannon duel continued for two straight days. During the fight Porter went out of his way to commend Captain Alfred Grayson of the U.S. Marines and "Captain Spencer of the U.S. Artillery late second in command at Fort Washington and now in command of the officers and men stationed there [who] were attached to my command by the War Department—they have given the most unquestionable proof that it was not want of courage on their part which caused the destruction of that Fort."[38]

One participant in this fight was Virginia militia captain Thomas Brown, an aide to General Hungerford. Brown slept on a pile of straw inside the White House and was frequently awakened when a cannonball or Congreve rocket crashed into the house or landed nearby. The bombardment caused General Hungerford to relocate his headquarters farther to the rear of the plantation. Even so, according to Brown, Hungerford was nearly killed as he sat on a pile of mattresses in his tent. Gordon's fire was so accurate that after forty-eight hours of continuous bombardment, every cannon in Porter's battery had been silenced. Moreover, Hungerford had fourteen men killed and another thirty-two wounded in the engagement. Gordon and his squadron were thus able to proceed downriver. One more effort to snag Gordon's squadron was made on 7 September, when a small battery, this time commanded by another American naval hero, Oliver Hazard Perry, attempted to engage Gordon near present-day Indian Head, Maryland. Perry later admitted that his guns were too small in caliber to have made much of a dent in Gordon's ships, and thus the British were able to get clean away.[39]

Two days after the British left Washington, but notably while Gordon and his squadron were still loitering around Alexandria, President Madison and most of his cabinet returned to D.C. Vehement recriminations about who was specifically responsible for the Bladensburg debacle began, but most of the blame seemed to attach itself to the acerbic secretary of war, John Armstrong. On 29 August 1814 Armstrong received word from the president that it would be best for everyone involved if the secretary resigned his office. In a 3 September letter to the editors of the *Baltimore Patriot*, Armstrong wrote that on the evening of the twenty-ninth, "the President called at my lodgings, and stated that a case of much delicacy had occurred; that a high degree of excitement had been raised among the militia of the District; that *he himself an object of their suspicions and menaces*; that an officer of that corps had given him notice, that they would no longer obey any order coming through me as Secretary of War." Armstrong stated he was not inclined to resign his post to "accommodate . . . the humors of a village mob." Nor, he continued, was the president inclined to accept his resignation under such circumstances. Nevertheless, both he and Madison agreed that he should leave Washington the following morning. Armstrong added that he had heard that the antiadministration Federalist newspaper editor Alexander C. Hanson may have played a role in his removal as secretary of war. He mentioned that the ubiquitous Hanson had met with Madison the morning of 29 August "by *deputation*, and had obtained from him a promise, that I should no longer direct the military defences of the district [emphasis in the original]." Armstrong wrote that the president "deemed it *prudent* to *sacrifice his authority*, in declining to support *mine* [emphasis in the original]."[40] The secretary then went on at length to refute the various charges that seemed to be leveled at him. No doubt, after this outburst, Madison was happy to see Armstrong go.

Secretary of State Monroe took over responsibility for the Department of War in addition to his duties at the State Department. During this transition, toward the end of August 1814, a small squadron under Captain Sir Peter Parker in the thirty-eight-gun frigate HMS *Menelaus* appeared off Kent Island, Maryland. This was the same squadron that had earlier appeared at the mouth of the Patapsco River and served to convince many that Baltimore, not Washington, was the true target of Cochrane's offensive. Rather than return empty-handed, Parker had received information that a two-hundred-man militia unit under the command of Lieutenant Colonel Philip Reed of the Twenty-First Maryland Regiment was gathered near Chestertown, Maryland. Reed was a veteran of the American Revolution and had served with distinction under Anthony Wayne at the Battle of Stony Point. Like his friend Samuel Smith, he also had served as a U.S. senator from 1806 to 1813.

Late in the evening of 30 August, Sir Peter landed approximately 125 sailors and marines near 2 farms called Waltham and Chantilly (accounts greatly vary as to the actual number landed by the British). At least 20 of the invaders carried pikes. At first Reed believed Parker and his men were there to raid farms, but later Reed discovered that he and his militia camp were the actual objective of the British night attack. Ordering his men to form a line near his campsite, on a slight rise at a location called Caulk's Field, Reed prepared to contest the progress of Parker's landing force.

There was a full moon that night, and Parker's landing force, led by a captured slave of dubious loyalty to the British cause, soon approached Reed's line of battle. Reed had taken the precaution of stationing five light cannon in the center of his line, and he deployed a company of riflemen under Captain Simon Wickes to act as skirmishers in a wood forward of his position. When Parker's column was about seventy paces distant, Reed had Wickes open fire. Parker immediately deployed his men into battle formation, and they drove the riflemen back toward the right of Reed's main line at Caulk's Field. Thinking that the Maryland militia was turning in its usual performance in battle, Parker and his men rolled toward Reed's men only to be greeted by blasts of grapeshot and musketry. Briefly repulsed, Parker's redcoats re-formed and attempted to turn Reed's left flank, but once again the Marylanders stood firm. The fighting continued for upward of an hour until both sides had nearly exhausted their supplies of ammunition. A critical turning point in the fighting occurred when Sir Peter himself was hit in the leg by a piece of buckshot. Believing that the wound was not serious, he continued to urge his men forward only to discover too late that the buckshot had nicked his femoral artery. He bled to death before his men could return him to their barges. Besides the death of Sir Peter Parker, British casualties for a fight of this size were fairly significant. They had approximately fourteen dead (nine of whom had been left on the field) and another twenty-seven men wounded, compared to none killed and only three wounded on the American side. For the British, except for the loss of Parker and thirteen of his men, the fight at Caulk's Field was largely meaningless. For the Americans, however, it demonstrated that the militia could perform well if it was professionally led; Revolutionary War veteran Philip Reed certainly answered that critical requirement.

Slowly but inexorably, Vice Admiral Cochrane gathered up the ships and detachments of his three-pronged offensive. While Captain James Gordon's Potomac River foray returned loaded down with goods seized at Alexandria, the northern prong returned the body of Sir Peter Parker, allegedly preserved in a whisky-filled coffin and eventually sent home to England for burial. Cochrane's main effort, led by Ross and Cockburn, returned to Benedict, Maryland, flush with victory over the Yankees at Bladensburg and encumbered with loot taken from the devastated city of Washington, D.C., and its surrounding southern Maryland suburbs.

When Ross' men arrived at Benedict, Maryland, at least a hundred of them remained unaccounted for. While some had been seriously wounded in the Bladensburg battle, others were deserters or the criminals who seemed to be part of every army of the era, more interested in theft than returning to the British ships on the Patuxent River. Not knowing what else to do about this situation, former Maryland governor Robert Bowie, sixty-five-year-old Dr. William Beanes of Academy Hill, and a few other leading citizens of Upper Marlboro armed themselves and placed any British stragglers they could find under arrest. At least one such straggler escaped, made his way to the town of Benedict, and informed Ross that Beanes and company were killing British stragglers in Upper Marlboro. While this was not true, the straggler's story convinced Ross to send sixty men on captured horses back to Upper Marlboro to investigate. Finding that the Americans had indeed captured some stragglers and were hiding quite a few deserters, the men threatened to burn Upper Marlboro to the ground unless the prisoners and deserters were delivered to them. Showing that they meant business, they took Beanes and two other men, Dr. William Hill and Philip Weems, prisoner and carried them off to Nottingham, Maryland. As the British prepared to leave the Patuxent River, they released Hill and Weems, but Beanes was placed in confinement on board Cochrane's flagship, HMS *Tonnant*, as a surety against further arrests of British stragglers by the Maryland citizenry.

Upon hearing of Beanes' arrest, Richard W. West, who lived near the Wood Yard in Prince George's County, appealed directly to Francis Scott Key, a Georgetown attorney of some local renown, to use his services to gain the doctor's release. Key agreed to the mission and was accompanied by fellow Prince Georgian, John S. Skinner, the government representative for prisoner exchange. Both men boarded a sloop at Baltimore under a flag of truce and headed to the Patuxent River, where they were sure to find the British invasion fleet. Intercepted by the HMS *Royal Oak*, the sloop was escorted to the *Tonnant*, then located farther south, off Tangier Island. Upon arrival, Key and Skinner were courteously received by Admiral Cockburn. The Americans had thoughtfully brought along letters from seriously wounded British soldiers from the Bladensburg battle that described their good treatment at the hands of the local residents. These letters served to offset Cockburn's bitter opposition to the release of any prisoner since it was apparent by this time that preparations on board the British ships for attacking Baltimore were well under way. Moreover, Cockburn believed that Beanes had purposefully deceived them by treating them with courtesy and respect when they had originally entered Upper Marlboro, only to deceitfully stab them in the back by arresting stragglers during their return march to Benedict, Maryland. Key observed that Beanes had not been treated like a POW but more like a culprit of some imagined crime.[41] Ross agreed to release Beanes but only after the impending attack on Baltimore was completed. Beanes, Key, and Skinner had seen too much. Key and Skinner were transferred to the frigate HMS *Surprize* to await further events.

7

————

THE BATTLE FOR BALTIMORE

In the two weeks that followed the destruction of Washington, D.C., Cochrane seemed to vacillate on his next target for the campaign. Writing to the first lord of the Admiralty, Dundas Melville, on 3 September 1814, Cochrane informed him that once he had all his troops reembarked and his fleet united in the bay, he intended to sail northward, attack Rhode Island, rest and refit there, return south in October, take Baltimore, proceed down the Carolina coast to Georgia, and ultimately end up at New Orleans. Hoping to avoid the mass illness Warren's men had experienced the previous year during August and September, known by native Marylanders as the "sickly season," Cochrane believed a change of venue would do his men some good.

Before he left the area, however, Cochrane hoped to do something about the city of Baltimore. Home to hundreds of privateers who had long plagued British commercial shipping and renowned as a pro-Madison Republican town (unlike most of the rest of the state), Baltimore, Cochrane bluntly told Lord Melville in London, "must be laid in ashes." The question in the admiral's mind was whether to attack now, while the Americans were still demoralized following the destruction of their national capital, or to attack later, after the proposed Rhode Island foray. Cockburn, of course, was in favor of an immediate attack on Baltimore. Ross, who had reembarked on board Cochrane's *Tonnant*, concurred with his commander in chief's plan to go north. This time Cockburn worried that he might not be able to convince both men that the time was right to go after Baltimore. Fortunately for Cockburn, the tides in September made it difficult to clear the Virginia Capes, so Cochrane changed his mind about Rhode Island and decided to attack Baltimore after all.

The Americans had had over a year to consider ways to improve Baltimore's defense. Much of this good fortune was because the state of Maryland had created a committee of safety with extensive centralized authority for improving local defense. Further, unlike in Bladensburg, all troops in the Baltimore region were commanded by the iron-willed major general of militia Samuel Smith. Granted, these troops were entirely made up of Maryland militiamen, but there were a lot more of them in Baltimore than anywhere else in the state.

During the 1813 scare Smith had been instrumental in making immediate improvements to Baltimore's principal defensive bastion, Fort McHenry. He also recognized that the primary land route into the city was likely the Patapsco Neck on the east side of the river. If the British landed troops anywhere near the city, it would be near the terminus of the neck at a place called North Point, off Old Roads Bay. Once the force had landed, it would simply be a matter of marching into the city from the east. Smith consequentially ordered entrenchments dug on high ground east of the harbor called Hampstead Hill. He did all this work in his role as a militia major general commanding the Third Militia Division.

Brigadier General William Winder was a regular Army officer who, unless Smith had been called into regular service as a volunteer, outranked the militia commander. Winder also firmly believed that as the commanding officer of the Tenth Military District, he was in command at Baltimore. This sticky command situation was deftly resolved by Winder's uncle, the governor of Maryland, Levin Winder, when he implied in a letter to Smith that the major general indeed had been called into federal service in July 1813. Smith accepted the governor's assumption, although there was no concrete evidence that this call to service had actually taken place. While Winder was not happy with being superseded, lacking the familial political support he had enjoyed before the debacle at Bladensburg, he acquiesced to Smith's claim to command without further protest.

The seaward approach to Baltimore's inner harbor was going to be a much more complex military problem for the British than the approach to Bladensburg. Baltimore's inner harbor forked into a V shape with Fort McHenry at the apex. The right side of the V was the Northwest Branch, which led directly into the inner harbor basin. The harbor channel was relatively shallow and would not safely admit a large ship of the line such as the HMS *Tonnant*, even in peacetime. Thus, in a waterborne assault on the city, Cochrane was forced to rely entirely on his bomb ships or lighter frigates to reduce Baltimore's principal defensive position—Fort McHenry. To make matters worse for the British, on the eastern bank of the Northwest Branch was a place called the Lazaretto. During peacetime people and goods were quarantined on the Lazaretto before they were landed in the city proper. There the land jutted out into the Northwest Branch like a dagger pointing toward Fort McHenry on Whetstone Point. During 1814 the Lazaretto was fortified with three guns behind a dirt wall and was under the command of the capable Lieutenant Solomon Frazier, formerly of Barney's flotilla. Frazier also commanded an additional 114 flotillamen to support the guns and to defend against a potential land assault. Merchant vessels were prepared to be sunk between the Lazaretto and Fort McHenry. Lieutenant Solomon Rutter positioned at least 8 barges immediately behind the proposed line of sunken hulls in the Northwest Branch. Each barge held 34 flotillamen and mounted either a single 8- or 12-pounder cannon in its bow.

Fort McHenry, or the Star Fort, as some called it, seemed to be a continual work in progress. From its beginning in 1794 as Fort Whetstone until 1803, the Star Fort slowly took its War of 1812 shape. The famous French military engineer John Jacob Ulrich Rivardi started its construction, but he did not see it to completion because he was called away to supervise what was thought to be more important work on a fort defending the vulnerable city of Norfolk, Virginia, to the south. At least three other engineers—Alexander De Leyritz, Major Louis Tousard, and John Foncin—contributed to improving the Star Fort. Built in the style of the great French military designer Vauban, Fort McHenry by 1814 had solid walls of stone, earth, and brick placed on stone foundations designed to make the fort extraordinarily resilient to naval gunfire. At least "600,000 bricks" were used to front the fort's walls and its five bastions. As was standard practice for such forts, a large ditch was dug in front of the walls to channel and trap any attacking infantry. The lack of bombproof shelters for support troops was a major design flaw that remained uncorrected until after the battle for Baltimore. The fort's ditch was at least five feet deep and approximately thirty feet wide. The 1814 fort was lower than it appears today—its walls were a mere fifteen feet high from the ditch to the top of the wall. The fort's designers went to the trouble to plant trees and sod on top of the earthen parapets to provide a bit of camouflage to the low-lying defensive work. The trees were planted about eighteen feet apart, and there were at least four of them on each of the five bastions. In addition to camouflage, they provided partial shade for those walking on the ramparts, and the sod soaked up rain that would otherwise have created a muddy mess of the earthen top portion of the walls. The greenery was also thought to have a positive effect on the health of the men stationed at the fort.[1]

In 1813 Colonel Joseph Swift recommended to Major Lloyd Beall, then Fort McHenry's commanding officer, that among other improvements, he erect "a Traverse inside the Fort in front of the gate-way, of brick, and also one in front of the magazine door, 12 feet long and 8 feet thick at the base, sloping two inches to each foot in height, the traverse in front of the magazine's door, as high as the top of the window over the door."[2] As noted by the U.S. Army inspector general, Colonel Abrams Y. Nicholls, Beall started work on the traverses, but there is debate over whether they were fully completed before the British bombardment.

Soon after Cockburn and a British squadron showed up in the Patapsco River roadstead on 16 April 1813, Major General Samuel Smith began to openly clash with Major Beall because of Beall's refusal to "incommode his own men" and admit Smith's militia into the fort's interior. Smith wrote to Secretary of War John Armstrong to strongly suggest that he replace the aging Beall with someone amenable. Smith bluntly asked the secretary, "Do you really believe that a gentleman of nearly 60 years of age, sorely affected with the gout and a young inexperienced officer of 20 is equal to the defenses of such a post[?] . . . I must tell you in the spirit of a friend that you take upon yourself a responsibility of a very serious nature." Later that year, when Congress was in session, Smith took his seat in the U.S. Senate and used his influence to hector the secretary of war for a command change at Fort McHenry. Finally giving in, Armstrong replaced Beall with Major George Armistead, who had briefly commanded the fort just a few years earlier. Smith was happy with the new arrangement. He believed Armistead was more flexible and apt to take the general's suggestions as to how and where his militia should be used around the fort. Moreover, unlike Beall, Armistead had a proven combat record, having distinguished himself during the assault on Fort George in Upper Canada. Almost immediately upon taking command at Fort McHenry, Armistead proved his worth to Smith by graciously accepting the services of Captain Joseph Nicholson's Baltimore Fencibles. This volunteer unit was made up of men from the upper tier of the Baltimore mercantile community, and by bringing them into the fold at Fort McHenry, Armistead improved the regular Army's standing with the local population.[3]

Smith was also active in recruiting Baltimore's maritime community to the cause. One such organization was the First Marine Artillery of the Union, more commonly called the Corps of Seamen. These men were under the command of Captain George Stiles, the owner of a sizable harbor wharf and a former commander during the Quasi-War with France. Smith noted,

> The whole [Corps of Seamen] are bound by written articles signed by each, to do duty either in boats or in fortifications for three months from the day of signing, unless sooner discharged, to conform and obey the command of their officers in the same manner as if they were in the actual service at sea, for which they are to receive Sixteen Dollars per month. This highly important corps have been employed in the Barges, in fixing the booms, transporting and mounting of cannons, placing the hulks, making wads for the guns, and in training to the exercise of the cannon.[4]

Smith divided these saltwater volunteers into two companies of about seventy-five men each under Stiles' overall command. One company was commanded by Lieutenant Solomon Rutter, the other by Captain Matthew Bunbury. Smith ordered Rutter to supervise the emplacement of a boom to extend from the Lazaretto (Gorsuch Point) to Whetstone Point by using old masts intertwined with heavy iron chains. The real issue for the defense of Baltimore in 1813 revolved around competition for available men. In response to the arrival of the British in the Patapsco River roadstead, various American military establishments had begun competing against each other for anyone willing to serve in their respective organizations. For example, when the U.S. Marine Corps sent Lieutenant Benjamin Hyde to Baltimore to recruit young men for the regular Marine Corps, he was forced to admit to the commandant, Lieutenant Colonel Franklin Wharton, that he was "sorry to say that I have not been able as yet to recruit a single man; the town at this time is so full of rendezvous recruiting for the army, particularly the 36th [Infantry] Regt. who are giving 40 Dollars Bounty and 8 Dollars per month pay and enlisting for only 12 months."[5] Hyde could do little to make service in the U.S. Marines more attractive.

In truth, with the exception of a single decrepit gunboat and Charles Gordon's aforementioned experiment with leased sloops, the only significant U.S. Navy vessels in port in 1813 were the still-to-be-completed sloops of war *Erie* and *Ontario* and the half-built USS *Java*. Hence, at that moment there was little need for U.S. Marines in Baltimore. Hyde did not mention that the Army also included a 160-acre land bounty as an additional recruiting incentive—something the sea services did not do, since Marines and sailors were eligible for prize money. With British blockade in full force, opportunities for taking prizes on the high seas were few. Further, as previously noted, the Baltimore Fencibles offered to pay sixteen dollars a month, and their service would clearly be local. Even the U.S. Army was a better deal. Most people understood that technically the newly organized 36th and 38th Infantry Regiments could be sent anywhere by the War Department, but all knew that they were destined for the defense of Maryland and would thus be kept home. On the other hand, a Marine recruited by Benjamin Hyde would likely be sent to various ships and posts out of the state. Given the less risky options that paid better and required shorter mandatory service, it is no wonder that Lieutenant Hyde could not attract any recruits.

By May 1814, thanks to the work of many contributors, Fort McHenry was as ready as it was likely going to be. Each of the five bastions mounted four 32-pounder guns and at least fourteen 24-pounder cannon. The fort also contained at least twelve 18-pounder guns on mobile carriages that could be shifted in an emergency to a threatened point of attack, such as the fort's weaker landward side. During an 1813 inspection Colonel Decius Wadsworth, the U.S. Army's commissary general of ordnance, pointed out some weaknesses that needed immediate correction, such as providing additional protection for the fort's pine door entranceway and improving the defenses of the largely unprotected water battery. Accordingly, Wadsworth ordered the construction of a "ravelin" in front of the entrance. The ravelin was a "triangular mound-like structure of earth and brick" that created a minifort in front of the main work; it was somewhat different from the structure that exists today. The ravelin was connected to the fort's sally port by a wooden drawbridge that spanned the ditch in front of the walls. The military road that led from the town ran through the left flank of the ravelin. Consequently, it was thought that at least one mobile 12-pounder gun was placed near this work to sweep the road.[6] The establishment of the ravelin was important because, as Decius Wadsworth noted in his 1813 report, the "Gate which opens towards the [water] battery is too much exposed, and a resolute Enemy getting possession of the Battery and turning some of its guns against the Gate, might open a passage so as to enter the Fort."[7]

Fort McHenry possessed an interior magazine to store its powder and other ordnance. The rectangular magazine had the capacity to store three hundred barrels of powder, and its interior in 1814 was approximately "10 feet wide by 26 feet." It was made of brick and mortar, and at the time of the battle, it was not arched. It was covered with wooden shingles and was "without a lightening rod." In reality, the magazine represented the single point of failure for the entire fort since it was not bombproof. The fort's interior had quarters for officers and barracks for the enlisted men, although its capacity for housing troops—which in peacetime never exceeded seventy men—was limited. The barracks was located uncomfortably close to the magazine, and the close quarters inside the fort made it an especially unhealthy place. By the 1830s the Army made it a policy to regularly evacuate the fort for health reasons several months each year.[8]

While Smith and Armistead worked to perfect Baltimore's land defenses, Commodore John Rodgers commanded all naval forces in the region. He had recently returned from Washington, D.C., where he had unsuccessfully tried to use fire rafts against James Gordon's Potomac River squadron following the British raid on Alexandria. Rodgers had previously ordered most of the sailors and all the U.S. Marines from his own ship, the newly built frigate USS *Guerriere*, to come to Baltimore. His rapidly growing naval force included surviving members of Barney's flotilla and other men from the Washington Navy Yard, such as the U.S. Marine contingent that had made the march from Bladensburg under the temporary command of quartermaster Captain Samuel Bacon. Rodgers assigned elements of his growing naval force to Captain David Porter and Captain Oliver Hazard Perry. Both men had, by that time, fully established reputations as experienced combatants. Perry was in Baltimore to take command of the nearly constructed frigate USS *Java*, then in the yards near Fells Point. However, he fell extremely ill and did not participate in any further military activity until after the battle for Baltimore was concluded.

At Smith's direction Rodgers' men formed a line of entrenchments and strongpoints complete with cannon from the Lazaretto to Samuel Smith's main line on Hampstead Hill. This area became known as Rodgers' Bastion, and to any approaching force, it must have looked quite formidable. Rodgers arranged a series of gun batteries beginning near the Sugar House on Harris Creek, which emptied into the Patapsco River. At the Sugar House he assigned a reliable midshipman named Salter along with twelve sailors to man a single gun battery. A short distance away, he positioned Sailing Master James Ramage from his own USS *Guerriere* with a five-gun battery to cover the Sparrows Point Road. Perhaps taking a page from Barney's success at Bladensburg, he placed another two-gun battery under Sailing Master George de la Roche from the USS *Erie* directly fronting the main road to Sparrows Point. At a crucial intersection of the Philadelphia and Sparrows Point Roads, Rodgers placed his heaviest concentration of artillery (seven guns) under the command of Lieutenant Thomas Gamble, his first officer from the *Guerriere*. In sum, Rodgers created artillery strongpoints so that they had interlocking fields of fire. He also posted the U.S. Marine detachment from the USS *Guerriere* under the command of First Lieutenant Joseph L. Kuhn, USMC, in a trench behind Gamble's main artillery emplacement. He stationed the First Maryland Regiment, under Colonel Henry Steiner, and some Pennsylvania riflemen, under Major Beale Randall, in the rear of the guns with orders to act as a mobile reserve if Rodgers' Bastion was approached by British infantry or the British attempted to make an amphibious assault against Frazier's guns and flotillamen at the Lazaretto. However, if British naval forces were able to break into the inner harbor, Rodgers and his men could be dislodged by enfilade fire coming from the Northwest Branch.[9]

Apparently the military transformation of the eastern side of the city was amazing. George Douglas, a transplanted New Yorker and immigrant from Northern Ireland who worked for the *Baltimore American and Commercial Daily Advertiser*, wrote to his friend Henry Wheaton in New York on 29 August 1814 about events unfolding as the British approached Baltimore following their success at Washington, D.C.:

Meanwhile, the people here seem to have recovered a new spirit, something like a confidence in their strength & resources. A great number of our county corps are arrived & are hourly arriving. Yesterday afternoon, I was delighted with the scene on the hills & high grounds above Fells Point & to the Eastward of this city [Hampstead Hill]. They are completely covered with tents, cannon & troops of all descriptions. I was particularly pleased with the *Marine* Corps under Captain Stiles. The multitude collected around them, saying "These are the men on whom we can depend." Com[modore] Rodgers, Porter & Perry are on the field, and on every spot were corps & regiments & artillery busily exercising.

Yesterday, from 7 in the morning to 6 in the evening, a vast entrenchment, at least a mile long, was raised, as if by magic; vast numbers busily at work, old & young, black & white. It was a most cheerful and animated scene. . . . It is evident that the Naval gentlemen have given a new turn to the spirit & exertions of our citizens. In another week, our whole city will be circumvallated, & all we shall want are some *heads* to conduct business properly if an attack on us be made.[10]

With the eastern approaches to the city well defended, the western half of the V in Baltimore Harbor held a bit more promise for a successful British forced entry. Known as the Ferry Branch, this part of the harbor approach was much broader. Here the Americans planned to sink additional obstructing hulks but did not complete the job before the British arrived on the scene. This did not matter since Rodgers did not have any more barges left to cover them anyway. During the months leading up to the appearance of the British at the harbor entrance, Beall and Armistead emplaced a number of heavy-caliber, long-range guns in front of Fort McHenry's walls and at the tip of Whetstone Point. Called the water battery, this emplacement had thirty-six guns, at least fifteen of which were long-range 36 pounders taken from a wrecked French ship of the line, the *L'Eole*, which had run aground off the Virginia Capes in 1806, was towed up the bay, and was ultimately abandoned in Baltimore Harbor. These guns were procured from the French ambassador and used to good effect at Fort McHenry. They could easily range any ship or barge attempting to enter the Ferry Branch. The water battery was manned by another contingent of flotillamen and fencibles and was locally commanded by Lieutenant Solomon Rodman, although the battery was under the overall command of the senior-ranking regular Army officer in command of Fort McHenry, Major George Armistead.

Even though the creation of the water battery had greatly improved the defensive arrangements of Baltimore's inner harbor, Samuel Smith was not one to leave anything to chance. Accordingly, he was instrumental in ordering the construction of three other small forts to cover the landward approach to Fort McHenry. Two of the forts were located on the north bank of the Ferry Branch and were known as Battery Babcock and Fort Covington. These defensive works were just over a mile and a quarter northwest of Fort McHenry. Battery Babcock had been hastily constructed during the 1813 scare and possessed six 18 pounders mounted in a four-foot-high semicircular sod earthwork. This work was manned by fifty-two flotillamen and commanded by Sailing Master John A. Webster of the Revenue Service. About another quarter mile farther away was Fort Covington. Completed in December 1813, this fort was a pie-shaped ten-foot-high brick wall demi-revetted for at least ten 18 pounders, although at that time the fort itself likely had far fewer than that number. Fort Covington was manned by eighty sailors from the USS *Guerriere* and commanded by Lieutenant Henry Newcomb of the same ship. A single gun, commanded by Sailing Master Leonard Hall (who passed away from natural causes just six days after the Battle of Baltimore), was emplaced on Federal Hill, overlooking the inner harbor. His lone 6-pounder gun played a critical role in signaling the movements of the British in the Patapsco River, and this was the position's true purpose. Indeed, Federal Hill was then, as it is now, a favorite location for viewing Baltimore's inner harbor and the river beyond.

A third supporting defensive structure on Whetstone Point was a half-moon-shaped earthwork called Fort Look-Out. This position was still being improved when the British arrived. Renamed Fort Wood immediately following the battle, Fort Look-Out was located on a prominent knoll not far from the rear of Fort McHenry (present-day Riverside Park in South Baltimore). Primarily intended as a fallback position for the defenders of Fort McHenry, this post was commanded by Lieutenant George Budd from the sloop of war USS *Ontario*. Fort Look-Out was designed by the ubiquitous engineer Captain Samuel Babcock and mounted at least seven 24-pounder naval guns. As bespoke its name, the fort was an excellent observation post for all activity taking place on either branch of the inner harbor and the river beyond.[11]

Early on the morning of 12 September, Leonard Hall spotted the British landing troops at North Point, more than twelve miles away, and fired three shots in quick succession from his 6-pounder gun. The gun signal brought out hundreds of Baltimore citizens who climbed to their rooftops to observe the coming onslaught, which was to take place in less than forty-eight hours.[12] The Maryland militia and U.S. Sea Fencibles were placed on heightened alert, and those sailors and soldiers in and near the various harbor forts, especially Fort McHenry, made ready to defend the city against a combined British land-sea assault they were sure was not long in coming.

Samuel Smith was busy turning Hampstead Hill into a veritable Gibraltar. He had already ordered out levies of local citizens who "worked in relays, depending on the ward where they lived. They reported at 6:00 AM and toiled until dark." He mercilessly drilled the various raw militia units arriving from Virginia and Pennsylvania, and they too worked from dawn to dusk. He was determined that there would be no repeat of the Bladensburg Races.

If Smith faced one persistent problem, it remained his confusing chain of command. Even though Smith was a militia major general, he was acknowledged by Governor Winder to have authority over regular U.S. troops in Baltimore owing to his dubious appointment as a "volunteer" in the regular establishment. Fortunately for Smith, acting secretary of war James Monroe later ratified Winder's unauthorized assumption of federal authority. Compounding the confusion, Smith commanded, either directly or indirectly, a virtual hodgepodge of disparate commands, including regular naval forces under John Rodgers, militia regiments from three states, independent Sea Fencibles, civilian levies, and supposedly Barney's veteran flotilla command. When Captain Robert Spence of the U.S. Navy, second in command at Rodgers' Bastion, attempted to exert control over Solomon Frazier's flotillamen at the Lazaretto, he was refused on the grounds that Barney's flotilla was technically not part of the regular Navy, or Army for that matter. Spence demanded that Frazier be court-martialed for refusing his orders. The wounded Barney weighed in and wrote a scathing letter to the Secretary of the Navy, blasting Spence as an "enemy of the Administration" and "a former party to the Burr Plot." Nonetheless, Barney offered to defuse the situation by recommending to the secretary that in the present emergency the flotillamen be temporarily placed under the control of John Rodgers.[13]

To ease some of this tension, Smith placed his largely untested Virginia militia in nearby support of Battery Babcock, Fort Look-Out, and Fort Covington. He initially assigned William Winder the mission of keeping an eye on this potential backdoor to Baltimore. However, unlike Smith, who had overall command of all forces in the area, Winder was made responsible for the Ferry Branch forts but not the sailors or flotillamen who manned these posts, only the militia. Moreover, everyone realized that if there was ground combat activity in the coming fight for Baltimore, it was going to take place east of the city near Hampstead Hill. Winder immediately penned a note to Smith protesting his assignment and requested that he be allowed to move toward the eastern side defenses. To Smith's credit, once it became clear that the main British land effort was indeed coming by way of Patapsco Neck, he allowed Winder and most of his troops to move to front the

Bel Air Road on the left flank of Hampstead Hill. By 10 September 1814 Smith could count on an aggregate of nearly 14,000 officers and men from three states to defend Baltimore against a maximum of 4,000 men that the British had available as a landing force.[14]

One such militia recruit was twenty-six-year-old Pennsylvania schoolteacher Lieutenant Francis R. Shunk. Shunk had been born in Trappe, Pennsylvania, and had enlisted in the First Brigade of Pennsylvania militia under the command of Colonel Maxwell Kennedy, then mustering at York, Pennsylvania. The scholarly Shunk soon found the life of a soldier more tedious than he had heretofore presumed. He wrote, "The life of a soldier when custom has dissolved it of novelty becomes dull & inset." He continued, "You will think in this multitude [the First Brigade] there must be always something to divert, something new, but it is mixed with so much wretchedness and confusion, so much groveling vice & low depravity that a person has more cause to weep than rejoice." Following the fighting, Shunk toured the North Point Battlefield. He noted that North Point "was [the] first ground I ever saw on which contending armies met." Shunk served for a total of six months. No longer naive about the realities of soldiering, he returned to his job as a schoolteacher on 5 March 1815.[15]

Fort McHenry was getting crowded and eventually grew to approximately a thousand men, mostly from militia and volunteer military organizations. Major Armistead originally had command of just sixty regulars of the U.S. Artillery Corps. Detachments from the regular regiments of the U.S. 36th, 38th, and 12th Infantry, under the command of Lieutenant Colonel William Stewart and Lieutenant Colonel Samuel Lane, were sent to augment Armistead's artillerymen and provide regular infantry support to Fort McHenry. Armistead posted these men along with Captain Matthew S. Bunbury's and Captain William H. Addison's U.S. Sea Fencibles in the dry moat outside the fort's brick walls. Other Baltimore volunteer units were crowded into or around the fort so that by 11 September 1814, Armistead had more than enough immediate infantry support.[16]

By 9 September 1814 scouts had informed Smith that the British invasion fleet had bypassed Annapolis and was headed directly for Baltimore. By this time Smith could count on three brigades of Maryland militia. The least ready was probably Brigadier General Thomas Forman's First Brigade. Most of these men were from the far northeastern part of the state (the Fortieth and Forty-Second Maryland Regiments from Harford County and the Thirtieth and Forty-Ninth

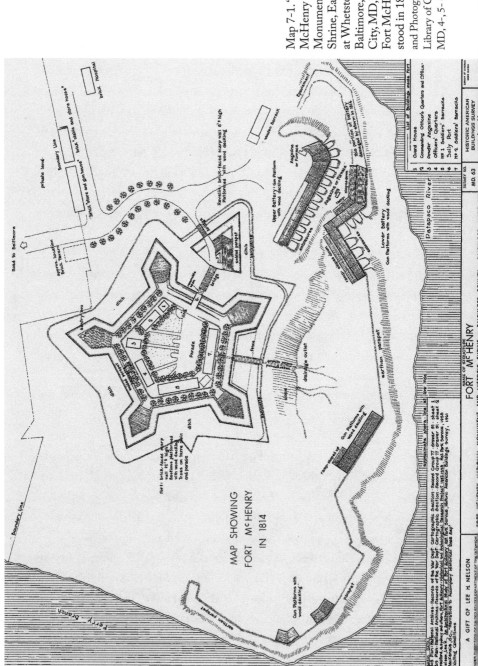

Map 7-1. "Fort McHenry National Monument and Historic Shrine, East Fort Avenue at Whetstone Point, Baltimore, Independent City, MD," showing Fort McHenry as it stood in 1814. Prints and Photographs Division, Library of Congress, HABS MD, 4-, 5- (sheet 1 of 11).

Maryland Regiments from Cecil County). Forman's men were short timers and had been drafted for only sixty days' active service. They had several Quakers in their ranks who immediately applied to General Smith for discharge on religious grounds. One of Forman's company commanders was nearly convicted of being away without proper leave, and his brigade was known to have a higher than normal desertion rate—a clear indication of poor leadership and unit morale. The Eleventh Brigade comprised Tobias Stansbury's Bladensburg veterans, who nearly all hailed from Baltimore County. His regiments, the Seventh, Fifteenth, Thirty-Sixth, Forty-First, and Forty-Sixth, were the same men who were so easily scattered by a Congreve barrage at Bladensburg. Despite this, Stansbury continued to enjoy a fairly good military reputation. Still, his men were not assembling as rapidly as he had hoped. However, Smith's Third "City" Brigade, commanded by Brigadier General John Stricker, seemed to be made of sterner stuff. Consisting of the battle-tested Fifth Maryland Regiment, which was one of the few militia units to perform fairly well at Bladensburg, Stricker's brigade also included the Sixth, Twenty-Seventh, Thirty-Ninth, and Fifty-First Regiments. More important, this brigade contained the First Artillery Regiment, the First Rifle Battalion, and the Fifth Regiment of Cavalry. In sum, Stricker's brigade was clearly the strongest and most capable of the three Maryland militia brigades, and this unit was Smith's obvious choice to deploy forward toward Bear Creek on Patapsco Neck.[17]

On 11 September the British invasion fleet could be seen from Federal Hill readying small landing craft to transport their troops ashore at North Point—exactly where Smith had long predicted the British would land. By 12 September they were coming ashore in force. Ross placed his three light infantry companies at the head of his column, just in front of his light brigade (the Eighty-Fifth Regiment of Foot), and they began the march up Long Log Lane toward eastern Baltimore. However, the day prior, Smith had ordered Stricker to prepare a defensive work near Bear Creek to delay the British should they advance up the neck. Stricker's troops were still engaged in building their entrenchments when the van of Ross' column suddenly appeared. Ross was in for a shock as Stricker had more than three thousand infantry on hand—nearly one-fourth of the total force at Smith's disposal.

Cavalry vedettes initially spotted the red-coated column marching up the single axis of advance—Long Log Lane. These men included at least eleven soldiers from Captain Henry Thompson's First Baltimore Horse Artillery (who also served as bodyguards and as couriers for General Smith). Near Cook's Tavern, Stricker had his aide-de-camp, Major George Stephenson, inform Smith that by 7:30 a.m. the British had advanced nearly to the Gorsuch Farm, about halfway up the neck. Stricker outlined his plans to resist the British advance as planned at his hastily dug entrenchments near Bear Creek. It was a good plan because the neck was narrowest at this particular location; this made it tougher for the British to maneuver around his flanks as they had so easily done around Winder's militia at Bladensburg.[18]

At around 9:00 a.m. on 12 September, Stricker had deployed Sterett's Fifth Maryland Regiment on the right of his line and extending left to touch the North Point Road. The Twenty-Seventh Maryland was next in line to the left of the road. Stricker placed his artillery between the two regiments astride the road. Directly behind the Fifth and Twenty-Seventh Maryland Regiments were the Fifty-First and Thirty-Ninth. About a half mile to the rear, Stricker held the Sixth Maryland in reserve. Members of the rifle battalion were used as skirmishers in some woods in front of Stricker's main line. However, before the British appeared, Captain W. B. Dyer, acting on a false rumor that the British had landed behind his men from the Back River, ordered the riflemen back to Stricker's main line before they could fire a shot. Upset at the unauthorized retreat and spotting an advance party of British soldiers loitering at the Gorsuch farmhouse, Stricker called for volunteers from the Fifth Maryland.

The volunteers were led by Major Richard Heath. Heath was accompanied by a party of 80 riflemen, under Captain Edward Aisquith, known as the Baltimore Sharpshooters; a small 4-pounder artillery piece; and 2 companies of infantry under Captain Aaron Levering and Captain Benjamin Howard. The term *riflemen* was likely a misnomer. Most, if not all, American troops around Baltimore called "riflemen" were actually armed with smoothbore muskets. In sum, Heath had a total of 250 men. This large reconnaissance in force momentarily outnumbered the British advance guard, which had made the mistake of getting too far out in front of its supporting main column.[19]

Heath's volunteers and the British advance party soon made contact and fired away at each other. Hearing the gunfire, Ross, who was nearby, spurred his horse forward to investigate. Seeing a force to his front larger and more determined than he had expected, he seemed about to turn his horse around to bring up reinforcements. At this moment he was shot through the chest by an American

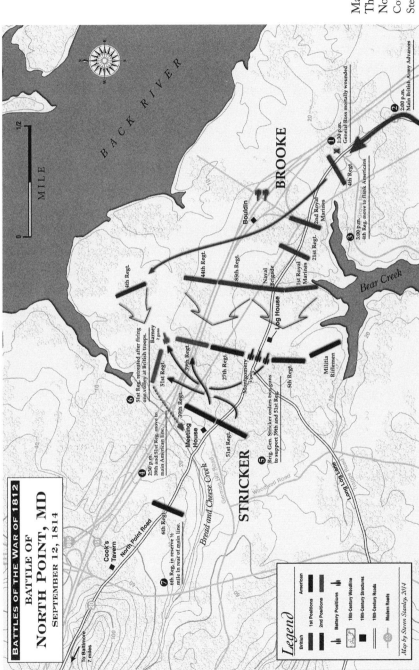

BATTLES OF THE WAR OF 1812
BATTLE OF
NORTH POINT, MD
SEPTEMBER 12, 1814

BACK RIVER

MILE
0   1/2

To Baltimore
7 miles

Cook's
Tavern

North Point Road

6th Regt.

⑦ 6th Reg. in reserve ¼
mile in rear of main line.

STRICKER

Bread and Cheese Creek

Woodbell Road

Long Log Lane

Gorsuch Road

④ 2:30 p.m.
39th and 51st Reg. move to
main American line.

⑥ 51st Reg. retreated after firing
one volley at British troops.

Meeting
House

39th Regt.

51st Regt.

51st Regt.

Barney
2 pm.

39th Regt.

27th Regt.

Montgomery
3 guns

⑤ Brig. Gen. Stricker orders two guns
to support 39th and 51st Reg.

5th Regt.

Militia
Riflemen

Log House

Naval
Brigade

1st Royal
Marines

Bear Creek

4th Regt.

44th Regt.

85th Regt.

Bouldin
2 pm

21st Regt.

2nd Royal
Marines

BROOKE

4th Regt.

① 1:30 p.m.
General Ross mortally wounded

② 2:00 p.m.
Main British Army Advances

③ 3:00 p.m.
4th Reg. move to flank Americans

Legend

British   American

1st Positions

2nd Positions

Battery Positions

19th-Century Woodline

19th-Century Structures

19th-Century Roads

Modern Roads

Map by Steven Stanley, 2014

Map 7-2.
The Battle of
North Point.
Courtesy of
Steven Stanley

rifleman. He died as he was being carried back to the landing site for medical treatment. His mortal wounding shocked the British troops nearby, and Colonel Arthur Brooke of the Forty-Fourth Regiment assumed command of the expedition. Brooke brought up reinforcements and drove Heath and his men back to Stricker's main line. Bringing up his own light artillery, Brooke perceived that Stricker had left a "several hundred yard gap" between the left of the Twenty-Seventh Maryland Regiment and the Back River. Seeing the British move a flanking column toward his left, Stricker ordered the Thirty-Ninth Maryland Regiment up to the left of the Twenty-Seventh and brought up the Fifty-First Maryland, telling the militiamen to form at a right angle to his main line (to protect his vulnerable left flank). Executing this battlefield maneuver under fire was clearly beyond the capabilities of the green militia regiment, and instead of forming where Stricker wanted them, the militiamen milled about in confusion.[20]

Militia major and later U.S. senator Robert Henry Goldsborough of Talbot County, Maryland, observed the action at North Point and claimed that Cochrane, upon learning of Ross' death, decided to ultimately withdraw "that part of the forces he controlled" (meaning the sailors and Royal Marines).[21] However, Goldsborough's account has not been corroborated. It doesn't appear that any detachment of forces occurred before Brooke decided to retreat down Patapsco Neck following the fighting at North Point. Nevertheless, Goldsborough wrote that during the fighting "the 5th Regiment and the 27th Regiment behaved well. The 51st commanded by Colonel Amy [Lieutenant Colonel Henry Amey] fired into one of our own troops of horse and killed and wounded 8 or 10 of them—they then took to their heels and ran off."[22]

Ross' untimely death was indeed a serious blow to British morale. Lieutenant G. G. MacDonald of the HMS *Diomede* recounted that Ross "received a rifle ball in his bridle arm [and it] enter[ed] his body. He instantly fell, and I not being far off, happened to be called with 12 of my men to take the General down to the beach." Lieutenant Gleig of the Eighty-Fifth Regiment of Foot recalled seeing the wounded Ross lying by the side of the road. "There were five English soldiers and three Yankees near him," he said. Two of the American casualties may have been teenage members of Aisquith's company, Private Henry Gough McComas and Private Daniel Wells. The third man was possibly the twenty-four-year-old Aquila Randall of the First Mechanical Volunteers. These casualties had likely been gathered by the British in their efforts to locate the perpetrators of the Ross ambush. Following the battle all three men were credited by local historians with killing the British commander. In reality, the actual shooter will likely never be known. Nonetheless, Lieutenant MacDonald stated that when his party carried Ross' body to the HMS *Tonnant*, lying off North Point, his death cast a pall over the entire operation. He flatly added, "These Americans are not to be trifled with."[23]

Having driven Heath's and Aisquith's men out of the woods, Brooke sensed the moment was right to continue the attack against Stricker's main line. At 2:50 p.m. he launched a furious assault against Stricker's left flank. Both sides fired volleys at each other. Heavy smoke from the gunfire obscured both lines until the Fifty-First Maryland Regiment broke and fled, taking part of the Thirty-Ninth along with them. Stricker's left flank rapidly crumbled in a galling fire from Brooke's Fourth Regiment. It was the same old story. But this time the more reliable troops on Stricker's right held firm. The British Twenty-First and Forty-Fourth Regiments slammed into the Fifth and Twenty-Seventh Maryland Regiments while Stricker's well-served artillery blasted back with grapeshot. North Point would not become another Bladensburg. However, after about an hour of heavy fighting, Stricker, whose orders were to fight a delaying action, directed that his forward regiments and artillery fall back to the Sixth Maryland and his second line near Cook's Tavern. While the British claimed that the Americans had been driven from the field and were flying in all directions, Stricker wrote in his report on the affair that most of his men calmly re-formed behind the Sixth Maryland. Brooke did not order his forces in pursuit but remained on the North Point Battlefield until the morning of 13 September. Stricker's losses were listed as 24 killed, 139 wounded, and 50 captured. Because they were on the offensive, the British suffered heavier losses, including their senior commander, Major General Robert Ross, and 38 others killed, 251 wounded, and another 50 missing. Although the British forces ultimately prevailed at North Point, it was a Pyrrhic victory.[24]

Smith ordered the remnants of Stricker's brigade to fall back toward Worthington's Mills, just beyond the left flank of his line. The general brought up the Virginia militia and other troops under Winder from the west side of town, along with a company of U.S. dragoons under Captain John Burd, and placed them on the left flank and at an angle from his main line—an ideal position from which to attack the flank of Brooke's men if they continued their advance on Hampstead

Hill. It rained heavily the night of 12–13 September, and damp, sodden conditions made the misery of the wounded on both sides even worse. Still, Brooke had his men moving by 5:30 a.m. toward Hampstead Hill. By 7:00 a.m. the colonel could distinctly hear Cochrane's bomb ships shelling Fort McHenry, although it was likely that the HMS *Terror* had fired ranging shots at the fort as early as 12 September and at least seven hours before the Battle of North Point. Emerging at the junction of Long Log Lane and the Philadelphia Road, Brooke had his first up close look at the American main line of resistance on Hampstead Hill, and he was stunned by what he saw. Thousands of dug-in American infantry supported by numerous artillery strongpoints crowned the crest of the hill. Brooke had hoped that Stricker's fleeing advance guard had infected the rest of the army, but taking one look at the hill to his front made him realize that he had been overly optimistic. The colonel tried to maneuver around the left of Smith's entrenchments but immediately ran into the prepared positions of Winder's and Stricker's men arrayed on high ground above the Bel Air Road. Once Brooke pulled back toward the Philadelphia Road area, Smith ordered Stricker and Winder to move even closer to the road in order to threaten Brooke's rear. By the afternoon of 13 September, Brooke was content with sending patrols forward to probe the center and left of Smith's line for any weaknesses. He also considered a risky night attack to mitigate Smith's artillery, and he hoped the Royal Navy had more success against Fort McHenry.[25]

By the early morning hours of 13 September 1814, Cochrane believed that if he could pound Baltimore's harbor defenses into submission, his frigates might possibly enter the harbor, enfilade Smith's and Rodgers' prepared defensive position with their naval guns, and assist Brooke in driving off the infantry so as to reenact the Bladensburg Races. James Gordon's light frigate, *Seahorse*, along with the HMS *Surprize* and *Severn*, led the way for Cochrane's powerful bomb ships— the *Terror*, *Aetna*, *Meteor*, *Volcano*, and *Devastation*—and a rocket ship—the HMS *Erebus*. This squadron moved within range to strike Fort McHenry, the water battery, and the Lazaretto. Cochrane transferred himself to the frigate *Surprize* so he would be in a position to better observe his bomb ships' effect on the fort while staying in communication with Cockburn, who was ashore with Ross and Brooke.

Cochrane's specialized bomb ships of the *Vesuvius* and *Hecla* classes were a sight to behold. They began firing shells from one 10-inch sea mortar and one 13-inch sea mortar per ship toward Fort McHenry and its supporting batteries from nearly 2.5 miles away. They also mounted two 6-pounder and eight 24-pounder guns, but these weapons were more likely for local defense. The heavy mortars weighed 3 tons apiece and could normally fire one 200-pound shell, or "carcass," every five minutes. These particular shells were about five times heavier than any other naval ordnance in Cochrane's inventory. Although the Americans attempted to return fire from some of their larger guns both in the fort and the water battery, it was quickly apparent that the bomb ships easily outranged the guns, and they ceased firing by 10:00 a.m. The hulls of the bomb ships were strongly reinforced to accept the heavy recoil of the mortars, and it was said that the ship "was forced two feet into the water" when the weapon was fired, "thus straining every part from stem to stern." These ships were considered so dangerous that they came with their own separate ammunition tender and were never fired near other vessels. Earlier versions of the bomb ship were ketches that proved to be poor sailors. The latest versions possessed by Cochrane retained their forward masts but substituted more durable chains instead of rope for their forward rigging to preserve their lines from the tremendous muzzle blast. The British continued their bomb ship attack against the fort for the next twenty-four hours. But by late morning Cochrane could tell that his weapons were not as effective as he had hoped and wrote to Cockburn, who was then ashore with Brooke's troops, "It is impossible for the Ships to render you any assistance, the Town is so far retired within the Forts. It is for Colonel Brooke to consider under such circumstances whether he has Force sufficient to defeat so large a number as it [is] said the Enemy has collected; say 20,000 strong or even less number & to take the Town; without this can be done it will be only throwing the Mens [land force] lives away and prevent us from going upon other services."[26]

Arthur Brooke later noted in his diary that this letter, which reached him on 13 September, caused him to reconsider a risky night attack against what he perceived was Smith's vulnerable right flank. Brooke lamented, "If I took the place, I should have been the greatest man in England. If I lost, My Military Character was gone forever." Brooke decided that he would retreat that evening, remain for some time on the North Point battleground, and "wait there some hours, in the hopes he [Smith] would follow, and give me an opportunity, of attacking him to more advantage, and after defeating him, of being able to follow him, into his works, but the lesson he got the day before [apparently at the Battle of North Point], had taught him to respect us, and thinks himself well off, by being allowed to remain in possession of his City, and entrenchments." Once it was apparent that Smith was not going to take the bait, Brooke moved his forces three more miles back down Patapsco Neck. By the late morning of 14 September, Brooke was back on board the HMS *Tonnant*.[27] Retreating British troops burned down the Todd farmhouse, the oldest known structure on Patapsco Neck. The Americans argued they did this out of spite. More likely, it was because the British did not wish to allow the Americans a convenient observation post from which they could view their reembarkation operations at North Point.

Throughout 13 September and into the next day, the British pounded Fort McHenry with all the available naval ordnance that could reach the structure. The HMS *Terror* was joined by Cochrane's bombardment frigates, the *Surprize*, *Madagascar*, *Severn*, *Havanna*, *Euryalus*, and *Hebrus*. The admiral also moved in lighter draught schooners and brigs. These vessels had only a few long-range guns but could maneuver close enough to hit the fort without too much damage being done in return. Cochrane also moved up the specialized rocket ship, the HMS *Erebus*, along with the other bomb ships, the *Meteor*, *Devastation*, *Aetna*, and *Volcano*. As previously noted, because of their superior range, the bomb ships were virtually invulnerable to American counterbattery fire.

What Sailing Master Beverly Diggs, in command of harbor gun barge No. 7, truly feared was that the bomb ships were actually there to provide suppressive fire so the frigate squadron could sail past Fort McHenry and break into the inner harbor. To preclude this possibility, Rodgers ordered Diggs, along with other local naval commanders in the harbor area, to "take such Vessels as were ballasted and could easily be Sunk without regards to whom the[y] might belong, and sink them in the River between Fort McHenry and the Lararetto." By this time landing operations were well under way at North Point. Rodgers had Lieutenant Solomon Rutter, formerly of Barney's Chesapeake flotilla, and Captain Robert Spence of the U.S. Navy sink at least twenty-four vessels in the Northwest Branch. Rutter lashed their masts together with a heavy chain and resumed his station on board the gun barges covering this ersatz boom. Many of the vessels belonged to the town's leading citizens, such as privateer investor Levi Hollingsworth and George Stiles, the commander of the First Marine Artillery of the Union. Even the commanding general Samuel Smith and his business partner James Buchanan contributed vessels to the effort.[28]

A View of the Bombardment of Fort McHenry, by John Bower, ca. 1814. Prints and Photographs Division, Library of Congress, LC-DIG-ppmsca-35544

The rocket ship HMS *Erebus* launched volley after volley of screaming Congreve rockets at the fort and its outer works. The *Erebus* was an impressive weapon of war—and exclusive to the Royal Navy. Congreve rockets had worked for the British at Copenhagen in 1807, were a renowned incendiary device, and had played a major role in the destruction of Havre de Grace the year before. Their effectiveness against the stone, earth, and brick fortification of Fort McHenry was limited, however. Moreover, the fort was located on a point of land that was still fairly distant from Baltimore's 1814 urban center. Unless a lucky shot hit the fort's magazine, the rockets did little damage at Fort McHenry and served only to inspire people like Francis Scott Key.

There can be no doubt that Rodgers' decision to block the Northwest Branch with hulks was crucial in determining the contest's eventual outcome. Soon after he had observed the hulks being sunk, Cochrane ordered the HMS *Terror* to drop out of the bombardment group. The ship's log from the *Terror* indicated that the vessel "at 1 [p.m.] came to and anchor[ed] off Patapsco Neck to cover the re-embarking of the troops." This was well before the bombardment of the fort by the other vessels was even half over. In fact, by this time, with Ross dead, the sunken hulks in the Northwest Branch, and the significant American military preparations on Hampstead Hill and at Rodgers' Bastion, Cochrane had come to realize that the prospects of a successful land assault were exceedingly remote. The early detachment of one of his valuable bomb ships is a good indication that he held out little hope that his ships could force their way into the harbor. On the afternoon of 13 September, both Cochrane and his fleet captain, Rear Admiral Edward Codrington, were on board the HMS *Surprize*. This ship was repositioned near Bear Creek for ease of communication with Ross' land forces, now led by senior-ranking colonel Arthur Brooke of the Forty-Fourth Regiment of Foot. Codrington lamented, "Heroism will do wonders . . . but I believe there is too much on hand for even that, and I wish the job were well over."[29]

Most likely, the demise of Ross and the intensity of American resistance encountered thus far—very different from that experienced at Washington, D.C.—had created a sense of pessimism that seemed to affect the British high command well before the full bombardment of Fort McHenry had reached its crescendo. Hence, the twenty-five-hour bombardment of the fort should be seen in a new light: as a forlorn hope that either the Americans would possibly buckle under the pounding or, barring that, the shelling would help cover the eventual withdrawal of ground forces—and Cochrane seemed inclined toward withdrawal as early as 1:00 p.m. on 13 September. In sum, the bombardment, intended to be a supporting operation, had become by the evening of 13 September the main effort.

The serious shelling of the fort began early on 13 September. Large bombs and shells fell inside the walls or exploded overhead, but the American troops seemed to stand it well. Captain Frederick Evans of the U.S. artillery saw two men killed by shrapnel as they hid under a heavy gun. He also stated that a female camp follower carrying water to the men was directly hit by a shell and instantly vaporized. He noted dud shells "as big as a flour barrel" fall nearby and fail to explode. At 2:00 p.m. another shell hit a gun; killed Lieutenant Levi Claggett and Sergeant John Clemm, members of Captain Nicholson's Baltimore Fencibles; and wounded a number of other nearby soldiers. Noticing the effect of the shell that killed Claggett and Clemm through his glass, Cochrane ordered his bomb ships to close the range on the fort. Unfortunately, this now put his ships within range of Armistead's larger guns, and nearly immediately, the *Devastation* and *Volcano* received some hits that wounded a sailor. The rocket ship *Erebus* was damaged so badly in its rigging that it had to be towed out of range by the frigate *Severn*. Cochrane wisely ordered all his ships to retire out of the fort's range once again.[30]

One soldier wounded during the prolonged shelling was Private William Williams of the U.S. 38th Infantry Regiment. Williams was most likely stationed in the dry moat in front of the fort's walls. He had enlisted as "No. 203, William Williams," but he was known as "Negro Frederick" or "Frederick Hall," a Prince George's County slave who had recently escaped from his owner, Benjamin Oden. Oden had placed an ad in the local newspaper the *American and Commercial Daily Advertiser* offering a forty dollar reward for his slave's return, but Private Williams was in the Army now, and no one seemed to be looking for him at that moment. Williams was awarded a fifty dollar enlistment bounty (most likely the most money he had ever had at any one time) and received the standard pay of an infantry private: eight dollars a month plus a daily ration. During the bombardment, Williams had "his leg blown off by a cannon ball," and he died several months later in a Baltimore hospital—most likely as a result of his wound. At that time disabled and discharged soldiers were entitled to a 160-acre land bounty, but obviously William Williams was not around to collect this entitlement. Nonetheless, in 1836 his former owner had the temerity to see if he could receive his slave's land. His request was denied by Congress on the grounds that Williams had fraudulently enlisted in the first place and that Oden had waited too long in trying to collect on the supreme sacrifice of his former slave who had so cleverly but briefly found a way to defeat the institution of slavery.[31]

Cochrane continued firing at long range into the night of 13 September and early morning hours of 14 September 1814. After having considered and rejected an amphibious assault on the Lazaretto, the admiral ordered Captain Napier of the HMS *Euryalis* to lead twenty boatloads of Royal Marines and sailors containing nearly twelve hundred men into the Ferry Branch, to enter Ridgely's Cove, and to attack Fort McHenry from its landward side. However, in a driving rain storm, eleven of Napier's boats became disconnected from the other nine and drifted toward the Lazaretto. Lieutenant Frazier alerted some nearby Pennsylvania riflemen to come to his aid, and once the wayward boats recognized what was about to happen, they pulled back toward the British ships and out of range. Napier's remaining boats persevered onward toward Ridgely's Cove. Not noticed at first by the gunners at Battery Babcock, the Americans eventually discovered Napier and his men. According to militia captain James Piper, Napier's boats "supposing themselves out of all danger; threw up a blue light rocket." This rocket tipped off

Battery Babcock. Sailing Master Webster fired his cannon first, but his blasts were quickly followed by Lieutenant Newcomb's guns at Fort Covington. Webster wrote, "I could hear the balls from our guns strike the barges. My men stated to me that they could hear the shrieks of the wounded. . . . During the firing of the enemy, I could distinctly see their barges by the explosion of their cannon which was a great guide to me to fire by." Captain Piper noted, "Neither boats, men or blue lights were ever afterwards heard of. No doubt the failure of this bold and daring enterprise contributed to some extent to put an end to all their hopes of possessing Baltimore." Other cannon positions in and around the fort, including at the Lazaretto, joined in, and Napier's Ferry Branch night assault was driven back down the river with a number of wounded and at least one sailor killed.[32]

In the night bombardment Major Armistead was allegedly one of the few people at Fort McHenry who knew that the magazine was not truly bombproof. A missile did penetrate its brick and masonry roof but failed to explode. Even this event was not overly worrisome to Armistead. He had had his men remove most of his powder barrels and spread them out over a wide expanse behind the fort so that if a barrel did happen to be hit, it would not cause catastrophic damage to the fort itself. By 4:00 a.m. the firing on the fort began to slacken. By 7:00 a.m. it ceased altogether. Soldiers on Hampstead Hill worried that the fort had possibly fallen. Armistead estimated, "During the bombardment, which lasted 25 hours (with two slight intermissions) from the best calculation I can make, from fifteen to eighteen hundred shells were thrown by the enemy." His figures were corroborated by the bomb-ship logs, which showed each of the 5 ships throwing approximately 275 rounds apiece—a combined weight of 133 tons of ordnance used against the fort. However, it was estimated that only 400 (22 percent) of the British shells actually landed in or near the fort's defensive works. While even a single shell could make a big impression on soldiers huddled in the fort's ditch or sailors manning the guns at the exposed water battery, the accuracy of these early nineteenth-century weapons left much to be desired. The real threat to the fort's defenders came from the exploding bombs that did not necessarily land but burst in the air, showering the area with pieces of iron shrapnel. They were more feared because the troops had no overhead cover in and around the fort. However, getting those particular shells to go off at the desired height and distance was still an inexact science, and they more often than not exploded too early or not at all.[33]

Despite the twenty-five hours of continuous intensive shelling, the fort had not surrendered. In fact, considering the amount of ordnance thrown at it, the actual damage to the stout fortification was astonishingly light. The fort's remarkable design and later prewar improvements did exactly what they were supposed to do. During the long bombardment, Georgetown lawyer Francis Scott Key, who had been a volunteer at the Battle of Bladensburg and knew firsthand what defeat looked like, had been taken on board a British "truce" vessel to negotiate the release of Dr. William Beanes, who had remained in captivity since the British retrograde movement from Upper Marlboro following the destruction of Washington, D.C. Key, Beanes, and Colonel John Skinner, the American agent for prisoner exchange, had a ringside seat for the nightlong British bombardment of the star-shaped fort. Fortunately for Key, once the British firing had ceased in the morning, he was able to spot the large fort flag (forty-two feet by thirty feet) still proudly flying from its mastlike flagpole. All three Americans on board then knew that Armistead and his men in the fort had prevailed. On the spot Key was inspired to write the words of the American national anthem, "The Star-Spangled Banner." Skinner and Key's mission to gain Beanes' release was ultimately successful.

Since Cochrane could not reduce the fort, Brooke had to either break into the city on his own or call the entire expedition off. Cochrane seemed to recognize these options long before Brooke did. During the bombardment of the fort, Brooke toyed with the idea of launching an attack against Hampstead Hill around 3:00 a.m. on 14 September. He still held out hope for this risky option because he believed a night assault would mitigate Smith's superiority in artillery. As previously noted, Brooke's other hope was that Smith would move out of his works and attack him in the open. But Smith was anything but a fool, and he kept his forces tightly closed up on Hampstead Hill and Rodgers' Bastion. He was later criticized for not attacking Brooke as he retreated back down Patapsco Neck. Yet the Royal Navy still controlled the Patapsco River and adjacent creeks all the way up to the harbor entrance. They could at any time land amphibious forces on the right or left flanks of an American force forward of Hampstead Hill. In hindsight, with Baltimore successfully defended, staying put was probably the right decision.

By 15 September Cochrane had all his ships drop down to Old Roads Bay, and he began to reembark Brooke's exhausted troops. It was over for the British in

The Star Spangled Banner, a painting of Francis Scott Key after the Battle of Baltimore, by Percy Moran. Prints and Photographs Division, Library of Congress, LC-DIG-ds-00032a

the Chesapeake for the rest of the season. Soon Cochrane was headed to Halifax, and Cockburn had departed for Bermuda. The British retained their naval base and a small contingent of colonial marines on Tangier Island until March of the following year, several months after peace had been declared, but they mostly had had enough of the Chesapeake Bay.

EPILOGUE

While Cochrane wrote in his official report that he never wanted to take Baltimore, the truth was that his senior land force commander, Major General Robert Ross, had been killed in action with more than fifty of his men, and he would have loved to have sacked America's third-largest city. What surprised him was that the Maryland militia's performance and the Americans' overall tenacity were more resolute at Baltimore than at Washington. The possible reasons for this are many and include Samuel Smith's iron discipline, his defense in depth, and the greater numbers of militiamen on hand in Baltimore. Or the British defeat may be related to Cochrane's inability to break into Baltimore's inner harbor to support the land assault. Regardless of the immediate reason, the Americans at Baltimore had decisively turned the British back after nearly an entire season of defeat and incompetence.

Nevertheless, the British did accomplish much of what they had set out to do. By August 1814 Cochrane and Cockburn had destroyed Barney's flotilla and completely eliminated any American naval presence from Annapolis to the Virginia Capes. Cochrane's colonial marine scheme initially met with some success. Nevertheless, the total number of escaped slaves willing to risk life and limb for the British military never came to full fruition. Large numbers did use the proximity of British military forces to self-liberate, but more often than not, slave owners circumvented this possibility by forcibly moving their slaves west until it was safe to return. Finally, at Bladensburg the British had completely embarrassed the Madison administration and caused the dismissal of Secretary of War John Armstrong. However, there is little indication that British pressure in the Chesapeake resulted in any sizable reduction of American force on the Canadian border.

201

In the end, because of the successful defense of the city of Baltimore, all the British operational success in Maryland meant little in the overall scheme of things. Now that the "sickly season" was fully under way, for reasons of health the British had to depart the Chesapeake as soon as they could clear the Virginia Capes. Cochrane decided that perhaps it was time to test American mettle at New Orleans. Here too he would ultimately meet with disappointment, and the British would lose another major general, Edward Pakenham, the Duke of Wellington's brother-in-law. In time, depredations caused by marauding armies would be repaired. Military reputations of people like William Winder had been shattered forever. Others like that of Samuel Smith, George Armistead, and John Stricker were enhanced. For years afterward, lasting until the 1880s, the city of Baltimore annually commemorated the "Old Defenders" while they still lived.

So what had each side accomplished during the two summer seasons of fighting in the Chesapeake region? First, while Cochrane, like his predecessor John Borlase Warren the previous year, sincerely believed that the British presence in the Chesapeake might relieve pressure on Canada, the Madison administration never gave much credence to this particular regional threat. Leaving the defense of Maryland and Virginia largely in the hands of the state governors was the sort of response typical of the Republican-minded James Madison, who believed local defense was nearly entirely a state-level responsibility. Although this strategy might have worked against landlocked eastern woodland tribes in the Ohio country, it was nearly disastrous for those states whose interior was bisected by one of the finest natural estuaries in the entire world. Next, the British strike force, often led by the aggressive and innovative Rear Admiral George Cockburn, expertly used its total control of the Chesapeake Bay and most of its tributaries to raid the Maryland and Virginia tidewater regions at will. Moreover, Cockburn's ability to strike at times and places of his choosing served to freeze the local militia in place at home. Consequently, when the militia was required to engage the British in battle, it was nearly always at a disadvantage, and even when the militiamen were more numerous and prepared, these citizen soldiers usually proved to be no match for the disciplined troops of Great Britain. However, the fighting at Craney Island and Caulk's Field and the Battle of North Point were notable exceptions to this trend, proving that when well led and properly motivated, the militia could perform quite well. Cockburn's easy naval success in the region made it all the more obvious that any future American Navy needed ships of the line to defend the American coast.

Alexander Cochrane's colonial marine policy was moderately successful. The British seaborne raid forces kept vulnerable Maryland and Virginia plantations in turmoil for most of two summers and served to assist in the liberation of hundreds of slaves suffering under the yoke of perpetual bondage. Moreover, many of those liberated chose to serve the Crown in a military capacity as marines or as guides, and this in turn enabled the British to raid farther inland than anyone on the American side had previously supposed. Unlike during the American Revolution, when the Americans legitimately claimed that liberated slaves were merely trading one master for another, this time the British went to great lengths to ensure that the former slaves ended up at a place of their own choosing. Many immigrated to Bermuda, Trinidad, Jamaica, or even Nova Scotia. Most had fled their former plantations with just the clothes on their backs, and some, like blacksmith Bartlet Shanklyn, did quite well after the war.

The British presence in the Chesapeake for two summers had embarrassed James Madison, destroyed the national capital, and caused the American government to precipitously flee. British raiding forces had caused hundreds of thousands of dollars in damage and turned a number of Maryland and Virginia towns, such as Havre de Grace, Hampton, Frenchtown, Georgetown, and Fredericktown, to ashes. While clearly the British campaign was designed to punish the Americans for similar activity in Canada, it was also supposed to cause an ostensibly panic-stricken Madison to order his veteran regiments from the St. Lawrence River. In this, British operations in the Chesapeake failed. They successfully held in place two green regiments (the 36th and 38th Infantry) that were intended to remain in Maryland all along, but otherwise, there were no significant troop movements from the frontier. The British naval blockade did do much to stop some (but not all) depredations caused by the Baltimore privateer fleet. It also caused the price of nearly everything to spike—at least temporarily. The British defeat at Baltimore at the end of the second summer (along with a near simultaneous victory at Plattsburg, New York) certainly helped strengthen the American hand in the peace negotiations then under way at Ghent. So other than burned build-ings and stolen crops and livestock, the British did not have much to show for their two-year investment in the region. Moreover, the 1814 campaign had cost them a promising major general (Ross) and a high-born naval captain (Sir Peter Parker). They were to lose a lot more to Andrew Jackson at New Orleans.

On 8 November 1814 the *Republican Star* ran the headline "A Brilliant Cruize." The story extolled the exploits of the now-legendary Baltimore privateer Thomas Boyle, who commanded "an elegant and fast sailing private armed brig Chasseur." Boyle had returned from the British Isles, lurked for a while off Halifax and Bermuda, and captured "18 prizes, manned 9 of them, burnt 4, and made cartels for prisoners of the remainder, and has on board a cargo of indigo, &c. taken out of one of her prizes valued at $70,000 dollars."[1]

Thomas Boyle was an extraordinary privateer and one of the most successful of the war. However, as previously noted, privateering was a risky business, and more often than not, both investors and sailors did not fare too well, especially after Great Britain tightened its blockade of most major American ports. Nevertheless, the presence of successful privateers like Thomas Boyle served to tie down dozens of vessels that could have otherwise been used elsewhere during the war. Boyle and his fellow investors had sold his *Comet* at auction in New York, but Thomas Kemp had quickly outfitted this skilled sailor with the amazingly swift *Chasseur*, which was also known informally as the *Pride of Baltimore*. At about the time the British were burning the White House, Boyle's *Chasseur* was raiding in British home waters. On 27 August 1814 Boyle captured the *Marquis of Cornwallis*. This vessel was of no value, but Boyle decided to use it as a cartel for the exchange of prisoners and to carry an audacious message to the Crown. He boldly declared the coast of Great Britain to be in "a state of strict and rigorous blockade." He said he did this in response to similar declarations by Admiral Warren and Admiral Cochrane "commanding small forces on the coast of the United States." Mimicking British language and phrases used in their own declarations, Boyle ensured that his message was posted at Lloyd's Coffee House in London. Within weeks the merchants and underwriters of Glasgow, Scotland, petitioned the king to do something about "the number of American privateers with which our channels have been infested, the audacity with which they have approached our coasts, and the success with which their enterprise had been attended, have proved injurious to our commerce, humbling to our pride and discreditable to the directors of the naval power of the British nation, whose flag till of late waved over every sea and triumphed over every rival."[2]

On 27 February 1815, near Cape Antonio, Cuba, Boyle's *Chasseur* engaged the former scourge of the Chesapeake Bay, the HMS *St. Lawrence*. The *St. Lawrence* had been the privateer *Atlas* when it was captured by Cockburn's forces during his brief foray to the Outer Banks of North Carolina in July 1813. The HMS *St. Lawrence* was often at the center of the fighting in the Chesapeake and frequently tangled with Barney's flotilla. Now caught alone and with its foretopmast damaged, the equally armed *St. Lawrence* had no choice but to fight it out with the *Chasseur*. It was a highly violent engagement. Like two bantam-weight boxers, the vessels circled each other. Boyle closed within ten yards, and the vessels traded broadsides. He noted that "blood [ran] freely from her scuppers." Boyle ordered his men to board the *St. Lawrence*, and as they jumped on board, the British commander, Lieutenant James E. Gordon, surrendered. Boyle later declared the *St. Lawrence* "to be a perfect wreck" and, instead of making her a prize, sent the vessel into Havana as a prisoner cartel. Informed by another American privateer of the signing of the Treaty of Ghent, Boyle passed Cape Henry on St. Patrick's Day and triumphantly entered Baltimore Harbor eight days later.[3]

The Treaty of Ghent, announcing that peace had been declared between Great Britain and the United States, was signed on Christmas Eve 1814. It would be Valentine's Day before the news reached the Chesapeake and the national capital. By then the British had fought and lost another meaningless campaign, sent another major general (Pakenham) home in a coffin, but launched the political career of Major General Andrew Jackson, who would dominate the American scene for the following quarter century. In addition to giving the country Jackson, the war gave the tiny U.S. Navy new respect. Although American naval forces would not rise to world power status until late in the nineteenth century, the first national heroes of the young republic were decidedly naval in orientation. John Rodgers, Stephen Decatur, William Bainbridge, Oliver Hazard Perry, Thomas Macdonough, and David Porter became household names throughout the country.

The treaty was greeted with great celebration by everyone. The War of 1812 had been a war of choice for America. Although bullied by Great Britain for years prior, the United States had not been forced to go to war. In the end the status quo antebellum was largely restored. The Americans had finally won a modicum of respect as an independent nation. Canada was never again seriously threatened by its aggressive southern neighbor, and a gradual rapprochement was established among the United States, Canada, and Great Britain through the rest of the nineteenth century. This peace ultimately paid dividends for all three nations in the twentieth century. Occupied territory was exchanged, and the British even evacuated Tangier Island in March 1815. Never again would a British man-of-war prowl the waters inside the Virginia Capes. The states of Maryland and Virginia could finally relax.

NOTES

CHAPTER 1. PRELUDE TO WAR

1. Tom Holmberg, "The Acts, Orders in Council, &c. of Great Britain [on Trade], 1793–1812," The Napoleon Series, last modified April 2003, accessed 1 April 2013, http://www.napoleon-series.org.

2. James Stephen, *War in Disguise; or, The Frauds of the Neutral Flags* (London, 1806), 9–10; Holmberg, "Acts, Orders in Council."

3. James Madison, *Examination of the British Doctrine Which Subjects to Capture a Neutral Trade, Not Open in Time of Peace* (microfiche), W 19, card 2 of 3, p. 171, American Pamphlets Collection, Alfred M. Gray Marine Corps Research Center, Quantico, VA.

4. William Wirt to Judge Carr, 15 February 1815, in John Pendleton Kennedy, *Memoirs of the Life of William Wirt* (Philadelphia: Lea and Blanchard, 1849), 1:367.

5. Christopher Robinson, ed., *Reports of Cases Argued and Determined in the High Court of Admiralty: Commencing with the Judgments of the Right Hon. Sir William Scott, Michaelmas Term 1798* (London: A. Strahan, 1801), 2:369.

6. Holmberg, "Acts, Orders in Council."

7. Bradford Perkins, *Prologue to War: England and the United States, 1805–1812* (Berkeley: University of California Press, 1963), 21; Jerome Alley, *A Vindication of the Principles and Statements Advanced in the Strictures of the Right Honorable Lord Sheffield* (London, 1806), 89–90.

8. Thomas Jefferson to William Duane, 13 November 1810, in *The Writings of Thomas Jefferson*, ed. Andrew A. Lipscomb and Albert E. Bergh (Washington, DC, 1903–4), 12:434.

9. "Report of Secretary of State James Monroe, 6 July 1812," in *American State Papers: Foreign Relations*, ed. Walter Lowrie and Matthew St. Clair Clarke (Washington, DC: Gales & Seaton, 1832), 3:583–85.

10. Thomas Jefferson to James Maury, 16 June 1815, Series 1, General Correspondence, 1651–1827, Thomas Jefferson Papers, Library of Congress, Washington, DC.

11. Perkins, *Prologue to War*, 27.
12. John H. Reinoehl, ed., "Some Remarks on the American Trade: Jacob Crowin-shield to James Madison, 1806," *William and Mary Quarterly*, 3rd ser., 16, no. 1 (January 1959): 85–88; Eli F. Heckscher, *The Continental System: An Economic Interpretation* (London, 1922), 103, 146.
13. Reinoehl, "Some Remarks," 85–88; Heckscher, *Continental System*, 103, 146.
14. Reinoehl, "Some Remarks," 92–93.
15. Ibid., 93–94.
16. Ibid., 96.
17. Garry Wills, *James Madison* (New York: Times Books, 2002), 52.
18. Sir John Nicholl to the Board of Trade, 20 March 1806, 80/116, Greenwich Hospital Miscellanea, Public Record Office, London; Perkins, *Prologue to War*, 82–84; "Protest of Boston Merchants," *New-York Evening Post*, 7 February 1806.
19. Denver Brunsman, *The Evil Necessity: British Naval Impressment in the Eighteenth-Century Atlantic World* (Charlottesville: University of Virginia Press, 2013), 132.
20. Anthony Steel, "Anthony Merry and the Anglo-American Dispute about Impressment, 1803–6," *Cambridge Historical Journal* 9, no. 3 (1949): 339; 5/104, 1 November 1806, Foreign Office Papers, Public Record Office, London.
21. James Madison, *All Impressments Unlawful and Inadmissible* (Boston: William Pelham, [1806]), 3–12. Available at https://ia600400.us.archive.org/5/items /allimpressmentsu00madi/allimpressmentsu00madi.pdf.
22. Donald R. Hickey, *Don't Give Up the Ship! Myths of the War of 1812* (Urbana: University of Illinois Press, 2006), 20.
23. Ibid., 18–19; Michael Lewis, *A Social History of the Navy, 1793–1815* (London: George Allen & Unwin, 2006), 420.
24. Hickey, *Don't Give Up the Ship*, 19.
25. Ibid., 19.
26. Brunsman, *Evil Necessity*, 304n16. Brunsman noted that in 1812 the U.S. government claimed that 6,257 Americans had been impressed, but this figure did not include those pressed before 1803 and after 1810. Including those sailors impressed during the wars of the French Revolution, historian Don Hickey concluded that the total number of Americans impressed from 1793 to 1812 is approximately 10,000 men. See Hickey, *Don't Give Up the Ship*, 21.
27. James F. Zimmerman, *Impressment of American Seamen* (Port Washington, NY: Kennikat Press, 1925), 41.
28. Ibid., 40–42; "Baltimore, June 25," *Jersey Chronicle*, 4 July 1795; "Boston, August 7. Extract of a Letter from a Gentleman at Newport, to His Friend in This Town," *Jersey Chronicle*, 22 August 1795; "Baltimore, March 1," *Jersey Chronicle*, 12 March 1796.
29. David M. Erskine, quoted in Donald R. Hickey, "The Monroe-Pinckney Treaty of 1806: A Reappraisal," *William and Mary Quarterly*, 3rd ser., 44, no. 1 (January

1987): 65; David M. Erskine to Lord Howick, 6 March 1807, 5/52, Foreign Office Papers.

30. Hickey, "Monroe-Pinkney Treaty," 67; "Treaty with England," *Columbian Centinel*, 21 March 1807; "Alexandria, Friday Morning, January 31," *Alexandria Daily Gazette*, 31 January 1812.

31. Hickey, "Monroe-Pinkney Treaty," 84.

32. Berkeley and Gallatin, quoted in Spencer C. Tucker and Frank T. Reuter, *Injured Honor: The* Chesapeake-Leopard *Affair, June 22, 1807* (Annapolis: Naval Institute Press, 1996), 62.

33. Ibid., 71–72.

34. Ibid.

35. Ibid., 75–76; Robert Malcomson, "Unturned Stones in the War of 1812 Studies," *War of 1812 Magazine*, no. 4 (September 2006), http://www.napoleon-series.org /military/Warof1812/2006/Issue4/c_editoriala.html.

36. Mariners' Museum, "Admiral Berkeley's Orders to Search the *Chesapeake*," Birth of the U.S. Navy, accessed November 19, 2014, http://www.marinersmuseum .org/sites/micro/usnavy/index.html.

37. Tucker and Reuter, *Injured Honor*, 72–73.

38. Ibid., 113–14.

39. Ibid., 115–16.

40. Phineas Bond to Lord Mulgrave, 3 December 1805, No. 20, 5/46, Foreign Office Papers; Steel, "Anthony Merry," 348.

41. Hickey, *Don't Give Up the Ship*, 25–26.

42. George Canning to David Erskine, 23 January 1809, in Bernard Mayo, ed., *Instructions to the British Ministers to the United States, 1791–1812* (New York: Da Capo Press, 1971), 261–67.

43. Samuel Smith, speech to the U.S. Senate, 19 March 1810, 20 *Annals of Cong.* 608 (1810), http://memory.loc.gov/cgi-bin/ampage?collId=llac&fileName=020 /llac020.db&recNum=299; John Pancake, "The Invisibles: A Chapter in the Opposition to President Madison," *Journal of Southern History* 21, no. 1 (February 1955): 29–30.

44. Hickey, *Don't Give Up the Ship*, 31.

45. Ibid., 36.

CHAPTER 2. THE WAR BEGINS

1. James Madison, "War Message to Congress," 1 June 1812, PresidentialRhetoric .com, accessed 4 February 2013, http://www.presidentialrhetoric.com/historic speeches/madison/warmessage.html.

2. George Cruikshank, "A Sketch for the Regents Speech on Mad-Ass-Son's Insanity," LC-USZC4-5917, British Cartoon Prints Collection, Prints and Photographs Division, Library of Congress, Washington, DC; Troy Bickham,

The Weight of Vengeance: The United States, the British Empire, and the War of 1812 (New York: Oxford University Press, 2012), 69.

3. Bickham, *Weight of Vengeance*, 69–71.

4. Donald R. Hickey and Connie D. Clark, *The Rockets' Red Glare: An Illustrated History of the War of 1812* (Baltimore: Johns Hopkins University Press, 2011), 27–28; John Randolph, 16 December 1811, 23 *Annals of Cong.* 533 (1811), http://memory.loc.gov/cgi-bin/ampage?collId=llac&fileName=023/llac023 .db&recNum=263; Noble E. Cunningham Jr., "Who Were the Quids?" *Mississippi Valley Historical Review* 50, no. 2 (September 1963): 252–63.

5. Henry Clay to Thomas Bodley, 18 December 1813, in Henry Clay, *The Papers of Henry Clay*, ed. James F. Hopkins and Mary W. M. Hargreaves (Lexington: University of Kentucky Press, 1959–92), 1:842.

6. *The War* (New York), 25 July 1812.

7. Sandy Antal, *A Wampum Denied: Procter's War of 1812* (Ottawa, ON: Carleton University Press, 1998).

8. James Madison, "Second Inaugural Address," 4 March 1813, Bartleby.com, accessed 8 May 2014, http://www.bartleby.com/124/pres19.html.

9. Bickham, *Weight of Vengeance*, 114–17.

10. "A Letter from Thomas Jefferson in the Early Weeks of the War of 1812," *War of 1812 Magazine*, no. 13 (June 2010), http://www.napoleon-series.org/military /Warof1812/2010/Issue13/c_Jefferson.html. Jefferson's letter referred to an earlier incendiary known as Jack the Painter. He envisioned releasing similar firebrands on the still largely wooden city of London in 1812 if the British torched Boston or New York.

11. Robert J. Brugger, *Maryland: A Middle Temperament, 1634–1980* (Baltimore: Johns Hopkins University Press, 1988), 176.

12. Richard Chew, "The Origins of Mob Town: Social Division and Racial Conflict in the Baltimore Riots of 1812," special edition, *Maryland Historical Magazine* 107 (2012): 7–35; "Hanson, Alexander Contee (1786–1819)," *Biographical Directory of the United States Congress*, accessed November 21, 2014, http://bio guide.congress.gov/scripts/biodisplay.pl?index=H000176%20P.

13. Alexander Hanson, Editorial, *Federal Republican* (Baltimore), 20 June 1812.

14. Paul A. Gilje, "The Baltimore Riots of 1812 and the Breakdown of the Anglo-American Mob Tradition," *Journal of Social History* 13, no. 4 (Summer 1980): 547–64.

15. Brugger, *Maryland*, 178; Bickham, *Weight of Vengeance*, 187.

16. Chew, "Origins of Mob Town," 18.

17. James McHenry to Robert Oliver, 24 June 1812, quoted in L. Marx Renzulli Jr., *Maryland: The Federalist Years* (Cranbury, NJ: Fairleigh Dickinson University Press, 1972), 265. Robert Oliver was likely a fellow Federalist since he owned the building that Hanson leased for his *Federal Republican* newspaper.

18. "The Unanimous Address of All the Federalists Who Met at the Late Session of the Legislature, to Their Constituents," *Maryland Gazette* (Annapolis), 2 July 1812; Renzulli, *Maryland*, 266–67; Gilje, "Baltimore Riots of 1812," 551.

19. John Lynn to Alexander C. Hanson, 20 July 1812, *Portrait of the Evils of Democracy* (pamphlet), 1816, War of 1812 Collection, Maryland Historical Society, Baltimore; "Cumberland, July 19th, 1812," *Poulson's American Daily Advertiser* (Philadelphia), August 13, 1812.

20. Gilje, "Baltimore Riots of 1812," 553–54.

21. Maryland General Assembly House of Delegates Committee on Grievances and Courts of Justice, *Report of the Committee of Grievances and Courts of Justice of the House of Delegates of Maryland: On the Subject of the Recent Mobs and Riots in the City of Baltimore, Together with the Depositions Taken before the Committee* (Annapolis: Jonas Green, 1813), 170, 48, 90; Gilje, "Baltimore Riots of 1812," 555.

22. John Thomson, *An Exact and Authentic Narrative, of the Events Which Took Place in Baltimore, on the 27th and 28th of July Last* (n.p.: Printed for the purchasers, 1812), http://archive.org/details/exactauthenticna01thom.

23. Otho Sprigg, deposition in ibid., 53.

24. John Thomson, deposition in ibid., 44; "Narrative of John Thomson," *Maryland Gazette*, 20 August 1812.

25. Thomson deposition, 46.

26. "Narrative of John Hall," *Maryland Gazette*, 3 September 1812.

27. Ibid.; Renzulli, *Maryland*, 278–79.

28. Gilje, "Baltimore Riots of 1812," 556–57.

29. Chew, "Origins of Mob Town," 27.

30. George C. Daughan, *1812: The Navy's War* (New York: Basic Books, 2011), 147–48.

31. Ibid., 123; Sir John Borlase Warren to Secretary of the Admiralty John W. Croker, 5 October 1812, in William S. Dudley, ed., *The Naval War of 1812: A Documentary History* (Washington DC: Naval Historical Center, 1985), 1:508–9.

32. Lord Dundas Melville to Sir John Borlase Warren, 26 March 1813, in Dudley, *Naval War of 1812*, 2:78–79. Melville underlined the word *paper* in his letter to make sure that Warren realized that the Admiralty wished for him to park actual ships off all American ports and trade routes. In the past the British had occasionally resorted to declaring a "paper blockade" owing to a lack of actual ships with which to enforce it. Even in 1812 paper blockades had dubious standing in international maritime law.

33. First Secretary of the Admiralty John W. Croker to Admiral Sir John B. Warren, 20 March 1813, in ibid., 2:75–76.

CHAPTER 3. THE BRITISH ARRIVE—1813

1. Robert Malcomson, "The Battle for Little York, 1813," *Military History Quarterly*, Autumn 2008, 42–43, 47–48. One reason the Americans gave for attacking York was a rumor that the British were building two brigs in York's nearby shipyard. As

it turned out, American intelligence was incorrect. There were no partially built brigs there, only the thirty-two-gun frigate HMS *Sir Isaac Brock*. The British were forced to burn the *Brock* as they retreated from the town. However, the Americans did capture an antiquated armed schooner, HMS *Duke of Gloucester*.

2. J. Dennis Robinson, *America's Privateer: Privateer* Lynx *and the War of 1812* (Newport Beach, CA: Lynx Educational Foundation, 2011), 61.

3. Geoffrey M. Footner, *Tidewater Triumph: The Development and Worldwide Success of the Chesapeake Bay Schooner* (Centerville, MD: Tidewater Publishing, 1998), 102.

4. Robinson, *America's Privateer*, 63. For greater detail on Baltimore clipper design and development, see Howard Irving Chapelle's *Search for Speed under Sail* (New York: W. W. Norton, 1967), as well his landmark book titled *The Baltimore Clipper: Its Origin and Development* (New York: Dover Publications, 2012), 81–82.

5. George Coggeshall, *History of the American Privateers and Letters-of-Marque, during Our War with England in the Years 1812, '13, and '14* (New York, 1856), 6.

6. Footner, *Tidewater Triumph*, 121.

7. Stephen Budiansky, *Perilous Fight: America's Intrepid War with Britain on the High Seas, 1812–1815* (New York: A. A. Knopf, 2010), 289.

8. Ibid., 288.

9. Ibid., 289, 290

10. Ibid., 289.

11. Fred W. Hopkins Jr., *Tom Boyle: Master Privateer* (Mattituck, NY: Amereon House, 1976), 2, 5, 9–11, 17.

12. Ibid., 17.

13. Ibid., 20–23, 25.

14. Jerome R. Garitee, *The Republic's Private Navy: The American Privateering Business as Practiced by Baltimore during the War of 1812* (Middletown, CT: Wesleyan University Press, 1977), 34–35.

15. Hopkins, *Tom Boyle*, 17–18.

16. Robinson, *America's Privateer*, 85.

17. John Armstrong, quoted in Christopher T. George, *Terror on the Chesapeake: The War of 1812 on the Bay* (Shippensburg, PA: White Mane Books, 2000), 1.

18. "Blockade of the Chesapeake," *The War*, 16 February 1813.

19. Jon Latimer, *1812: War with America* (Cambridge, MA: Belknap Press of the Harvard University Press, 2007), 155–56; William B. Crane and John P. Cranwell, *Men of Marque: A History of Private Armed Vessels out of Baltimore during the War of 1812* (New York: W. W. Norton, 1940), 182–83, 185–86.

20. Crane and Cranwell, *Men of Marque*, 82–83.

21. Robinson, *America's Privateer*, 87.

22. Ibid., 88–90.

23. Glenn F. Williams, *USS* Constellation: *A Short History of the Last All-Sail Warship Built by the United States Navy* (Virginia Beach, VA: Donning, 2000), 7.

24. Many postwar sources have wrongly indicated that the Independent Foreigners were called "Canadian Chasseurs" or "Chasseurs Britanique." Some of this confusion was caused by Sir Sidney Beckwith himself, who called these men "Canadian Chasseurs" in a dispatch printed in the *Times* (London), 16 August 1813. Later historians believed that since they were French, they must have been French Canadian in origin. All such appellations are incorrect. These men were actually recruited during Wellington's Iberian Peninsula campaign from the large number of French army deserters or prisoners who fell into British hands in 1812. It is not surprising that many deserted at their first opportunity. It also was apparent that wherever they went (Bermuda, Hampton, or Halifax), they caused trouble, as we will see in chapter 4.

25. Master Commandant Charles Gordon to Secretary of the Navy William Jones, 16 February and 13 March 1813, in Dudley, *Naval War of 1812*, 2:331–32; Secretary of the Navy Jones to Captain Charles Gordon, 15 April 1813, in ibid., 348–52.

26. William L. Calderhead, "Naval Innovation in Crisis: War in the Chesapeake, 1813," *American Neptune: A Quarterly Journal of Maritime History* 36 (July 1976): 211.

27. Ibid., 212–13.

28. Frank A. Cassell, "Baltimore in 1813: A Study of Urban Defense in the War of 1812," *Military Affairs* 33 (December 1969): 351–58. These men were maritime workers and commercial sailors. Although they had the word *marine* in their title, they should not be confused with U.S. Marines.

29. Hollingsworth to Tobin, 18 May 1813, MS 1849, Lydia Hollingsworth Letters, Maryland Historical Society, Baltimore; Barbara Weeks, "This Present Time of Alarm," *Maryland Historical Magazine* 84 (Fall 1989): 260.

30. Weeks, "This Present Time of Alarm," 260–261; David Hoffman to Virgil Maxey, 17 April 1813, MS 1846, War of 1812 Collection.

31. George, *Terror on the Chesapeake*, 27; Donald G. Shomette, *Lost Towns of Tidewater Maryland* (Centreville, MD: Tidewater Publishers, 2000), 254–57; "Admiralty-Office, July 10, 1813: Copy of a Letter from Admiral Sir John Borlase Warren, Bart, and K. B. &c. to John Wilson Croker, Esq. dated at Bermuda, the 28th May, 1813," *London Gazette*, 6 July 1813. Several schooners the British used in the Frenchtown raid, such as the *Dolphin* and *Racer*, had been captured during the 3 April 1813 Rappahannock River raid. Once again, the captured *Highflyer* played a central role.

32. Frederick Chamier, quoted in Latimer, *1812*, 159. In 1833 Chamier published a book, *Life of a Sailor*, in which he accused Cockburn of "human rights abuses" during the 1813–14 Chesapeake campaigns. His version of events was strongly disputed, most notably by Cockburn's aide-de-camp James Scott, who challenged Chamier to a "hostile meeting" over the matter. The duel never occurred. See ibid., 474.

33. Charles Napier, *Life and Opinions of General Sir Charles Napier*, ed. by W. F. P. Napier, 2nd ed. (London: J. Murray, 1857), 1:225; Frederick Chamier, *The Life of a Sailor by a Captain in the Navy* (New York: J. & J. Harper, 1833), 1:201. Also see George, *Terror on the Chesapeake*, 29.

34. Chamier, *Life of a Sailor*, 1:201.

35. "The Conflagration of Havre de Grace," *North-American Review and Miscellaneous Journal* 5 (July 1817): 159. A famous contemporary cartoon shows the British looting the town of Havre de Grace. Centrally featured and apparently directing the activity is a British officer with his arm in a sling. This officer is likely Cockburn's favorite naval commando, First Lieutenant George Westphal, whom Cockburn describes in his report to Warren as having been shot through the hand.

36. Blaine Taylor, "May 3, 1813: Cockburn vs. O'Neill at Havre de Grace Britain's Sea-Going Commando Burns the Harbor of Mercy," *Harford Historical Bulletin*, no. 43 (Winter 1990): 9–17; James Jones Wilmer, *Narrative Respecting the Conduct of the British* (Baltimore: P. Mauro, 1813), 5–6, 16.

37. Brigadier General Henry Miller to Sir J. B. Warren, 8 May 1813, and Sir J. B. Warren to Henry Miller, 10 May 1813, *The Sun* (Dover, NH), 22 May 1813.

38. George, *Terror on the Chesapeake*, 34.

39. "Letter of Rear Admiral George Cockburn to Admiral John B. Warren, 3 May 1813," *London Gazette*, 6 July 1813.

40. Shomette, *Lost Towns of Tidewater Maryland*, 278–80. Colonel T. W. Veazey became governor of Maryland in the 1830s.

41. J. Thomas Scharf, *History of Maryland: From the Earliest Period to the Present Day* (Baltimore: J. B. Piet, 1879), 3:44; Shomette, *Lost Towns of Tidewater Maryland*, 285–90; *The Reporter* (Lexington, KY), 26 June 1813.

42. George Douglas to Henry Wheaton, 24 August 1813, in John Gordon Freymann, "A View of the War and the World from Baltimore, 1813–1815," *Maryland Historical Magazine* 107 (Winter 2012): 487.

43. J. Mackay Hitsman and Alice Sorby, "Independent Foreigners or Canadian Chasseurs," *Military Affairs* 25 (Spring 1961): 12–14.

44. R. Maurice Hill, "A Short History of the New South Wales Corps, 1789–1818," *Journal of the Society for Army Historical Research* 13, no. 51 (Autumn 1934): 136–40; Robert Marrion and Reginald L. Campbell, "The 102nd Regiment of Foot, 1814," *Military Collector and Historian* 33, no. 2 (Summer 1981): 74–75.

CHAPTER 4. THE CAMPAIGN TO TAKE NORFOLK

1. Napier, *Life and Opinions*, 1:211.

2. John M. Hallahan, *The Battle of Craney Island* (Portsmouth, VA: St. Michael's Press, 1986), 39.

3. Amy W. Yarsinke, *The Elizabeth River* (Charleston, SC: History Press, 2007), 132; Rene Chartrand, *Forts of the War of 1812* (Oxford: Osprey Publishing, 2012), 21–22.

4. George, *Terror on the Chesapeake*, 7.

5. Robert Taylor, quoted in Hallahan, *Battle of Craney Island*, 46; Charles Stewart to Secretary of the Navy William Jones, 17 March 1813, in Dudley, *Naval War of 1812*, 2:315.

6. Charles Stewart to William Jones, 22 March 1813, in Dudley, *Naval War of 1812*, 2:317.

7. Orderly Sergeant James Jarvis, quoted in Parker Rouse Jr., "Low Tide at Hampton Roads," *U.S. Naval Institute Proceedings* 95 (July 1969): 80.

8. Brigadier General Robert B. Taylor to the Governor of Virginia, 21 March 1813, in *Calendar of Virginia State Papers*, ed. W. P. Palmer, Sherwin McRae, and H. W. Flournoy (Richmond, VA, 1892), 10:331–32.

9. Yarsinke, *Elizabeth River*, 156.

10. Williams, *USS* Constellation, 7; Sergeant James Jarvis, quoted in Latimer, *1812*, 171; Yarsinke, *Elizabeth River*, 155–56.

11. Yarsinke, *Elizabeth River*, 155.

12. "From Our Correspondent, Norfolk, June 22," *Eastern Shore General Advertiser* (Easton, MD), 29 June 1813; John Cassin to the Secretary of the Navy, "Operations of the Blockading Squadron," 21 June 1813, in *The Historical Register of the United States: Part II, From the Declaration of War in 1812, to January 1, 1814*, ed. Thomas H. Palmer, 2nd ed. (Philadelphia: G. Palmer, 1814), 2:257–58.

13. Cassin to the Secretary of the Navy.

14. Hallahan, *Battle of Craney Island*, 66; Benson J. Lossing, *The Pictorial Field Book of the War of 1812* (New York: Harper & Brothers, 1868), 678. We have Lossing to thank for many of the first-person accounts from the War of 1812. In the 1850s he traveled to wartime locations to interview many of the participants and their survivors. The "alert sentry" was named, according to Lossing, William Shutte. Lossing stated that Shutte was "stationed upon a small island that once lay near the mouth of Wise's Creek. Shutte made the usual challenge, and, receiving no answer, fired, and continued to fire until the camp was fully aroused."

15. Sergeant William Young, quoted in Rouse, "Low Tide at Hampton Roads," 81.

16. Rouse, "Low Tide at Hampton Roads," 68–70.

17. Ibid., 70–72.

18. Ibid., 73.

19. Captain John Cassin to Secretary of the Navy Jones, 23 June 1813, in Dudley, *Naval War of 1812*, 2:360; Latimer, *1812*, 171; "Copy of a Letter from Com. Cassin to the Secretary of the Navy, 23 June 1813," *Baltimore Patriot*, 30 June 1813.

20. "By This Evening's Mail," *Baltimore Patriot*, 30 June 1813.

21. Vice Admiral John Borlase Warren, quoted in Alistair J. Nichols, "Desperate Banditti? The Independent Companies of Foreigners, 1812–14," *Journal of the Society for Army Historical Research*, no. 79 (2001): 282–83.

22. Major Stapleton Crutchfield, letter, in Parker Rouse Jr., ed., "The British Invasion of Hampton in 1813: The Reminiscences of James Jarvis," *Virginia Magazine of History and Biography* 76, no. 3 (July 1968): 322.

23. George, *Terror on the Chesapeake*, 50; "Brought by Express to the Executive, This Morning at 1 O'clock," *Baltimore Patriot*, 28 June 1813.

24. Nichols, "Desperate Banditti?" 279–80, 283.

25. Hitsman and Sorby, "Independent Foreigners," 11–17.

26. "Enquirer Office, July 16," *Enquirer* (Richmond, VA), 16 July 1813; Rouse, "British Invasion of Hampton," 318–36. Parker italicized the noted uniform colors to indicate that some of the depredations had been committed by British soldiers vice, as was later claimed by Admiral Warren and Sir Sidney Beckwith, by the green-coated companies of Independent Foreigners.

27. Napier, *Life and Opinions*, 1:221–22; Rouse, "British Invasion of Hampton," 318–36; Hitsman and Sorby, "Independent Foreigners," 11–17.

28. "Extracts from the Communication of James Jarvis, Esq. to Leopold P. C. Cowper, 12 February 1849," doc. no. 75, in Virginia General Assembly, House of Delegates, *Report of the Select Committee . . . in Reference to the Defense of Craney Island . . . 22nd of June 1813* (Richmond, VA, 1848), 17–19.

29. *Norfolk Herald*, 24 July 1813.

30. *Baltimore Whig*, 25 July 1813.

31. George, *Terror on the Chesapeake*, 56; Wade G. Dudley, *Splintering the Wooden Wall: The British Blockade of the United States, 1812–1815* (Annapolis: Naval Institute Press, 2003), 97.

32. "From the Virginia Argus: Outrages at Hampton," *Green-Mountain Farmer* (Bennington, VT), 27 July 1813; *Boston Daily Advertiser*, 30 July 1813; "The Monsters!!" *Baltimore Patriot*, 19 July 1813; U.S. Navy Department, *Ships Data US Naval Vessels* (Washington, DC: Government Printing Office, 1929), 353.

33. National Park Service, "Fort Warburton," accessed 20 February 2011, http://www.nps.gov/fowa/historyculture/warburton.htm.

34. George, *Terror on the Chesapeake*, 58.

35. Donald G. Shomette, *Flotilla: The Patuxent Naval Campaign in the War of 1812*, rev. ed. (Baltimore: Johns Hopkins University Press, 2009), 14–18.

36. Commodore Joshua Barney to Secretary of the Navy William Jones, 4 July 1813, in Dudley, *Naval War of 1812*, 2:373–74.

37. Ibid., 376.

38. "To the Public," *Eastern Shore General Advertiser*, 14 September 1813. One of the problems that the Federalists had with Barney was that following the conclusion of the American Revolution, with the Continental navy no longer in existence, professional combat commanders like Barney sought work with foreign navies. Like John Paul Jones, Barney ultimately wound up serving in the French navy from 1794 to 1800 (a period that included the Quasi-War with France). Many

in the Federalist Party (Lemuel Taylor clearly being one) believed that Barney's French navy service, especially during the undeclared war with France, made him untrustworthy and unworthy of a new command in the reconstituted U.S. Navy.

39. Secretary of the Navy Jones to Acting Master Commandant Joshua Barney, 27 August 1813, in Dudley, *Naval War of 1812*, 2:377–78.
40. Acting Master Commandant Joshua Barney to Secretary of the Navy Jones, 31 August 1813, in Dudley, *Naval War of 1812*, 2:379.
41. "Extract of a Letter to a Gentleman in This City, Dated Centervile (within 14 Miles of Kent Island) Eastern Shore of Maryland, August 9, 1813," *Baltimore Patriot*, 16 August 1813; "Jacob Gibson," *Hagers-Town Gazette*, 11 May 1813.
42. Scharf, *History of Maryland*, 3:50–51.
43. Harry C. Rhodes, *Queenstown: The Social History of a Small American Town* (Queenstown, MD: Queen Anne Press, 1985), 68–71; Ralph E. Eshelman, Scott S. Sheads, and Donald R. Hickey, *The War of 1812 in the Chesapeake: A Reference Guide to Historic Sites in Maryland, Virginia and the District of Columbia* (Baltimore: Johns Hopkins University Press, 2010), 179–82.
44. Calderhead, "Naval Innovation in Crisis," 217–18. Another reason for the Balti-more leadership's failure to readily embrace the torpedo concept was the opposition of conservative but highly respected Commodore John Rodgers.
45. Ibid., 218; *Norfolk Herald*, 27 July 1813; *Niles' Weekly Register* (Baltimore), 7 August 1813.
46. William L. Calderhead, "A Strange Career in a Young Navy: Captain Charles Gordon, 1778–1816," *Maryland Historical Magazine* 72 (Fall 1977): 377–80.
47. Ibid., 380–84; William L. Calderhead, "U. S. F. Constellation in the War of 1812—An Accidental Fleet-in-Being," *Military Affairs* 40 (April 1976): 81–82. The unlucky Charles Gordon Jr. died of dysentery during a diplomatic mission to Algeria and was interred in the American cemetery at Messina, Sicily, on 6 September 1816. His body remains there in an unmarked grave to this day. The son of Maryland loyalist Charles Gordon Sr. of Cecil County, Maryland, Charles Jr. had been forced to live in poverty after the Revolution. His financial situation and perhaps a desire to atone for the unfortunate politics of his father may have caused young Gordon to seek a commission as a U.S. Navy midshipman in 1799 during the Quasi-War with France. Bad timing and worse luck seemed to plague young Gordon from the moment he set foot on the USS *Chesapeake* in 1807. Nevertheless, he served ably and credibly throughout his naval career.
48. Cassell, "Baltimore in 1813," 349–61; Calderhead, "Naval Innovation in Crisis," 211–14.

CHAPTER 5. THE BRITISH RETURN—1814

1. Roger Morris, *Cockburn and the British Navy in Transition* (Columbia: University of South Carolina Press, 1997), 97.

2. Vice Admiral Alexander Cochrane to Lord Dundas Melville, 17 July 1814, quoted in ibid., 97–98.

3. Secretary of the Navy William Jones to Acting Master Commandant Joshua Barney, 18 February 1814, in *The Naval War of 1812: A Documentary History*, ed. Michael J. Crawford (Washington, DC: Naval Historical Center, 2002), 3:33–34.

4. Acting Master Commandant Joshua Barney to Secretary of the Navy Jones, 1 March 1814, in ibid., 35.

5. Vice Admiral Sir Alexander Cochrane to Governor-General Sir George Prevost, 11 March 1814, in ibid., 38–40.

6. Cochrane Proclamation, 2 April 1814, Adm. 1/508, 587, Admiralty Archives, Public Record Office, London; Christopher T. George, "Mirage of Freedom: African Americans in the War of 1812," *Maryland Historical Magazine* 107 (Spring 2012): 43.

7. Lord Bathurst to Sir Sidney Beckwith, 20 March 1813, Thomas Brisbane Papers, 1813–1815, William L. Clements Library, University of Michigan, Ann Arbor; George, "Mirage of Freedom," 40.

8. Matthew Mason, "The Battle of the Slaveholding Liberators: Great Britain, the United States, and Slavery in the Early Nineteenth Century," *William and Mary Quarterly*, 3rd ser., 59, no. 3 (July 2002): 671–76; Gerald T. Altoff, *Amongst My Best Men: African-Americans and the War of 1812* (Put-in-Bay, OH: Perry Group, 1996), 125.

9. Alan Taylor, *The Internal Enemy: Slavery and War in Virginia, 1772–1832* (New York: W. W. Norton, 2013), 279–80.

10. Ibid., 279–84; Captain Robert Barrie to George Cockburn, 1 June 1814, in Crawford, *Naval War of 1812*, 3:111–14.

11. Captain Robert Barrie, RN, to Admiral Sir John B. Warren, 14 November 1813, Adm. 1/505, 131–133, Admiralty Archives.

12. Bartlet Shanklyn to Abraham B. Hooe, 21 May 1820, RG 76, entry 190, box 3, case 177 (Abraham B. Hooe), National Archives, College Park, MD; Taylor, *Internal Enemy*, 3–6.

13. Thomas Malcomson, "Freedom by Reaching the Wooden World," *Northern Mariner* 22, no. 4 (October 2012): 387, 390.

14. Rear Admiral George Cockburn to Vice Admiral Alexander Cochrane, 2 April 1814, in Crawford, *Naval War of 1812*, 3:43–45. By the end of April 1814, the British had not generated the number of colonial marine recruits that they had hoped for. Cockburn reported that only about a hundred total former slaves and their families had made it to the relative safety of Tangier Island. However, better results were produced once Cochrane emitted a proclamation that guaranteed runaway slaves safe haven. See Alexander Cochrane, *The Fighting Cochranes* (London: Quiller Press, 1983), 255.

15. Shomette, *Flotilla*, 57–59.

16. Joshua Barney to Secretary of the Navy William Jones, 11 May 1814, in Crawford, *Naval War of 1812*, 3:58–59.

17. Joshua Barney to Secretary of the Navy William Jones, 9 June 1814, in ibid., 84–85.

18. Joshua Barney to Secretary of the Navy William Jones, 16 June 1814, in ibid., 101–2.

19. Shomette, *Flotilla*, 105–10; Shomette, *Lost Towns of Tidewater Maryland*, 124–25.

20. Shomette, *Lost Towns of Tidewater Maryland*, 150–51.

21. Secretary of the Navy William Jones to Joshua Barney, 20 June 1814, in Crawford, *Naval War of 1812*, 3:107.

22. George, *Terror on the Chesapeake*, 76.

23. Ibid., 77.

24. Shomette, *Flotilla*, 154–55; Joshua Barney to Louis Barney, 27 June 1814, in Crawford, *Naval War of 1812*, 3:123–24.

25. Captain Samuel Miller to Commandant of the Marine Corps, Lieutenant Colonel Franklin Wharton, USMC, 27 June 1814, in *Daily National Intelligencer* (Washington, DC), 7 July 1814.

26. Shomette, *Flotilla*, 158.

27. Ibid., 158–59.

28. Thomas King to Benjamin King, 14 July 1814, quoted in ibid., 165.

CHAPTER 6. THE PATUXENT RIVER AND BLADENSBURG

1. W. A. Maguire, "Major General Robert Ross and the Burning of Washington," *Irish Sword: The Journal of the Military History Society of Ireland* 14, no. 55 (Winter 1980): 117–19.

2. "Secret Letter from Rear Admiral George Cockburn to Vice Admiral Alexander Cochrane, 17 July 1814," *Maryland Historical Magazine* 6, no. 1 (March 1911): 16–17.

3. Ibid., 17–18.

4. Ibid., 18–19.

5. Rear Admiral George Cockburn to Captain Robert Barrie, 16 July 1814, quoted in Morris, *Cockburn and the British Navy*, 99.

6. "Copy of a Letter from Vice Admiral Cochrane to Mr. Monroe," *Hallowell Gazette* (Hallowell, ME), 21 September 1814; "Copy of a Letter from Mr. Monroe to Sir Alexander Cochrane Vice Admiral &c.," *Washingtonian* (Windsor, VT), 10 October 1814; Lowrie and Clarke, *American State Papers*, 3:88–89. Various American newspapers debated whether Madison and Monroe were aware of Cochrane's intentions before or after the burning of Washington. Democratic newspapers argued that Madison received this information after Washington had been burned. Federalist newspapers point to the date of Cochrane's letter as

prima facie evidence that Madison had this information in hand before the burning of the national capital. The Windsor, Vermont, *Washingtonian* stated that the government was aware of Cochrane's threat before the burning of Washington but kept this information "a state secret until the enemy had left the Potomac."

7. "Copy of a Letter from Vice Admiral Cochrane"; "Copy of a Letter from Mr. Monroe"; Lowrie and Clarke, *American State Papers*, 3:88–89.

8. James J. Willes, Entries of 20, 23, 26 and 30 July 1814, "Diary of Lieutenant James J. Willes, Adjutant, 3rd Battalion Royal and Colonial Marines," Royal Marines Museum, Eastney, UK; "Extract of a Letter from Colonel Richard Parker to the Adjutant General, 24 July 1814," *Eastern Shore General Advertiser*, 9 August 1814.

9. Charles Ball, *Slavery in the United States: A Narrative of the Life and Adventures of Charles Ball, a Black Man* (New York: Negro Universities Press, 1969), 469.

10. Lord Bathurst to Colonel Sir Sidney Beckwith, 20 March 1813, Thomas Brisbane Papers; George, "Mirage of Freedom," 40.

11. Ball, *Slavery in the United States*, 471–73; George, "Mirage of Freedom," 41–42.

12. George, *Terror on the Chesapeake*, 80; Morris, *Cockburn and the British Navy*, 102.

13. "Kinsale, 8th August, 1814," *Daily National Intelligencer*, 13 August 1814.

14. George Robert Gleig, *The Campaigns of the British Army at Washington and New Orleans in the Years 1814–1815* (London: W. Clowes and Sons, 1836), 88–89.

15. "Official Report of Rear Admiral George Cockburn," quoted in Scharf, *History of Maryland*, 3:74.

16. Secretary of the Navy Jones to Master Commandant John O. Creighton, 22 August 1814, in Crawford, *Naval War of 1812*, 3:199–200.

17. Vice Admiral Sir Alexander F. I. Cochrane to Rear Admiral George Cockburn, 22 August 1814 and Rear Admiral George Cockburn to Vice Admiral Alexander F. I. Cochrane, 23 August 1814, in ibid., 197–98.

18. Robert S. Quimby, *The U.S. Army in the War of 1812: An Operational and Command Study* (East Lansing: Michigan State University Press, 1997), 2:663–65.

19. Private John P. Kennedy, quoted in Charles G. Muller, *The Darkest Day: 1814* (Philadelphia: J. B. Lippincott, 1963), 104, 107.

20. George, *Terror on the Chesapeake*, 91.

21. Lossing, *Pictorial Field Book*, 2:923.

22. Walter Lord, *The Dawn's Early Light* (New York: W. W. Norton, 1972), 93–98.

23. Ibid., 102–5.

24. Lt. George Robert Gleig, quoted in Glenn F. Williams, "The Bladensburg Races," *Military History Quarterly* 12, no. 1 (1999): 64.

25. Pvt. Henry Fulford, quoted in Shomette, *Flotilla*, 315.

26. Lord, *Dawn's Early Light*, 130.

27. Shomette, *Flotilla*, 322–23.

28. Letter of Captain Samuel Bacon, 16 September 1814, in John Ockerbloom, "The Discovery of a U.S. Marine Officer's Account of Life, Honor, and the

Battle of Bladensburg, Washington and Maryland, 1814," *Military Collector and Historian* 61, no. 4 (Winter 2009): 260; Capt. Alfred Grayson to Lt. Col. Franklin Wharton, 28 August 1814, in ibid., 261. After the war Bacon resigned his commission, studied law, became an ordained Episcopal minister, and played an active role in the American Colonization Society. He was commissioned by the Monroe administration to escort eighty-five freed slaves to the west coast of Africa. Bacon and company had established a base in what became known as Monrovia, Liberia, when a fever swept through his camp. He was among the first victims of the disease and died on 2 May 1820.

29. Gordon S. Brown, *The Captain Who Burned His Ships: Captain Thomas Tingey, USN, 1750–1829* (Annapolis: Naval Institute Press, 2011), 127–28.
30. Mordecai Booth to Thomas Tingey, 22 August 1814, in Crawford, *Naval War of 1812*, 3:202, 205.
31. C. B. Judge, "Navy Powder Goes on a Journey: An Episode of the War of 1812," *U.S. Naval Institute Proceedings* 69 (September 1943): 1223–28.
32. Mordecai Booth to Thomas Tingey, 22 August 1814, in Crawford, *Naval War of 1812*, 3:202, 205.
33. Mordecai Booth to Thomas Tingey, 24 August 1814, in ibid., 212–13.
34. Brown, *Captain Who Burned His Ships*, 132–34.
35. Charles G. Muller, "Fabulous Potomac Passage," *U.S. Naval Institute Proceedings* 90 (May 1964): 85–88. Many historians believe that the biography of Captain James Gordon was used by contemporary novelist Patrick O'Brien for his main character, Captain Jack Aubrey, in his multivolume series on the Royal Navy during the Napoleonic era.
36. Ibid., 85–88; *Baltimore Patriot*, 19 November 1814.
37. Muller, "Fabulous Potomac Passage," 85–88.
38. Captain David Porter to Secretary of the Navy William Jones, 7 September 1814, in Crawford, *Naval War of 1812*, 3:255.
39. Bertram H. Groene, "A Trap for the British: Thomas Brown and the Battle of the 'White House,'" *Virginia Cavalcade* 18, no. 1 (1968): 13–19. After the war Brown was elected to two terms in the Virginia House of Delegates for Fauquier County. In 1827 Brown moved to Florida (near Tallahassee) and was governor of the state from 1849 to 1853.
40. Secretary of War John Armstrong to the editors of the *Baltimore Patriot, The Sun*, 17 September 1814.
41. Caleb Clarke Magruder Jr., "Dr William Beanes, the Incidental Cause of the Authorship of the Star-Spangled Banner," *Records of the Columbia Historical Society* 22 (1919): 217–18; Eugene H. Conner, "Notes and Events: William Beanes, M.D. (1749–1829) and the Star-Spangled Banner," *Journal of the History of Medicine and Allied Sciences* 34, no. 2 (1979): 224–29.

CHAPTER 7. THE BATTLE FOR BALTIMORE

1. Richard Walsh, "The Star Fort: 1814," *Maryland Historical Magazine* 54 (September 1959): 298–99.
2. Joseph Swift to Lloyd Beall, 27 March 1813, RG 77, Records of the War Department, National Archives, Washington, DC; Scott Sheads, "Defending Baltimore in the War of 1812: Two Sidelights," *Maryland Historical Magazine* 84 (Fall 1989): 252.
3. Samuel Smith to John Armstrong, 21 April 1813, Samuel Smith Papers, Library of Congress, Washington, DC; Sheads, "Defending Baltimore," 254; Scott Sheads, *The Rocket's Red Glare: The Maritime Defense of Baltimore in 1814* (Centreville, MD: Tidewater Publishers, 1986), 14–18.
4. Samuel Smith, quoted in Sheads, *Rocket's Red Glare*, 20.
5. Benjamin Hyde, quoted in ibid., 26–30.
6. Walsh, "Star Fort," 299–300.
7. Decius Wadsworth to Secretary of War John Armstrong, 18 March 1813, Samuel Smith Papers; Sheads, "Defending Baltimore," 253.
8. Walsh, "Star Fort," 300, 305.
9. Franklin R. Mullaly, "The Battle of Baltimore," *Maryland Historical Magazine* 54 (March 1959): 65–66.
10. George Douglas to Henry Wheaton, 29 August 1814, in Freymann, "View of the War," 502. The marine corps Douglas refers to is likely the Baltimore Sea Fencibles, not the U.S. Marine Corps, since he mentions they were under the command of Captain Stiles, a renowned local militia leader.
11. S. Sydney Bradford, "Fort McHenry: 1814: The Outworks in 1814," *Maryland Historical Magazine* 54 (June 1959): 207–8; Scott Sheads, "Baltimore's Riverside Park during the War of 1812," My Locust Point, accessed 11 April 2014, http://mylocustpoint.wordpress.com/history/history-notes/baltimores-riverside-park-during-the-war-of-1812/.
12. Sheads, "Defending Baltimore," 256–57.
13. Mullaly, "Battle of Baltimore," 70.
14. Lord, *Dawn's Early Light*, 235; Mullaly, "Battle of Baltimore," 70–71.
15. Meredith Eliassen, "A Soldier's Dilemma: Francis R. Shunk's Account for the Battle for Baltimore, 1814," *Maryland Historian* 31, no. 2 (Fall 2007): 72–75, 78. Shunk was later elected governor of Pennsylvania—a long climb from a militia private during the War of 1812.
16. Quimby, *U.S. Army in the War*, 2:715.
17. Mullaly, "Battle of Baltimore," 71–73.
18. Nelson Mott Bolton and Christopher T. George, "Captain Henry Thompson's First Baltimore Horse Artillery in the Defense of Baltimore in the War of 1812," *Maryland Historical Magazine* 108 (Winter 2013): 431–32.
19. Mullaly, "Battle of Baltimore," 85.

20. Ibid., 87.
21. Robert Henry Goldsborough to Henrietta Maria Nicols Goldsborough [?], 21 September 1814, *Maryland Historical Magazine* 107 (Spring 2012): 120–21.
22. Ibid., 121.
23. Christopher T. George, "Militia Redeemed before Baltimore," *Military History* 22, no. 6 (September 2005): 42–43.
24. Mullaly, "Battle of Baltimore," 90–91; Joseph A. Whitehorne, *Battle for Baltimore 1814* (Baltimore: Nautical & Aviation, 1997), 183.
25. Whitehorne, *Battle for Baltimore 1814*, 184; Scott Sheads, "H. M. Bomb Ship *Terror* and the Bombardment of Fort McHenry," *Maryland Historical Magazine* 103 (Fall 2008): 259.
26. Sheads, "H. M. Bomb Ship *Terror*," 258–59; Vice Admiral Cochrane to Rear Admiral Cockburn, 13 September 1814, quoted in ibid., 262.
27. Christopher T. George, "The Family Papers of Major General Robert Ross, the Diary of Colonel Arthur Brooke, and the British Attacks on Washington and Baltimore of 1814," *Maryland Historical Magazine* 88 (Fall 1993): 311.
28. Sheads, "H. M. Bomb Ship *Terror*," 259–60; Christopher T. George, "Sunk to Save Baltimore: Compensating the Owners of Ships Sunk in Baltimore Harbor during the War of 1812," *Journal of the War of 1812* 14 (Summer 2011): 13–14. The sunken vessels were all removed by 1815. Some, such as those owned by Smith, were raised earlier than the others. The owners tried for decades to get appropriate compensation from Congress for their particular contribution to the defense of Baltimore. See George, "Sunk to Save Baltimore," 16–21. Although some drawings and artist's renditions show the Ferry Branch also being blocked with sunken vessels, War of 1812 historians generally agree that this activity was not completed until after the British had departed the area for good.
29. Sheads, "H. M. Bomb Ship *Terror*," 262.
30. Whitehorne, *Battle for Baltimore 1814*, 187–88; George, "Militia Redeemed before Baltimore," 44.
31. Scott Sheads, "A Black Soldier Defends Fort McHenry, 1814," *Military Collector and Historian* 41, no. 1 (Spring 1989): 20–21.
32. Sailing Master John A. Webster, quoted in George, *Terror on the Chesapeake*, 152; Captain James Piper to Brantz Mayer, Esq., 20 April 1854, *Maryland Historical Magazine* 107 (Spring 2012): 108.
33. Major George Armistead to Acting Secretary of War James Monroe, 24 September 1814, *Niles' Weekly Register*, 1 October 1814; Sheads, "H. M. Bomb Ship *Terror*," 258–62.

EPILOGUE

1. "New York, Oct. 31, A Brilliant Cruize," *Republican Star* (Easton, MD), 8 November 1814.
2. Hopkins, *Tom Boyle*, 42–47.
3. Ibid., 52–53.

BIBLIOGRAPHY

DIARIES AND PERSONAL ACCOUNTS

Ball, Charles. *Slavery in the United States: A Narrative of the Life and Adventures of Charles Ball, a Black Man.* New York: Negro Universities Press, 1969.

Chamier, Frederick. *The Life of a Sailor by a Captain in the Navy.* 2 vols. New York: J. & J. Harper, 1833.

Gleig, George Robert. *The Campaigns of the British Army at Washington and New Orleans in the Years 1814–1815.* London: W. Clowes and Sons, 1836.

———. *A Narrative of the Campaigns of the British Army at Washington and New Orleans under Generals Ross, Pakenham, and Lambert, in the Years 1814 and 1815, with Some Account of the Countries Visited.* London: J. Murray, 1821.

James, William. *A Full and Correct Account of the Military Occurrence of the Late War between Great Britain and the United States of America.* vols. 1–2. London: Black, Kingsbury, Parbury & Allen, 1818.

Napier, Charles. *Life and Opinions of General Sir Charles Napier.* Edited by W. F. P. Napier. 2nd ed. 4 vols. London: J. Murray, 1857.

Thomson, John. *An Exact and Authentic Narrative, of the Events Which Took Place in Baltimore, on the 27th and 28th of July Last.* N.p.: Printed for the purchasers, 1812. http://archive.org/details/exactauthenticna01thom.

Willes, James J. "Diary of Lieutenant James J. Willes, Adjutant, 3rd Battalion Royal and Colonial Marines." Royal Marines Museum, Eastney, UK.

Wilmer, James Jones. *Narrative Respecting the Conduct of the British.* Baltimore: P. Mauro, 1813.

NEWPAPERS

Alexandria Daily Gazette
American and Commercial Daily Advertiser (Baltimore)
American Farmer (Baltimore)
Baltimore Commercial and Daily Advertiser

Baltimore Patriot
Baltimore Whig
Boston Daily Advertiser
Boston Gazette
Columbian Centinel (Boston, MA)
Daily National Intelligencer (Washington, DC)
Eastern Shore General Advertiser (Easton, MD)
Enquirer (Richmond, VA)
Federal Republican (Baltimore)
Green-Mountain Farmer (Bennington, VT)
Hagers-Town Gazette
Hallowell Gazette (Hallowell, ME)
Independent Chronicle (Boston, MA)
Jersey Chronicle
London Gazette
London Times
Maryland Gazette (Annapolis)
New-York Evening Post
Niles' Weekly Register (Baltimore)
Norfolk Herald
Nova Scotia Royal Gazette
Poulson's American Daily Advertiser (Philadelphia)
The Reporter (Lexington, KY)
Republican Star (Easton, MD)
The Sun (Dover, NH)
The War (New York)
Washingtonian (Windsor, VT)

PAPERS, ARCHIVES, AND OTHER PRIMARY SOURCES

Admiralty Archives. Public Record Office, London.
Alley, Jerome. *A Vindication of the Principles and Statements Advanced in the Strictures of the Right Honorable Lord Sheffield*. London, 1806.
American Pamphlets Collection. Alfred M. Gray Marine Corps Research Center, Quantico, VA.
Annals of Congress: Debates and Proceedings in the Congress of the United States, 1789–1824. 42 vols. Washington, DC: Gales & Seaton, 1834–56. http://memory.loc.gov/ammem/amlaw/lwaclink.html.
Barney, Joshua. Papers. Dreer Collection. Pennsylvania Historical Society, Philadelphia.
Brisbane, Thomas. Papers, 1813–1815. William L. Clements Library, University of Michigan, Ann Arbor.

Browne, William Hand, ed. Maryland State Archives. Vols. 21, 22, 26, and 39. Baltimore: Maryland Historical Society.

Clay, Henry. *The Papers of Henry Clay*. Edited by James F. Hopkins and Mary W. M. Hargreaves. 11 vols. Lexington: University of Kentucky Press, 1959–92.

Cockburn, George. Papers, 1788–1847. Library of Congress, Washington, DC.

Codrington, Edward. Papers. National Maritime Museum, Greenwich, UK.

Crawford, Michael J., ed. *The Naval War of 1812: A Documentary History*. Vol. 3. Washington, DC: Naval Historical Center, 2002.

Cruikshank, George. "A Sketch for the Regents Speech on Mad-Ass-Son's Insanity." LC-USZC4-5917, British Cartoon Prints Collection, Prints and Photographs Division, Library of Congress, Washington, DC.

Dudley, William S., ed. *The Naval War of 1812: A Documentary History*. Vols. 1–2. Washington, DC: Naval Historical Center, 1985–92.

Foreign Office Papers. Public Record Office, London.

Greenwich Hospital Miscellanea. Public Record Office, London.

Hamilton, Stanislaus M., ed. *The Writings of James Monroe*. Vol. 5. New York: G. P. Putnam's Sons, 1901.

Hollingsworth, Lydia. Letters. Maryland Historical Society, Baltimore.

House of Delegates Committee on Grievances and Courts of Justice. *Report of the Committee of Grievances and Courts of Justice of the House of Delegates of Maryland: On the Subject of the Recent Mobs and Riots in the City of Baltimore, Together with the Depositions Taken Before the Committee*. Annapolis: Jonas Green, 1813.

Jefferson, Thomas. Papers. Library of Congress, Washington, DC.

———. *The Writings of Thomas Jefferson*. Edited by Andrew A. Lipscomb and Albert E. Bergh. Vol. 12. Washington, DC, 1903–4.

Lowrie, Walter, and Matthew St. Clair Clarke, eds. *American State Papers: Foreign Relations*. Vol. 3. Washington, DC: Gales & Seaton, 1832.

Madison, James. *All Impressments Unlawful and Inadmissible*. Boston: W. Pelham, [1806]. https://ia600400.us.archive.org/5/items/allimpressmentsu00madi/allimpressmentsu00madi.pdf.

———. Papers. Library of Congress, Washington, DC.

Mariners' Museum. "Admiral Berkeley's Orders to Search the *Chesapeake*." Birth of the U.S. Navy. Accessed November 19, 2014. http://www.marinersmuseum.org/sites/micro/usnavy/index.html.

Maryland General Assembly House of Delegates Committee on Grievances and Courts of Justice. *Report of the Committee of Grievances and Courts of Justice of the House of Delegates of Maryland: On the Subject of the Recent Mobs and Riots in the City of Baltimore, Together with the Depositions Taken before the Committee*. Annapolis: Jonas Green, 1813.

Mayo, Bernard, ed. *Instructions to the British Ministers to the United States, 1791–1812*. New York: Da Capo Press, 1971.

National Archives, College Park, MD.

Palmer, Thomas H., ed. *The Historical Register of the United States: Part II, From the Declaration of War in 1812, to January 1, 1814.* 2nd ed. Vol. 2. Philadelphia: G. Palmer, 1814.

Palmer, W. P., Sherwin McRae, and H. W. Flournoy, eds. *Calendar of Virginia State Papers.* 11 vols. Richmond, VA, 1892.

Records of the War Department. National Archives, Washington, DC.

Robinson, Christopher, ed. *Reports of Cases Argued and Determined in the High Court of Admiralty: Commencing with the Judgments of the Right Hon. Sir William Scott, Michaelmas Term 1798.* 6 vols. London: A. Strahan, 1801.

Smith, Samuel. Papers. Library of Congress, Washington, DC.

U.S. Navy Department. *Ships Data US Naval Vessels.* Washington, DC: Government Printing Office, 1929.

Virginia General Assembly, House of Delegates. *Report of the Select Committee . . . in Reference to the Defense of Craney Island . . . 22nd of June 1813.* Richmond, VA, 1848.

War of 1812 Collection. Maryland Historical Society, Baltimore.

ARTICLES

Bolton, Nelson Mott, and Christopher T. George. "Captain Henry Thompson's First Baltimore Horse Artillery in the Defense of Baltimore in the War of 1812." *Maryland Historical Magazine* 108 (Winter 2013): 420–44.

Bradford, S. Sydney. "Fort McHenry: 1814: The Outworks in 1814." *Maryland Historical Magazine* 54 (June 1959): 188–209.

Calderhead, William L. "Naval Innovation in Crisis: War in the Chesapeake, 1813." *American Neptune: A Quarterly Journal of Maritime History* 36 (July 1976): 206–21.

———. "A Strange Career in a Young Navy: Captain Charles Gordon, 1778–1816." *Maryland Historical Magazine* 72 (Fall 1977): 373–86.

———. "U. S. F. Constellation in the War of 1812—An Accidental Fleet-in-Being." *Military Affairs* 40 (April 1976): 79–83.

Cassell, Frank A. "Baltimore in 1813: A Study of Urban Defense in the War of 1812." *Military Affairs* 33 (December 1969): 349–61.

Chew, Richard. "The Origins of Mob Town: Social Division and Racial Conflict in the Baltimore Riots of 1812." Special edition, *Maryland Historical Magazine* 107 (2012): 7–35.

"The Conflagration of Havre de Grace." *North-American Review and Miscellaneous Journal* 5 (July 1817): 157–63.

Conner, Eugene H. "Notes and Events: William Beanes, M.D. (1749–1829) and the Star-Spangled Banner." *Journal of the History of Medicine and Allied Sciences* 34, no. 2 (1979): 224–29.

Cunningham, Noble E., Jr. "Who Were the Quids?" *Mississippi Valley Historical Review* 50, no. 2 (September 1963): 252–63.

Eliassen, Meredith. "A Soldier's Dilemma: Francis R. Shunk's Account for the Battle for Baltimore, 1814." *Maryland Historian* 31, no. 2 (Fall 2007): 67–80.

Freymann, John Gordon. "A View of the War and the World from Baltimore, 1813–1815." *Maryland Historical Magazine* 107 (Winter 2012): 484–518.

George, Christopher T. "The Family Papers of Major General Robert Ross, the Diary of Colonel Arthur Brooke, and the British Attacks on Washington and Baltimore of 1814." *Maryland Historical Magazine* 88 (Fall 1993): 300–316.

———. "Militia Redeemed before Baltimore." *Military History* 22, no. 6 (September 2005): 38–45.

———. "Mirage of Freedom: African Americans in the War of 1812." *Maryland Historical Magazine* 107 (Spring 2012): 36–55.

———. "Sunk to Save Baltimore: Compensating the Owners of Ships Sunk in Baltimore Harbor during the War of 1812." *Journal of the War of 1812* 14 (Summer 2011): 10–23.

Gilje, Paul A. "The Baltimore Riots of 1812 and the Breakdown of the Anglo-American Mob Tradition." *Journal of Social History* 13, no. 4 (Summer 1980): 547–64.

Groene, Bertram H. "A Trap for the British: Thomas Brown and the Battle of the 'White House.'" *Virginia Cavalcade* 18, no. 1 (1968): 13–19.

Hickey, Donald R. "The Monroe-Pinckney Treaty of 1806: A Reappraisal." *William and Mary Quarterly*, 3rd ser., 44, no. 1 (January 1987): 65–88.

Hill, R. Maurice. "A Short History of the New South Wales Corps, 1789–1818." *Journal of the Society for Army Historical Research* 13, no. 51 (Autumn 1934): 136–40.

Hitsman, J. Mackay, and Alice Sorby. "Independent Foreigners or Canadian Chasseurs." *Military Affairs* 25 (Spring 1961): 12–14.

Judge, C. B. "Navy Powder Goes on a Journey: An Episode of the War of 1812." *U.S. Naval Institute Proceedings* 69 (September 1943): 1223–28.

"A Letter from Thomas Jefferson in the Early Weeks of the War of 1812." *War of 1812 Magazine*, no. 13 (June 2010). http://www.napoleon-series.org/military/Warof1812/2010/Issue13/c_Jefferson.html.

Magruder, Caleb Clarke, Jr. "Dr William Beanes, the Incidental Cause of the Authorship of the Star-Spangled Banner." *Records of the Columbia Historical Society* 22 (1919): 207–25.

Maguire, W. A. "Major General Robert Ross and the Burning of Washington." *Irish Sword: The Journal of the Military History Society of Ireland* 14, no. 55 (Winter 1980): 117–19.

Malcomson, Robert. "The Battle for Little York, 1813." *Military History Quarterly*, Autumn 2008, 40–49.

———. "Unturned Stones in the War of 1812 Studies." *War of 1812 Magazine*, no. 4 (September 2006). http://www.napoleon-series.org/military/Warof1812/2006/Issue4/c_editoriala.html.

Malcomson, Thomas. "Freedom by Reaching the Wooden World." *Northern Mariner* 22, no. 4 (October 2012): 361–92.

Marrion, Robert, and Reginald L. Campbell. "The 102nd Regiment of Foot, 1814." *Military Collector and Historian* 33, no. 2 (Summer 1981): 74–75.

Mason, Matthew. "The Battle of the Slaveholding Liberators: Great Britain, the United States, and Slavery in the Early Nineteenth Century." *William and Mary Quarterly*, 3rd ser., 59, no. 3 (July 2002): 665–96.

Mullaly, Franklin R. "The Battle of Baltimore." *Maryland Historical Magazine* 54 (March 1959): 61–101.

Muller, Charles G. "Fabulous Potomac Passage." *U.S. Naval Institute Proceedings* 90 (May 1964): 85–91.

Nichols, Alistair J. "Desperate Banditti? The Independent Companies of Foreigners, 1812–14." *Journal of the Society for Army Historical Research*, no. 79 (2001): 278–94.

Ockerbloom, John. "The Discovery of a U.S. Marine Officer's Account of Life, Honor, and the Battle of Bladensburg, Washington and Maryland, 1814." *Military Collector and Historian* 61, no. 4 (Winter 2009): 258–63.

Pancake, John. "The Invisibles: A Chapter in the Opposition to President Madison." *Journal of Southern History* 21, no. 1 (February 1955): 17–37.

Reinoehl, John H., ed. "Some Remarks on the American Trade: Jacob Crowinshield to James Madison, 1806." *William and Mary Quarterly*, 3d ser., 16, no. 1 (January 1959): 83–118.

Rouse, Parker, Jr. "The British Invasion of Hampton in 1813: The Reminiscences of James Jarvis." *Virginia Magazine of History and Biography* 76, no. 3 (July 1968): 318–36.

———. "Low Tide at Hampton Roads." *U.S. Naval Institute Proceedings* 95 (July 1969): 79–86.

"Secret Letter from Rear Admiral George Cockburn to Vice Admiral Alexander Cochrane, 17 July 1814." *Maryland Historical Magazine* 6 (March 1911): 16–19.

Sheads, Scott S. "A Black Soldier Defends Fort McHenry, 1814." *Military Collector and Historian* 41, no. 1 (Spring 1989): 20–21.

———. "Defending Baltimore in the War of 1812: Two Sidelights." *Maryland Historical Magazine* 84 (Fall 1989): 252–57.

———. "H. M. Bomb Ship *Terror* and the Bombardment of Fort McHenry." *Maryland Historical Magazine* 103 (Fall 2008): 257–67.

Steel, Anthony. "Anthony Merry and the Anglo-American Dispute about Impressment, 1803–6." *Cambridge Historical Journal* 9, no. 3 (1949): 331–51.

Taylor, Blaine. "May 3, 1813: Cockburn vs. O'Neill at Havre de Grace Britain's Sea-Going Commando Burns the Harbor of Mercy." *Harford Historical Bulletin*, no. 43 (Winter 1990): 9–17.

Walsh, Richard. "The Star Fort: 1814." *Maryland Historical Magazine* 54 (September 1959): 296–309.

Weeks, Barbara. "This Present Time of Alarm." *Maryland Historical Magazine* 84 (Fall 1989): 257–66.

Williams, Glenn F. "The Bladensburg Races." *Military History Quarterly* 12, no. 1 (1999): 58–65.

SECONDARY SOURCES

Adams, Henry. *History of the United States of America during the Administrations of James Madison*. New York: Literary Classics of the United States, 1986.

Altoff, Gerald T. *Amongst My Best Men: African-Americans and the War of 1812*. Put-in-Bay, OH: Perry Group, 1996.

Antal, Sandy. *A Wampum Denied: Procter's War of 1812*. Ottawa, ON: Carleton University Press, 1998.

Bickham, Troy. *The Weight of Vengeance: The United States, the British Empire, and the War of 1812*. New York: Oxford University Press, 2012.

Black, Jeremy. *The War of 1812 in the Age of Napoleon*. Norman: University of Oklahoma Press, 2009.

Brant, Irving. *James Madison, Secretary of State, 1800–1809*. Indianapolis: Bobbs-Merrill, 1953.

Brown, Gordon S. *The Captain Who Burned His Ships: Captain Thomas Tingey, USN, 1750–1829*. Annapolis: Naval Institute Press, 2011.

Brugger, Robert J. *Maryland: A Middle Temperament, 1634–1980*. Baltimore: Johns Hopkins University Press, 1988.

Brunsman, Denver. *The Evil Necessity: British Naval Impressment in the Eighteenth-Century Atlantic World*. Charlottesville: University of Virginia Press, 2013.

Budiansky, Stephen. *Perilous Fight: America's Intrepid War with Britain on the High Seas, 1812–1815*. New York: A. A. Knopf, 2010.

Carter, Thomas. *Historical Record of the Forty-Fourth, or East Essex Regiment of Foot*. London: W. O. Mitchell, 1864.

Chapelle, Howard Irving. *The Baltimore Clipper: Its Origin and Development*. New York: Dover Publications, 2012.

———. *The History of the American Sailing Navy: The Ships and Their Development*. New York: W. W. Norton, 1949.

———. *Search for Speed under Sail*. New York: W. W. Norton, 1967.

Chartrand, Rene. *Forts of the War of 1812*. Oxford: Osprey Publishing, 2012.

Cochrane, Alexander. *The Fighting Cochranes*. London: Quiller Press, 1983.

Coggeshall, George. *History of the American Privateers and Letters-of-Marque, during Our War with England in the Years 1812, '13, and '14*. New York, 1856.

Coles, Harry L. *The War of 1812*. Chicago: University of Chicago Press, 1965.

Crane, William B., and John P. Cranwell. *Men of Marque: A History of Private Armed Vessels out of Baltimore during the War of 1812*. New York: W. W. Norton, 1940.

Daughan, George C. *1812: The Navy's War*. New York: Basic Books, 2011.

Dudley, Wade G. *Splintering the Wooden Wall: The British Blockade of the United States, 1812–1815*. Annapolis: Naval Institute Press, 2003.

Elting, John R. *Amateurs to Arms! A Military History of the War of 1812*. Chapel Hill, NC: Algonquin Books, 1991.

Eshelman, Ralph E., and Burton K. Kummerow. *In Full Glory Reflected: Discovering the War of 1812 in the Chesapeake*. Baltimore: Maryland Historical Trust Press, 2012.

Eshelman, Ralph E., Scott S. Sheads, and Donald R. Hickey. *The War of 1812 in the Chesapeake: A Reference Guide to Historic Sites in Maryland, Virginia and the District of Columbia*. Baltimore: Johns Hopkins University Press, 2010.

Footner, Geoffrey M. *Tidewater Triumph: The Development and Worldwide Success of the Chesapeake Bay Schooner*. Centreville, MD: Tidewater Publishing, 1998.

Footner, Hulbert. *Sailor of Fortune: The Life and Adventures of Commodore Joshua Barney, USN*. New York: Harper & Brothers, 1940.

Fredriksen, John C. *Resource Guide for the War of 1812*. Los Angeles: Subia, 1979.

———. *The United States Army in the War of 1812: Concise Biographies of Commanders and Operational Histories of Regiments, with Bibliographies of Published and Primary Resources*. Jefferson, NC: McFarland, 2009.

Garitee, Jerome R. *The Republic's Private Navy: The American Privateering Business as Practiced by Baltimore during the War of 1812*. Middletown, CT: Wesleyan University Press, 1977.

George, Christopher T. *Terror on the Chesapeake: The War of 1812 on the Bay*. Shippensburg, PA: White Mane Books, 2000.

Glatfelter, Heidi L. *Havre de Grace in the War of 1812: Fire on the Chesapeake*. Charleston, SC: History Press, 2013.

Graves, Donald E. *Sir William Congreve and the Rocket's Red Glare*. Alexandria Bay, NY: Museum Restoration Service, 1989.

Hallahan, John M. *The Battle of Craney Island*. Portsmouth, VA: St. Michael's Press, 1986.

Healey, David. *1812: Rediscovering the Chesapeake Bay's Forgotten War*. Rock Hill, SC: Bella Rosa Books, 2005.

Heckscher, Eli F. *The Continental System: An Economic Interpretation*. London, 1922.

Heidler, David S., and Jeanne T. Heidler, eds. *Encyclopedia of the War of 1812*. Annapolis: Naval Institute Press, 1997.

Herrick, Carole L. *August 24, 1814: Washington in Flames*. Reston, VA: Higher Education Publications, 2005.

Hickey, Donald R. *Don't Give Up the Ship! Myths of the War of 1812*. Urbana: University of Illinois Press, 2006.

Hickey, Donald R., and Connie D. Clark. *The Rockets' Red Glare: An Illustrated History of the War of 1812*. Baltimore: Johns Hopkins University Press, 2011.

Hitsman, Mackay. *The Incredible War of 1812*. Toronto: University of Toronto Press, 1965.

Hopkins, Fred W., Jr. *Tom Boyle: Master Privateer.* Mattituck, NY: Amereon House, 1976.

Kennedy, John Pendleton. *Memoirs of the Life of William Wirt.* Vol. 1. Philadelphia: Lea and Blanchard, 1849.

Langguth, A. J. *Union 1812: The Americans Who Fought the Second War of Independence.* New York: Simon & Schuster, 2006.

Latimer, Jon. *1812: War with America.* Cambridge, MA: Belknap Press of the Harvard University Press, 2007.

Lewis, Michael. *A Social History of the Navy, 1793–1815.* London: George Allen & Unwin, 2006.

Lloyd, Alan. *The Scorching of Washington: The War of 1812.* Washington, DC: R. B. Luce, 1974.

Lord, Walter. *The Dawn's Early Light.* New York: W. W. Norton, 1972.

Lossing, Benson J. *The Pictorial Field Book of the War of 1812.* New York: Harper & Brothers, 1868.

Malcomson, Robert. *Capital in Flames: The American Attack on York, 1813.* Annapolis: Naval Institute Press, 2008.

———. *Lords of the Lake: The Naval War on Lake Ontario, 1812–1814.* Toronto: Robin Brass Studio, 1998.

Marine, William M. *The British Invasion of Maryland, 1812–1815.* Bowie, MD: Heritage Books, 1998.

Morgan, James Dudley. *Historic Fort Washington on the Potomac.* Washington, DC, 1904.

Morris, Roger. *Cockburn and the British Navy in Transition.* Columbia: University of South Carolina Press, 1997.

Muller, Charles G. *The Darkest Day: 1814.* Philadelphia: J. B. Lippincott, 1963.

Norton, Louis A. *Joshua Barney: Hero of the Revolution and 1812.* Annapolis: Naval Institute Press, 2000.

Perkins, Bradford. *Prologue to War: England and the United States, 1805–1812.* Berkeley: University of California Press, 1963.

Perrett, Bryan. *The Real Hornblower: The Life of Admiral Sir James Gordon, GCB.* Annapolis: Naval Institute Press, 1997.

Pitch, Anthony. *The Burning of Washington: The British Invasion of 1814.* Annapolis: Naval Institute Press, 1998.

Quimby, Robert S. *The U.S. Army in the War of 1812: An Operational and Command Study.* 2 vols. East Lansing: Michigan State University Press, 1997.

Renzulli, L. Marx, Jr. *Maryland: The Federalist Years.* Cranbury, NJ: Fairleigh Dickinson University Press, 1972.

Rhodes, Harry C. *Queenstown: The Social History of a Small American Town.* Queenstown, MD: Queen Anne Press, 1985.

Robinson, J. Dennis. *America's Privateer: Privateer* Lynx *and the War of 1812.* Newport Beach, CA: Lynx Educational Foundation, 2011.

Rutland, Robert A. *The Presidency of James Madison*. Lawrence: University Press of Kansas, 1990.

Scharf, J. Thomas. *History of Maryland: From the Earliest Period to the Present Day*. Vol. 3. Baltimore: J. B. Piet, 1879.

Sheads, Scott S. *Fort McHenry*. Baltimore: Nautical & Aviation, 1995.

———. *The Rocket's Red Glare: The Maritime Defense of Baltimore in 1814*. Centreville, MD: Tidewater Publishers, 1986.

Shomette, Donald G. *Flotilla: The Patuxent Naval Campaign in the War of 1812*. Rev. ed. Baltimore: Johns Hopkins University Press, 2009.

———. *Lost Towns of Tidewater Maryland*. Centreville, MD: Tidewater Publishers, 2000.

Stephen, James. *War in Disguise; or, The Frauds of the Neutral Flags*. London, 1806.

Taylor, Alan. *The Civil War of 1812*. New York: Vintage Books, 2010.

———. *The Internal Enemy: Slavery and War in Virginia, 1772–1832*. New York: W. W. Norton, 2013.

Tucker, Spencer C., and Frank T. Reuter. *Injured Honor: The* Chesapeake-Leopard *Affair, June 22, 1807*. Annapolis: Naval Institute Press, 1996.

Vogel, Steve. *Through the Perilous Fight: Six Weeks That Saved the Nation*. New York: Random House, 2013.

Whitehorne, Joseph A. *The Battle for Baltimore 1814*. Baltimore: Nautical & Aviation, 1997.

Williams, Glenn F. *USS* Constellation: *A Short History of the Last All-Sail Warship Built by the United States Navy*. Virginia Beach, VA: Donning, 2000.

Wills, Garry. *James Madison*. New York: Times Books, 2002.

Yarsinke, Amy W. *The Elizabeth River*. Charleston, SC: History Press, 2007.

Zimmerman, James F. *Impressment of American Seamen*. Port Washington, NY: Kennikat Press, 1925.

INDEX

Alexandria, 98, 151, 165, 168–69, 172, 180

American Indian tribes, 31–32, 33–34, 37–42, 118

Annapolis: bypassing of, 185; campaign to take, 99, 111, 115, 139–40; defense of, 97, 98, 104, 137–38, 140, 201; target of raids, creation of confusion about, 146–47, 152–53

Armistead, George, 72, 177, 185, 199, 202

Armstrong, John: Bladensburg defeat, responsibility for, 162–63, 170–71; British naval task force in Chesapeake, response to, 63; dismissal of, 201; focus of war effort at Canadian border, 112; Fort McHenry commander, assignment of, 177; Fort Washington, improvements to, 98; portrait of, 128; resignation of, 170–71; St. Leonard's Creek battles, 125; target of raids, creation of confusion about, 152–53, 155, 162; Washington, evacuation of, 163; Washington defense, militia units for, 97

Army, British: Craney Island assault, 87, 89; force strength of, 113, 115; looting and burning by, 93–96, 216n26; Norfolk campaign, 67–68, 82, 121; performance of troops, dissatisfaction with, 121; Queenstown raid, 105–6; Regiment of Foot, 102nd, 67–68, 81, 82, 87, 95, 105–6, 121; Washington defenses, testing of, 96–97

Army, U.S., 70, 88, 111–12, 125–26, 128–33, 179

Bacon, Samuel, 161–62, 180, 220–21n28

Baltimore: attack on, preparations for, 173; attack on, release of prisoners after, 173; British arrival in area, 178, 185; campaign to take, 99, 111, 115, 139–40; Charles Street house, mob activity around, 46–49, 53; Cockburn operations in preparation for raid on, 70–71, 72, 79–80, 112; decision to attack, 174; defeat of British at, 203; defense of, 43, 55, 58, 68–73, 104, 111, 112, 137–38, 175–87, 202; defense of, chain of command for, 175, 184; defense of, force strength for, 185; defense of, preparations for, 79–81; defense of, success of, 195–99, 200, 201; economic importance of, 42–43; growth of population of, 42; investigation of mob activity, 52–53; jail, mob activity around, 49–52; Lazaretto, 116, 176, 178, 180, 184, 192, 194, 197; mob activity and riots in, 44–53; Mob Town title, 42, 53; naval defense of, 107–9, 110–11, 180–81; Old Defenders, commemoration of, 202; painting of, 116; political divisiveness in, 43–53, 210n17; privateers based in, 58–66, 204–5; raid on, 201; raid on, British force strength for, 185; shallow waters in harbor, 70, 175; ships for defense of, 69–70, 71, 112; sunken ships for defense of, 72, 194, 195–96, 223n28; target of raids, creation of confusion about, 142, 171; torpedoes and defense of, 107–9, 217n44

ABOUT THE AUTHOR

Dr. Charles P. Neimeyer is the director of Marine Corps History and the Gray Research Center at Marine Corps University, Quantico, Virginia. Prior to coming to Quantico, Dr. Neimeyer was the dean of academics at the Naval War College and Forrest Sherman Chair of Public Diplomacy in Newport, Rhode Island, and a vice president of academic affairs at Valley Forge Military Academy and College. He also previously served as a history professor at the U.S. Naval Academy and the University of Central Oklahoma. During his twenty-year career as a military officer, Dr. Neimeyer served in a variety of posts and stations in the Marine Corps, including tours in all three active Marine divisions and service at the White House. He is the author of *America Goes to War: A Social History of the Continental Army, 1775–1783* (New York University Press, 1996) and *The Revolutionary War* (Greenwood Press, 2007). He edited a volume published by the Naval Institute Press in 2008 titled *On the Corps: USMC Wisdom from the Pages of* Leatherneck, Marine Corps Gazette, *and* Proceedings.

The Naval Institute Press is the book-publishing arm of the U.S. Naval Institute, a private, nonprofit, membership society for sea service professionals and others who share an interest in naval and maritime affairs. Established in 1873 at the U.S. Naval Academy in Annapolis, Maryland, where its offices remain today, the Naval Institute has members worldwide.

Members of the Naval Institute support the education programs of the society and receive the influential monthly magazine *Proceedings* or the colorful bimonthly magazine *Naval History* and discounts on fine nautical prints and on ship and aircraft photos. They also have access to the transcripts of the Institute's Oral History Program and get discounted admission to any of the Institute-sponsored seminars offered around the country.

The Naval Institute's book-publishing program, begun in 1898 with basic guides to naval practices, has broadened its scope to include books of more general interest. Now the Naval Institute Press publishes about seventy titles each year, ranging from how-to books on boating and navigation to battle histories, biographies, ship and aircraft guides, and novels. Institute members receive significant discounts on the Press's more than eight hundred books in print.

Full-time students are eligible for special half-price membership rates. Life memberships are also available.

For a free catalog describing Naval Institute Press books currently available, and for further information about joining the U.S. Naval Institute, please write to:

Member Services
U.S. NAVAL INSTITUTE
291 Wood Road
Annapolis, MD 21402-5034
Telephone: (800) 233-8764
Fax: (410) 571-1703
Web address: www.usni.org